Junior
Worldmark
Encyclopedia
of the
States

VOLUME **2**

Junior Worldmark Encyclopedia of the States

States

VOLUME 2

Indiana to Nebraska

U·X·L®

AN IMPRINT OF GALE

an International Thomson Publishing company I(T)P®

JUNIOR WORLDMARK ENCYCLOPEDIA OF THE STATES

Timothy L. Gall and Susan Bevan Gall, *Editors*
Rosalie Wieder, *Senior Editor*
Deborah Baron and Daniel M. Lucas, *Associate Editors*
Brian Rajewski and Deborah Rutti, *Graphics and Layout*
Cordelia R. Heaney, *Editorial Assistant*
Dianne K. Daeg de Mott, Janet Fenn, Matthew Markovich,
    Ariana Ranson, and Craig Strasshofer, *Copy Editors*
Janet Fenn and Matthew Markovich, *Proofreaders*
University of Akron Laboratory for Cartographic and
    Spatial Analysis, Joseph W. Stoll, Supervisor;
    Scott Raypholtz, Mike Meger, *Cartographers*

U•X•L Staff

Jane Hoehner, *U•X•L Developmental Editor*
Carol DeKane Nagel, *Managing Editor*
Thomas L. Romig, *U•X•L Publisher*
Mary Beth Trimper, *Production Director*
Evi Seoud, *Assistant Production Manager*
Shanna Heilveil, *Production Associate*
Cynthia Baldwin, *Product Design Manager*
Barbara J. Yarrow, *Graphic Services Supervisor*
Mary Krzewinski, *Cover Designer*

♾™ This book is printed on acid-free paper that meets the minimum requirements of American National Standard for Information Sciences——Permanence Paper for Printed Library Materials, ANSI Z39.48-1984.

Library of Congress Cataloging-in-Publication Data
Junior Worldmark encyclopedia of the states / edited by Timothy Gall
    and Susan Gall.
        p.   cm.
    Includes bibliographical references and index.
    ISBN 0-7876-0736-3 (set)
    1. United States—Encyclopedia.   I. Gall, Susan B.   II. Title.
E156.G35   1996
973'.03—dc20   95-36740
                                                                        CIP

ISBN 0-7876-0736-3 (set)
ISBN 0-7876-0737-1 (vol. 1)
ISBN 0-7876-0738-X (vol. 2)
ISBN 0-7876-0739-8 (vol. 3)
ISBN 0-7876-0740-1 (vol. 4)

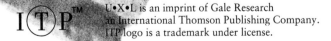

I(T)P™ U•X•L is an imprint of Gale Research,
        an International Thomson Publishing Company.
        ITP logo is a trademark under license.

CONTENTS

READER'S GUIDE

Junior Worldmark Encyclopedia of the States presents profiles of the 50 states of the nation, the District of Columbia, Puerto Rico, and the U.S. dependencies, arranged alphabetically in four volumes. *Junior Worldmark* is based on the third edition of the reference work, *Worldmark Encyclopedia of the States.* The *Worldmark* design organizes facts and data about every state in a common structure. Every profile contains a map, showing the state and its location in the nation.

For this first *Junior* edition of *Worldmark,* facts were updated and many new graphical elements were added, including photographs. Recognition is due to the many tourist bureaus, convention centers, press offices, and state agencies that contributed the photographs that illustrate this encyclopedia. This edition also benefits from the work of the many article reviewers listed at the end of this Reader's Guide. The reviewers contributed insights, updates, and substantive additions that were instrumental to the creation of this work. The editors are extremely grateful for the time and effort these distinguished reviewers devoted to improving the quality of this encyclopedia.

Sources

Due to the broad scope of this encyclopedia many sources were consulted in compiling the information and statistics presented in these volumes. Of primary importance were the following publications from the U.S. Bureau of the Census: *1990 Census of Population, 1990 Census of Manufacturers, 1992 Census of Wholesale Trade, 1992 Census of Retail Trade, 1992 Census of Service Industries,* and the *1992 Census of Agriculture.* More recent economic statistics on the labor force, income, and earnings were obtained from files posted as of January 1996 by the Economics and Statistics Administration of the U.S. Department of Commerce on *The Economic Bulletin Board,* an electronic information retrieval service. The most recent agricultural statistics on crops and livestock were obtained from files posted by the U.S. Department of Agriculture on its gopher server and its world-wide web site at http://www.econ.ag.gov. Finally, many fact sheets, booklets, and state statistical abstracts were used to update data not collected by the federal government.

Profile Features

The *Junior Worldmark* structure—40 numbered headings—allows students to compare two or more states in a variety of ways.

Each state profile begins by listing the origin of the state name, its nickname, the capital, the date it entered the union, the state song and motto, and a description of the state coat of arms. The profile also presents a picture and textual description of both the state seal and the state flag (a key to the flag color symbols appears on page xii of each volume). Next, a listing of the official state animal, bird, fish, flower, tree, gem, etc. is given. The introductory information ends with the standard time given by time zone in relation to Greenwich mean time (GMT). The world is divided into 24 time zones, each one hour apart. The Greenwich meridian, which is 0 degrees, passes through Greenwich, England, a suburb of London. Greenwich is at the center of the initial time zone, known as Greenwich mean time (GMT). All times given are converted from noon in this zone. The time reported for the state is the official time zone.

The body of each country's profile is arranged in 40 numbered headings as follows:

1 LOCATION AND SIZE. The state is located on the North American continent. Statistics are given on area and boundary length. Size comparisons are made to the other 50 states of the United States.

2 TOPOGRAPHY. Dominant geographic features including terrain and major rivers and lakes are described.

3 CLIMATE. Temperature and rainfall are given for the various regions of the state in both English and metric units.

4 PLANTS AND ANIMALS. Described here are the plants and animals native to the state.

5 ENVIRONMENTAL PROTECTION. Destruction of natural resources—forests, water supply, air—is described here. Statistics on solid waste production, hazard-ous waste sites, and endangered and extinct species are also included.

6 POPULATION. 1990 Census statistics as well as 1995 state population estimates are provided. Population density and major urban populations are summarized.

7 ETHNIC GROUPS. The major ethnic groups are ranked in percentages. Where appropriate, some description of the influence or history of ethnicity is provided.

8 LANGUAGES. The regional dialects of the state are summarized as well as the number of people speaking languages other than English at home.

9 RELIGIONS. The population is broken down according to religion and/or denominations.

10 TRANSPORTATION. Statistics on roads, railways, waterways, and air traffic, along with a listing of key ports for trade and travel, are provided.

11 HISTORY. Includes a concise summary of the state's history from ancient times (where appropriate) to the present.

12 STATE GOVERNMENT. The form of government is described, and the process of governing is summarized.

13 POLITICAL PARTIES. Describes the significant political parties through history, where appropriate, and the influential parties in the mid-1990s.

14 LOCAL GOVERNMENT. The system of local government structure is summarized.

15 JUDICIAL SYSTEM. Structure of the court system and the jurisdiction of courts in each category is provided. Crime rates as reported by the Federal Bureau of Investigation (FBI) are also included.

[16] **MIGRATION.** Population shifts since the end of World War II are summarized.

[17] **ECONOMY.** This section presents the key elements of the economy. Major industries and employment figures are also summarized.

[18] **INCOME.** Personal income and the poverty level are given as is the state's ranking among the 50 states in per person income.

[19] **INDUSTRY.** Key industries are listed, and important aspects of industrial development are described.

[20] **LABOR.** Statistics are given on the civilian labor force, including numbers of workers, leading areas of employment, and unemployment figures.

[21] **AGRICULTURE.** Statistics on key agricultural crops, market share, and total farm income are provided.

[22] **DOMESTICATED ANIMALS.** Statistics on livestock—cattle, hogs, sheep, etc.—and the land area devoted to raising them are given.

[23] **FISHING.** The relative significance of fishing to the state is provided, with statistics on fish and seafood products.

[24] **FORESTRY.** Land area classified as forest is given, along with a listing of key forest products and a description of government policy toward forest land.

[25] **MINING.** Description of mineral deposits and statistics on related mining activity and export are provided.

[26] **ENERGY AND POWER.** Description of the state's power resources, including electricity produced and oil reserves and production, are provided.

[27] **COMMERCE.** A summary of the amount of wholesale trade, retail trade, and receipts of service establishments is given.

[28] **PUBLIC FINANCE.** Revenues, expenditures, and total and per person debt are provided.

[29] **TAXATION.** The state's tax system is explained.

[30] **HEALTH.** Statistics on and description of such public health factors as disease and suicide rates, principal causes of death, numbers of hospitals and medical facilities appear here. Information is also provided on the percentage of citizens without health insurance within each state.

[31] **HOUSING.** Housing shortages and government programs to build housing are described. Statistics on numbers of dwellings and median home values are provided.

[32] **EDUCATION.** Statistical data on educational achievement and primary and secondary schools is given. Per person state spending on primary and secondary education is also given. Major universities are listed, and government programs to foster education are described.

[33] **ARTS.** A summary of the state's major cultural institutions is provided together

with the amount of federal and state funds designated to the arts.

34 LIBRARIES AND MUSEUMS. The number of libraries, their holdings, and their yearly circulation is provided. Major museums are listed.

35 COMMUNICATIONS. The state of telecommunications (television, radio, and telephone) is summarized.

36 PRESS. Major daily and Sunday newspapers are listed together with data on their circulations.

37 TOURISM, TRAVEL, AND RECREATION. Under this heading, the student will find a summary of the importance of tourism to the state, and factors affecting the tourism industry. Key tourist attractions are listed.

38 SPORTS. The major sports teams in the state, both professional and collegiate, are summarized.

39 FAMOUS PEOPLE. In this section, some of the best-known citizens of the state are listed. When a person is noted in a state that is not the state of his of her birth, the birthplace is given.

40 BIBLIOGRAPHY. The bibliographic listings at the end of each profile are provided as a guide for further reading.

Because many terms used in this encyclopedia will be new to students, each volume includes a glossary and a list of abbreviations and acronyms. A keyword index to all four volumes appears in Volume 4.

Acknowledgments

Junior Worldmark Encyclopedia of the States draws on the third edition of the *Worldmark Encyclopedia of the States*. Readers are directed to that work for a complete list of contributors, too numerous to list here. Special acknowledgment goes to the government officials throughout the nation who gave their cooperation to this project.

Reviewers

The following individuals reviewed state articles. In all cases the reviewers added important information and updated facts that might have gone unnoticed. The reviewers were also instrumental in suggesting changes and improvements.

Patricia L. Harris, Executive Director, Alabama Public Library Service

Patience Frederiksen, Head, Government Publications, Alaska State Library

Jacqueline L. Miller, Curator of Education, Arizona State Capitol Museum

John A. Murphey, Jr., State Librarian, Arkansas State Library

Eugene Hainer, School Library Media Consultant, Colorado State Library

Susan Cormier, Connecticut State Library

Dr. Annette Woolard, Director of Development, Historical Society of Delaware

Reference Staff, State Library of Florida

Cheryl Rogers, Consultant, Georgia Department of Education, Public Library Services

Lorna J. T. Peck, School Library Services, Specialist, State of Hawaii Department of Education

Marcia J. Beckwith, Director, Information Services/Library, Centennial High School, Boise, Idaho

Karen McIlrath-Muskopf, Youth Services Consultant, Illinois State Library

Cordell Svengalis, Social Science Consultant, Iowa Department of Education

Marc Galbraith, Director of Reference Services, Kansas State Library

James C. Klotter, State Historian, Kentucky Historical Society

Virginia R. Smith, Head, Louisiana Section, State Library of Louisiana

Ben Keating, Division Director, Maine State Library

Patricia V. Melville, Director of Reference Services, Maryland State Archives

Brian Donoghue, Reference Librarian, Massachusetts Board of Library Commissioners

Denise E. Carlson, Head of Reference, Minnesota Historical Society

Ronnie Smith, Reference Specialist, Mississippi Library Commission

Darlene Staffeldt, Director, Statewide Library Resources, Montana State Library

Rod Wagner, Director, Nebraska Library Commission

Reference Services and Archives Staff, Nevada State Library & Archives

Kendall F. Wiggin, State Librarian, New Hampshire State Library

John H. Livingstone, Acting Assistant Commissioner and State Librarian, New Jersey State Library

Robert J. Torrez, State Historian, New Mexico State Records and Archives

R. Allan Carter, Senior Librarian, New York State Library

Staff, Information Services and State Archives Research, State Library of North Carolina

Doris Daugherty, Assistant State Librarian, North Dakota State Library

Carol Brieck and Audrey Hall, Reference Librarians, State Library of Ohio

Audrey Wolfe-Clark, Edmond, Oklahoma

Paul Gregorio, Assistant Professor of Education, Portland State University, Portland, Oregon

Alice L. Lubrecht, Acting Bureau Director, State Library of Pennsylvania

Barbara Weaver, Director, Department of State Library Services, Rhode Island

Michele M. Reid, Director of Public Services, South Dakota State Library

Dr. Wayne C. Moore, Archivist, Tennessee State Library and Archives

Douglas E. Barnett, Managing Editor, New Handbook of Texas, Texas State Historical Association

Lou Reinwand, Director of Information Services, Utah State Library

Paul J. Donovan, Senior Reference Librarian, Vermont Department of Libraries

Catherine Mishler, Head, Reference, Library of Virginia

Gayle Palmer, Senior Library Information Specialist, Washington/Northwest Collections, Washington State Library

Karen Goff, Head of Reference, West Virginia Library Commission

Richard L. Roe, Research Analyst, Wisconsin Legislative Reference Bureau

Priscilla Golden, Principal Librarian, Wyoming State Library

Staff, Washingtoniana Division, Martin Luther King Memorial Library, Washington, D.C.

Advisors

The following persons were consulted on the content and structure of this encyclopedia. Their insights, opinions, and suggestions led to many enhancements and improvements in the presentation of the material.

Mary Alice Anderson, Media Specialist, Winona Middle School, Winona, Minnesota

Pat Baird, Library Media Specialist and Department Chair, Shaker Heights Middle School, Shaker Heights, Ohio

Pat Fagel, Library Media Specialist, Shaker Heights Middle School, Shaker Heights, Ohio

Nancy Guidry, Young Adult Librarian, Santa Monica Public Library, Santa Monica, California

Ann West LaPrise, Children's Librarian, Redford Branch, Detroit Public Library, Detroit, Michigan

Nancy C. Nieman, Teacher, U.S. History, Social Studies, Journalism, Delta Middle School, Muncie, Indiana

Madeleine Obrock, Library Media Specialist, Woodbury Elementary School, Shaker Heights, Ohio

Ernest L. O'Roark, Teacher, Social Studies, Martin Luther King Middle School, Germantown, Maryland

Ellen Stepanian, Director of Library Services, Shaker Heights Board of Education, Shaker Heights, Ohio

Mary Strouse, Library Media Specialist, Woodbury Elementary School, Shaker Heights, Ohio

Comments and Suggestions

We welcome your comments on the *Junior Worldmark Encyclopedia of the States* as well as your suggestions for features to be included in future editions. Please write: Editors, *Junior Worldmark Encyclopedia of the States,* U•X•L, 835 Penobscot Building, Detroit, Michigan 48226-4094; or call toll-free: 1-800-877-4253.

Guide to State Articles

All information contained within a state article is uniformly keyed by means of a boxed number to the left of the subject headings. A heading such as "Population," for example, carries the same key numeral (6) in every article. Therefore, to find information about the population of Alabama, consult the table of contents for the page number where the Alabama article begins and look for section 6.

Introductory matter for each state includes: Origin of state name
Nickname
Capital
Date and order of statehood
Song
Motto
Flag
Official seal
Symbols (animal, tree, flower, etc.)
Time zone.

Flag color symbols

| Yellow | Red | Green | Blue | Orange | Brown | White | Black |

Sections listed numerically

1   Location and Size
2   Topography
3   Climate
4   Plants and Animals
5   Environmental Protection
6   Population
7   Ethnic Groups
8   Languages
9   Religions
10 Transportation
11 History
12 State Government
13 Political Parties
14 Local Government
15 Judicial System
16 Migration
17 Economy
18 Income
19 Industry
20 Labor
21 Agriculture
22 Domesticated Animals
23 Fishing
24 Forestry
25 Mining
26 Energy and Power
27 Commerce
28 Public Finance
29 Taxation
30 Health
31 Housing
32 Education
33 Arts
34 Libraries and Museums
35 Communications
36 Press
37 Tourism, Travel, and Recreation
38 Sports
39 Famous Persons
40 Bibliography

Alphabetical listing of sections

Agriculture	21	Labor	20
Arts	33	Languages	8
Bibliography	40	Libraries and Museums	34
Climate	3	Local Government	14
Commerce	27	Location and Size	1
Communications	35	Migration	16
Domesticated Animals	22	Mining	25
Economy	17	Plants and Animals	4
Education	32	Political Parties	13
Energy and Power	26	Population	6
Environmental Protection	5	Press	36
Ethnic Groups	7	Public Finance	28
Famous Persons	39	Religions	9
Fishing	23	Sports	38
Forestry	24	State Government	12
Health	30	Taxation	29
History	11	Topography	2
Housing	31	Tourism, Travel, and Recreation	37
Income	18	Transportation	10
Industry	19		
Judicial System	15		

Explanation of symbols

A fiscal split year is indicated by a stroke (e.g. 1994/95).
Note that 1 billion = 1,000 million = 10^9.
The use of a small dash (e.g., 1990–94) normally signifies the full period of calendar years covered (including the end year indicated).

INDIANA

State of Indiana

ORIGIN OF STATE NAME: Named "land of Indians" for the many Indian tribes that formerly lived in the state.

NICKNAME: The Hoosier State.

CAPITAL: Indianapolis.

ENTERED UNION: 11 December 1816 (19th).

SONG: "On the Banks of the Wabash, Far Away."

MOTTO: The Crossroads of America.

FLAG: A flaming torch representing liberty is surrounded by 19 gold stars against a blue background. The word "Indiana" is above the flame.

OFFICIAL SEAL: In a pioneer setting, a farmer fells a tree while a buffalo flees from the forest and across the prairie; in the background, the sun sets over distant hills. The words "Seal of the State of Indiana 1816" surround the scene.

BIRD: Cardinal.

FLOWER: Peony.

TREE: Tulip tree (yellow poplar).

STONE: Indiana limestone.

POEM: "Indiana."

TIME: 7 AM EST = noon GMT; 6 AM CST = noon GMT.

1 LOCATION AND SIZE

Situated in the eastern north-central US, Indiana is the smallest of the 12 midwestern states and ranks 38th in size among the 50 states. Indiana's total area is 36,185 square miles (93,720 square kilometers). The state extends about 160 miles (257 kilometers) east-west and about 280 miles (451 kilometers) north-south. The total boundary length of Indiana is 1,696 miles (2,729 kilometers).

2 TOPOGRAPHY

Indiana has two principal types of terrain: slightly rolling land in the northern half of the state, and rugged hills in the southern, extending to the Ohio River. The highest point in the state is 1,257 feet (383 meters) above sea level. The lowest point, on the Ohio River, is 320 feet (98 meters).

Four-fifths of the state's land is drained by the Wabash River and by its tributaries, the White, Eel, Mississinewa, and Tippecanoe rivers. The northern region is drained by the Maumee, Calumet, and Kankakee rivers. In the southwest, the two White River forks empty into the Wabash, and in the southeast, the Whitewater River flows into the Ohio.

In addition to Lake Michigan on the northwestern border, there are more than 400 lakes in the northern part of the state. The largest lakes include Wawasee, Maxinkuckee, Freeman, and Shafer. There are mineral springs at French Lick and West Baden in Orange County.

3 CLIMATE

Temperatures vary from the extreme north to the extreme south of the state. The annual mean temperature is 49°F–58°F (9°C–12°C) in the north and 57°F (14°C) in the south. The average temperatures in January range between 17°F (–8°C) and 35°F (2°C). Average temperatures during July vary from 63°F (17°C) to 88°F (31°C). Rainfall is distributed fairly evenly throughout the year, although drought sometimes occurs in the southern region. The average annual precipitation in the state is 40 inches (102 centimeters), ranging from about 35 inches (89 centimeters) near Lake Michigan to 45 inches (114 centimeters) along the Ohio River. The annual snowfall in Indiana averages less than 22 inches (56 centimeters).

4 PLANTS AND ANIMALS

There are 124 native tree species, including 17 varieties of oak, as well as black walnut, sycamore, and the tulip tree (yellow poplar), the state tree. Fruit trees—apple, cherry, peach, and pear—are common. American elderberry and bittersweet are common shrubs, while various jack-in-the-pulpits and spring beauties are among the indigenous wildflowers. The peony is the state flower. Mountain laurel

Indiana Population Profile

Estimated 1995 population:	5,688,000
Population change, 1980–90:	1.0%
Leading ancestry group:	German
Second leading group:	Irish
Foreign born population:	1.7%
Hispanic origin†:	1.8%
Population by race:	
White:	90.6%
Black:	7.8%
Native American:	0.2%
Asian/Pacific Islander:	0.7%
Other:	0.7%

Population by Age Group

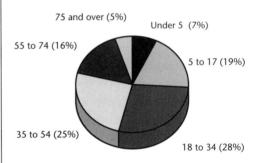

75 and over (5%)
Under 5 (7%)
55 to 74 (16%)
5 to 17 (19%)
35 to 54 (25%)
18 to 34 (28%)

Top Cities with Populations Over 25,000

City	Population	National rank	% change 1980–90
Indianapolis	757,275	12	na
Fort Wayne	173,717	101	0.5
Evansville	127,566	145	–3.2
Gary	116,702	157	–23.2
South Bend	105,942	188	–3.8
Hammond	84,256	264	–10.1
Muncie	72,419	318	–8.0
Bloomington	61,503	392	16.5
Anderson	60,360	399	–8.1
Terre Haute	59,196	411	–6.0

Notes: †A person of Hispanic origin may be of any race. NA indicates that data are not available.
Sources: Economic and Statistics Administration, Bureau of the Census. *Statistical Abstract of the United States, 1994–95.* Washington, DC: Government Printing Office, 1995; Courtenay M. Slater and George E. Hall. *1995 County and City Extra: Annual Metro, City and County Data Book.* Lanham, MD: Bernan Press, 1995.

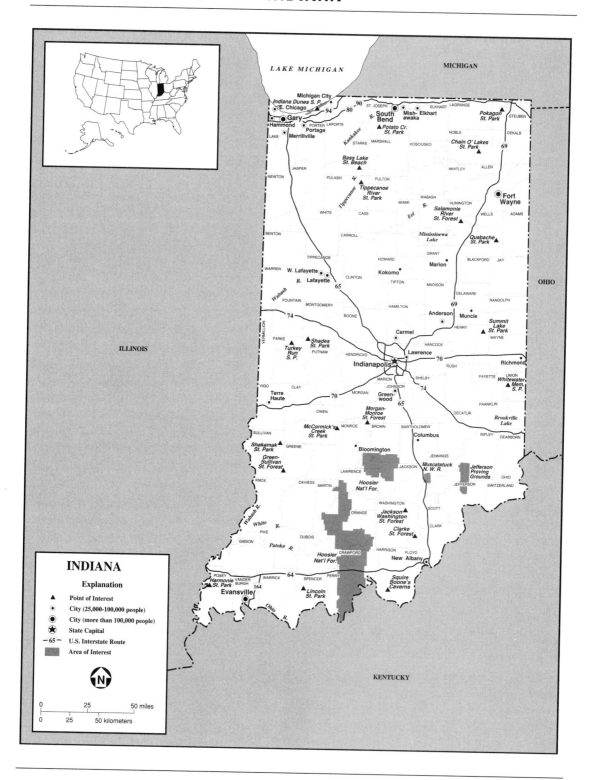

LAKE MICHIGAN

MICHIGAN

ILLINOIS

OHIO

KENTUCKY

INDIANA

Explanation

▲   Point of Interest

⊙   City (25,000-100,000 people)

◉   City (more than 100,000 people)

✪   State Capital

— 65 —   U.S. Interstate Route

▨   Area of Interest

0	25	50 miles
0	25	50 kilometers

is considered threatened, and the prairie white-fringed orchid is endangered.

Although the presence of wolves and coyotes has been reported occasionally, the red fox is Indiana's only common carnivorous mammal. Other native mammals include the common cottontail, muskrat, and raccoon. Many waterfowl and marsh birds, including the black duck and great blue heron, inhabit northern Indiana, while the field sparrow, yellow warbler, and red-headed woodpecker nest in central Indiana. Catfish, pike, bass, and sunfish are native to state waters. Among endangered species for which the state provides protection are the bobcat, badger, otter, and big-eared bat.

5 ENVIRONMENTAL PROTECTION

The Indiana Department of Environmental Management (IDEM) was established in April 1986, with a legislative order to protect public health through various environmental programs.

In 1990, IDEM spearheaded landmark legislation requiring counties to form solid waste management districts to develop plans for meeting statewide waste reduction goals. Most of those districts are now working toward achieving a 50% reduction by the year 2000.

In March 1990, Indiana's Water Pollution Control Board adopted some of the strictest water quality standards in the nation for more than 90 chemicals, and included almost all water bodies for protection of aquatic life and recreational use. Indiana is the tenth largest producer of hazardous waste in the country. IDEM devotes much attention to identifying, cleaning up, and lessening all forms of toxic contamination.

Some of the state's most serious environmental challenges lie in Lake and Porter counties in Northwest Indiana. A century of spills, emissions, and discharges to the environment there require comprehensive, regionally coordinated programs. The Northwest Indiana Remedial Action Plan (RAP) is a three-phased program designed especially for the Grand Calumet River and the Indiana Harbor Ship Canal. Both waterways are heavily contaminated and, if left at their current state, would degrade the waters of Lake Michigan, the primary source of drinking water for the Northwest Indiana area. In 1994, there were 33 hazardous waste sites in the state.

6 POPULATION

In 1990, Indiana had a population of 5,544,149 and ranked 14th in population among the 50 states. The population density was 155 persons per square mile (59.5 persons per square kilometer). The 1995 projection shows a population of 5,688,000, a five-year growth of 9.7%. Of the 1990 census population, 64.9% lived in urban areas and 35.1% resided in rural areas. Indianapolis, the capital and largest city, had a population of 757,275 in 1992, and its metropolitan area had a population of over 1,250,000. Other cities with 1992 populations of more than 100,000 were Fort Wayne, 173,717; Evansville, 127,566; Gary, 116,702; and South Bend, 105,942.

7 ETHNIC GROUPS

Restrictions on foreign immigration and the availability of jobs spurred the migration of black Americans to Indiana after World War I. By 1990, the state had 432,000 blacks, representing about 7.8% of the total population. In 1990, approximately 1.8% (99,000) of Indiana's population was of Hispanic origin. That year, Indiana's Asian residents included 6,093 Indians, 6,128 Chinese, 5,354 Filipinos, 6,298 Koreans, 6,338 Japanese, and 2,420 Vietnamese. In 1990, there were 13,000 Native Americans.

8 LANGUAGES

Most Indiana speech is basically that of the South Midland pioneers from south of the Ohio River, with a transition to North Midland north of Indianapolis.

In 1990, 95.2% of all Hoosiers five years old and older spoke only English at home. Other languages spoken at home (and number of speakers) include Spanish (90,146), German (46,034), French (20,578), and Polish (11,552). Chinese, Indic, Greek, Italian, and Korean were also reported.

9 RELIGIONS

In addition to a sizable Roman Catholic population, the largest Protestant denominations were United Methodist Church, Churches of Christ, American Baptist Churches in USA, Lutheran Church–Missouri Synod, and Presbyterian Church (USA). The estimated Jewish population of the state was 20,314 as of 1990. A group of religious dissidents founded the Pentecostal Church of God at Beaver Dam

in 1881. The world headquarters of the church, which had 22,569 adherents in 1990, is now at Anderson.

10 TRANSPORTATION

Indiana's central location in the US and its position between Lake Michigan to the north and the Ohio River to the south gave the state its motto, "The Crossroads of America." Historically, the state took advantage of its strategic location by digging canals to connect Indiana rivers and by building roads and railroads to provide farmers access to national markets. In December 1992, there were 29 railroads operating on 4,185 rail miles (6,734 kilometers) of track. Regularly scheduled Amtrak passenger trains served Indianapolis and 13 other stations in the state, with a total of 205,835 riders in Indiana during 1991/92. The South Shore commuter railroad connects South Bend, Gary, and East Chicago with Chicago, Illinois.

In 1993, Indiana had 1,138 miles (1,831 kilometers) of interstate highways—more than other states of comparable size. In that year, there were 11,362 miles (18,281 kilometers) of state highways and 81,012 miles (130,348 kilometers) of country and municipal roads. In 1993, motor vehicle registrations totaled 4,670,301, including 3,413,908 passenger cars and 1,233,503 trucks.

The transport of freight via Lake Michigan and the Ohio River helped to spark Indiana's industrial development. The deepwater port of Burns Harbor on Lake Michigan, which became operational in 1970, provided access to world markets

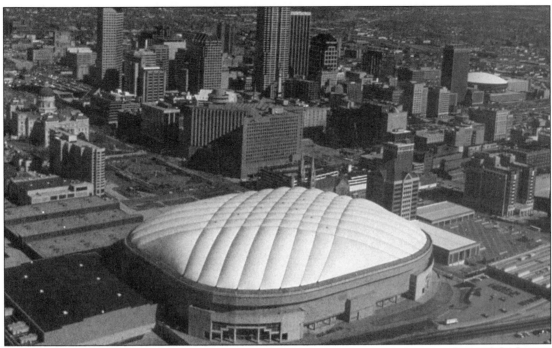

Photo credit: Rob Banayote.

The Indianapolis skyline featuring the Indiana Convention Center & RCA Dome. The RCA Dome is the home of the Indianapolis Colts professional football team.

via the St. Lawrence Seaway. Indiana Harbor handled 13.7 million tons of goods in 1991, and the tonnage at the port of Gary was over 9.5 million tons. In 1991, there were 576 public and private airports in the state. The number of active general aviation aircraft in Indiana was 3,460.

11 HISTORY

The first Native Americans to be seen by Europeans in present-day Indiana were probably the Miami and Potawatomi tribes. The first European penetration was made in the 1670s by the French explorers Father Jacques Marquette and Robert Cavelier, Sieur de la Salle. After the founding of Detroit, Michigan, in 1701, the Maumee-Wabash river route to the lower Ohio was discovered. The first French fort was built farther down the Wabash among the Wea tribe, near present-day Lafayette, in 1717.

By 1765, Indiana had fallen to the English. The pre-Revolutionary turmoil in the colonies on the Atlantic was hardly felt in Indiana. However, the region did not escape the Revolutionary War itself. Colonel George Rogers Clark, acting for Virginia, captured Vincennes from a British garrison early in 1779. Following the war, the area northwest of the Ohio River was granted to the new nation by treaty in 1783.

The first US town plotted in Indiana was Clarksville, established in 1784. A government for the region was established by the Continental Congress under the Northwest Ordinance of 1787. Known as the Northwest Territory, it included present-day Indiana, Ohio, Illinois, Michigan, Wisconsin, and part of Minnesota. After continued Native American unrest, General Anthony Wayne was put in command of an enlarged army, which ended the disturbance in 1794 at Fallen Timbers (near Toledo, Ohio).

Statehood

In 1800, as Ohio prepared to enter the Union, the rest of the Northwest Territory was set off and called Indiana Territory, with its capital at Vincennes. After Michigan Territory was detached in 1805, and Illinois Territory in 1809, Indiana assumed its present boundaries (having added about 10 miles to its northern border in 1816). William Henry Harrison was appointed first governor and, with a secretary and three appointed judges, constituted the government of Indiana Territory. When the population totaled 60,000—as it did in 1815—the voters were allowed to elect delegates to write a state constitution and to apply for admission to the Union. Indiana became the 19th state on 11 December 1816.

After the War of 1812, new settlers began pouring into the state from the upper South and in fewer numbers from Ohio, Pennsylvania, New York, and New England. In 1816, Thomas Lincoln brought his family from Kentucky, and his son Abe grew up in southern Indiana from age 7 to 21. Unlike most other frontier states, Indiana was settled from south to north. Central and northern Indiana were opened up as land was purchased from the Native Americans. Railroads began to tie Indiana commercially with the East. Irish immigrants dug canals and laid the rails, and German immigrants took up woodworking and farming. Levi Coffin, a Quaker who moved to Fountain City in 1826, operated the Underground Railroad, a network of people dedicated to help escaping slaves from the South.

Civil War

Hoosiers (as Indianans are called) showed considerable sympathy with the South in the 1850s. However, Indiana remained staunchly in the Union under Governor Oliver P. Morton, sending some 200,000 soldiers to the Civil War. The state suffered no battles, but General John Hunt Morgan's Confederate cavalry raided the southeastern sector of Indiana in July 1863.

After the Civil War, small local industries expanded rapidly. Discovery of natural gas in several northeastern counties in 1886, and the resultant low fuel prices, spurred the growth of energy-intensive glass factories. As America became captivated by the automobile, a racetrack for testing cars was built outside Indianapolis in 1908, and the famous 500-mile (805-kilometer) race on Memorial Day weekend began in 1911. Five years earlier, US Steel had constructed a steel plant at the south end of Lake Michigan. The town built by the company to house the workers was called Gary, and it grew rapidly with

Photo credit: Northern Indiana Historical Society.

The Oliver chilled plow developed by James Oliver, an industrialist who came to South Bend, Indiana, in the 1850s. A superior farm plow made of chilled and hardened steel, it revolutionized farming in the later half of the 19th century.

the help of the company and the onset of World War I.

World Wars

Although many Hoosiers of German and Irish descent favored neutrality when World War I began, Indiana industries boomed with war orders, and public sympathy swung heavily toward the Allies. Indiana furnished 118,000 men and women to the armed forces and suffered the loss of 3,370.

After 1920, only about a dozen makes of cars were still being manufactured in Indiana, and those factories steadily lost out to the three largest car makers in Detroit. Auto parts continued to be a big business, however, along with steelmaking and oil-refining in the Calumet region. Elsewhere there was manufacturing of machinery, farm implements, railway cars, furniture, and pharmaceuticals. Meat-packing, coal-mining, and limestone-quarrying continued to be important. With increasing industrialization, cities grew, particularly in the northern half of the state, and the number of farms diminished. The balance of rural and urban population, about even in 1920, tilted in favor of urban dwellers.

World War II had a greater impact on Indiana than did World War I. Most factories converted to production of war materials, and 300 of them held defense orders in 1942. Military training facilities were created. Camp Atterbury covered 100 square miles (259 square kilometers) in Bartholomew County, and two air stations trained aviators. Two large ammunition depots loaded and stored shells, and the enormous Jefferson Proving Grounds tested ammunition and parachutes.

Post-War Period

After the war, many small local industries were taken over by national corporations, and their plants were expanded. By 1984, the largest employer in Indiana was General Motors, with 47,800 employees in six cities. Inland Steel, with 18,500 workers, was second, followed by US Steel with 13,800 workers.

Nostalgia for an older, simpler, rural way of life pervades much Hoosier thinking. The state's conservation efforts were guided by Richard Lieber, a state official during 1915–33. During the 1930s and 1940s, Lieber nationally promoted the preservation of land for state parks and recreational areas as well as for state and federal forests.

Hoosiers enjoy politics and participate intensively in conventions and elections. The percentage of registered voters who vote has generally exceeded the national average by a wide margin. The state legislature was dominated by rural interests until a 1966 reorganization gave urban counties more representation.

12 STATE GOVERNMENT

The Indiana general assembly consists of a 50-member senate elected to four-year terms, with half the senators elected every two years, and a 100-member house of representatives elected to two-year terms. The state's chief executive is the governor, elected to a four-year term. The governor may call special sessions of the legislature and may veto bills passed by the legislature, but his veto can be overridden by a majority vote in each house.

Indiana's other top elected officials are the lieutenant governor, secretary of state, treasurer, auditor, attorney general, and superintendent of public instruction. Each is elected to a four-year term. The lieutenant governor is constitutionally empowered to preside over the state senate and to act as governor if that office should become vacant or the governor is unable to discharge his duties. Legislation may be introduced in either house of the general assembly, although bills for raising revenue must originate in the house of representatives.

13 POLITICAL PARTIES

After voting Republican in four successive presidential elections, Indiana voted Democratic in 1876 and became a swing state. More recently, a Republican trend has been evident: the state voted Republican in 13 out of 14 presidential elections between 1940 and 1992.

In 1992, Indiana gave 43% of the vote to Republican George Bush, 37% to Democrat Bill Clinton, and 20% to Independent Ross Perot. Democrat Evan Bayh was elected to his second term as governor. Richard Lugar, a Republican, won election to his fourth term in the Senate in 1994, and Daniel Coats, also a Republican, was reelected in 1992. Indiana's 1994 delegation to the US House of Representatives included seven Democrats and three Republicans. In the state senate, Republicans numbered 28; Democrats, 22. In the state house, there were 55 Democrats and 45 Republicans.

14 LOCAL GOVERNMENT

Counties in Indiana have traditionally provided law enforcement in rural areas, operated county courts and institutions, maintained county roads, administered public welfare programs, and collected taxes. In 1984, counties were given the power to impose local income taxes. The county's business is conducted by a Board of County Commissioners, consisting of three members elected to four-year terms.

Townships provide assistance for the poor and assess taxable property. Each township is administered by a trustee elected to a four-year term. Indiana had 566 municipal governments in 1992. They are governed by elected city councils varying in membership from five to 25 persons.

15 JUDICIAL SYSTEM

The Indiana supreme court consists of five justices who are appointed by the governor. The state court of appeals consists of 15 justices. The court exercises appeals jurisdiction under rules set by the state supreme court. Superior courts, probate courts, and circuit courts all function as general trial courts and are presided over by 242 judges who serve a term of six years. Indiana had 14,470 prisoners in state and federal correctional facilities in 1993. For 1994, the FBI Crime Index reported 30,205 instances of violent crime, or 525.1 per 100,000.

16 MIGRATION

The principal migratory pattern since 1920 has been within the state, from the farms to the cities. Since World War II, Indiana has lost population through a growing migratory movement to other states, mostly to Florida and the Southwest. From 1985 to 1990, however, there was a net gain in migration of over 35,000, 90% of whom came from abroad. As of 1990, 71.1% of all state residents had been born in Indiana.

17 ECONOMY

Indiana is both a leading agricultural and industrial state. The state's industrial development in Indianapolis, Gary, and

Indiana Presidential Vote by Political Parties, 1948–92

YEAR	INDIANA WINNER	DEMOCRAT	REPUBLICAN	PROGRESSIVE	PROHIBITION
1948	Dewey (R)	807,833	821,079	9,649	14,711
1952	*Eisenhower (R)	801,530	1,136,259	1,222	15,335
1956	*Eisenhower (R)	783,908	1,182,811	—	6,554
1960	*Nixon (R)	952,358	1,175,120	—	6,746
1964	*Johnson (D)	1,170,848	911,118	—	8,266
				AMERICAN IND.	
1968	*Nixon (R)	806,659	1,067,885	243,108	4,616
				PEOPLE'S	SOC. WORKERS
1972	*Nixon (R)	708,568	1,405,154	4,544	5,575
				AMERICAN	
1976	Ford (R)	1,014,714	1,185,958	14,048	5,695
				CITIZENS	LIBERTARIAN
1980	*Reagan (R)	844,197	1,255,656	4,852	19,627
1984	*Reagan (R)	841,481	1,377,230	—	6,741
				NEW ALLIANCE	
1988	*Bush (R)	860,643	1,297,763	10,215	—
1992	Bush (R)	848,420	989,375	455,934	7,936

* Won US presidential election.

other cities was based on its plentiful natural resources—coal, natural gas, timber, stone, and clay—and on good transportation facilities. The northwestern corner of the state is the site of one of the world's greatest concentrations of heavy industry, especially steel.

The largest employers among the manufacturing industries in 1992 included electric and electronic equipment, with 75,300 workers; primary metals, with 66,100 employees; and machinery (except electrical), with 65,200 on its payroll. In 1992, manufacturing companies earned $23,534 million, or 30.8% of the total earnings of private industries. Indiana ranks first in the production of raw steel, limestone, mobile homes, radios and television sets, and engine electronic equipment.

18 INCOME

In 1994, Indiana ranked 28th among the 50 states in individual personal income, with an average of $20,262 per capita (per person). Total earned income in 1994 amounted to $116.5 billion. About 704,000 persons (12.2% of the population) had incomes below the federal poverty level in 1993.

19 INDUSTRY

The industrialization of Indiana that began in the Civil War era was spurred by technological advances in processing agricultural products, manufacturing farm equipment, and improving transportation facilities. Meat-packing plants, textile mills, furniture factories, and wagon works—including Studebaker wagons—

were soon followed by metal foundries, machine shops, farm implement plants, and various other durable-goods plants.

In 1991, the estimated total value of shipments by manufacturers in Indiana was $97.2 billion. Among the leading industry groups in 1991 were transportation equipment, primary metal products, chemicals, food products, and electrical equipment. Indiana is a leading producer of storage batteries, small motors and generators, mobile homes, household furniture, burial caskets, and musical instruments. Most manufacturing plants are located in and around Indianapolis and in the Calumet region.

20 LABOR

In 1994, the state's civilian labor force totaled 3,056,000 persons. In 1994, Indiana had an unemployment rate of 4.9%.

In 1994, 19.3% of all workers were members of unions. Thirteen national labor unions were operating in the state in 1993.

21 AGRICULTURE

Agriculture remains vital to the state's economy, and nearly 68% of its total area is farmland. There were 63,000 farms being worked in 1994, when farmland totaled 15.6 million acres (6.3 million hectares). In 1994, Indiana ranked 12th among the 50 states in cash farm receipts. The state's total farm marketings that year were valued at $4.8 billion. The leading crops were corn and soybeans.

In 1994, Indiana ranked fourth in bushels of soybeans produced, and fifth in production of corn for grain. Corn and soybeans, respectively, accounted for 28% and 26% of total agricultural receipts in 1994. Indiana's principal field crops were as follows:

CROPS	ACREAGE (1,000)	PRODUCTION	
Corn	5,960.0	858,240,000	bushels
Soybeans	4,680.0	219,960,000	bushels
Wheat	630.0	38,430,000	bushels
Hay	650.0	2,110,000	tons
Tobacco	7.1	15,265,000	tons
Oats	35.0	1,855,000	bushels

22 DOMESTICATED ANIMALS

In 1994, hog production accounted for 13.8% of total agricultural receipts. In that year, about 36.5% of the state's farm income came from the sale of livestock and livestock products, which amounted to $1.76 billion.

In 1994, dairy farms accounted for 6.1% of agricultural receipts. The numbers of livestock on Indiana farms at the end of 1994 were hogs, 4,500,000; cattle, 1,170,000; milk cows 145,000; and sheep, 75,000. Indiana poultry farmers raised 26,400,000 chickens in 1994. Other animal products are honey, beeswax, and wool.

23 FISHING

Fishing is not of commercial importance in Indiana. In 1992, only 1,358,000 pounds of fish valued at $2,550,000 were landed. Fishing for bass, pike, perch, catfish, and trout is a popular sport with Indiana anglers.

24 FORESTRY

About 19% of Indiana land is forested. Indiana has 4,439,200 acres (1,820,072 hectares) of forestland. Indiana has always been noted for the quality of its hardwood forests and the trees it produces. It presently is the third leading producer of hardwood lumber, following Pennsylvania and North Carolina. In the southern half of Indiana, oak, hickory, beech, maple, yellow poplar, and ash predominate in the uplands. Soft maple, sweetgum, pin oak, cottonwood, sycamore, and river birch are the most common species found in wetlands and drainage corridors.

Approximately 49,000 Hoosiers are employed in Indiana's wood-using industry, which pays over $800 million in wages annually. Indiana's wood-using industries manufacture everything from the "crinkle" center lining in cardboard boxes to the finest furniture in the world. Products such as pallets, desks, fancy face veneer, millwork, flooring, mobile homes and even recreational vehicles use about 500 million board feet of lumber each year.

25 MINING

The value of nonfuel mineral production in Indiana in 1994 was about $517 million, the highest ever recorded in the state. The state's top two mineral commodities, crushed stone and cement, each accounted for approximately 35% of Indiana's total nonfuel value. Indiana was among the nation's top ten states in output of both of these commodities, and seventh in production of crude gypsum in 1992. In 1992, Indiana was the leading producer of dimension stone in the United States, with

20% of the nation's dimension stone being quarried in Indiana.

26 ENERGY AND POWER

In 1992, Indiana's gross energy consumption totaled 2,408 trillion Btu, of which 51% was provided by coal, 31% by petroleum products, 17% by dry natural gas, and 1% by other sources. The state has no nuclear power plants. Per capita (per person) energy consumption in the state in 1992 was 425.5 million Btu. Indiana ranks high in energy expenditures per capita—$2,051 in 1992.

Electric power produced in Indiana in 1993 totaled 100 billion kilowatt hours.

Indiana's estimated proved reserves of petroleum totaled 16 million barrels; production of crude petroleum totaled three million barrels. In 1992 Indiana's coal production was estimated at 32 million short tons of coal, ninth in the US. Recoverable reserves totaled 10.1 billion short tons.

27 COMMERCE

Wholesale sales in 1992 totaled $52.4. billion; retail sales in 1993 totaled $45.8 billion; and service establishment receipts in 1992 were $19.6 billion. Indiana ranked 16th among the 50 states in exports during 1992, when its farm products shipped abroad were valued at $6.2 billion.

28 PUBLIC FINANCE

The State Budget Agency acts as a watchdog over state financial affairs.

Photo credit: South Bend/Mishawaka Convention and Visitors Bureau.

A kayaker looking at Century Center, South Bend.

The total estimated revenues for fiscal year 1989/90 were $16,396.9 million; expenditures were $15,309.9 million.

The total indebtedness of the state government was nearly $5.5 billion in 1993. This debt amounted to $957 per capita (per person). Indiana has a constitutional prohibition against the state government directly carrying debt. Therefore, the state uses entities tied with the private sector to issue bonds.

29 TAXATION

Indiana imposes property, gasoline, income, and sales taxes, as well as taxes on the manufacture and sale of alcoholic beverages. In 1994, the state sales tax was 5%, and the state tax on cigarettes was 15.5 cents per pack. The state's personal income tax was 3.4% of adjusted gross income. In the 1991 fiscal year, Indiana's state tax revenue totaled $6 billion, of which the tax per capita (per person) was about $1,102. The total federal income tax burden in Indiana amounted to $9.2 billion.

30 HEALTH

In 1992 the principal causes of death were heart disease, cancer, cerebrovascular diseases, pulmonary diseases, accidents, and suicide. Indiana had 115 community hospitals in 1993, with 21,300 beds. The state had 9,600 nonfederal physicians and about 39,600 nurses in that year. The average expense for care per patient day came to $898, or $5,677 per stay. Some 11.9% of Indianans did not have health insurance coverage in 1993.

31 HOUSING

The great majority of Indiana families enjoy adequate housing, particularly in newly built suburbs, but inadequate housing exists in the deteriorating central cores of large cities. In 1993, the state had an estimated 2,329,000 housing units. The median monthly payment for mortgage and other selected costs was $561, and the median monthly cost for owners without a mortgage was $188. Median monthly rent was $374. In 1993, 30,803 new housing units were authorized for construction, at an estimated value of $2.8 billion.

Photo credit: South Bend/Mishawaka Convention and Visitors Bureau.

University of Notre Dame, Hesburgh Library.

32 EDUCATION

In 1990, 76% of those aged 25 years and over were high school graduates, and 15% had completed four years of college. In the fall of 1993, Indiana had about 965,000 pupils enrolled in public elementary and secondary schools. As of 1993/94, total nonpublic school enrollment came to 101,416. In 1993/94, Indiana spent more than $4.3 billion on public schools, or about $5,439 per pupil (24th in the nation).

In the 1992/93 academic year there were 384,842 students attending colleges and universities in the state. Indiana University, the state's largest institution of higher education, is one of the largest state universities in the US, with a total 1992/93 enrollment on seven campuses of 121,290. The Bloomington campus alone had 45,455 students. Other major state universities are Purdue University (Lafayette), Ball State University (Muncie), and Indiana State University (Terre Haute). Well-known private universities in the state include Notre Dame University (South Bend) and Butler University (Indianapolis). Small private schools include DePauw University (Greencastle) and Earlham College (Richmond).

33 ARTS

Indianapolis remains the state's cultural center, especially after the opening in the late 1960s of the Lilly Pavilion of the Decorative Arts; the Krannert Pavilion; the Clowes Art Pavilion; and the Grace Showalter Pavilion of the Performing Arts. Since 1969, the Indiana Arts Commission has taken art—and artists—into many Indiana communities; the commission also sponsors biennial awards to artists in the state.

Amateur theater has been popular since the founding in 1915 of the nation's oldest amateur drama group, the Little Theater Society, which later became the Civic Theater of Indianapolis. The Indiana Repertory Theatre's Junior Works Program received $85,000 from the National Endowment for the Arts (NEA). Music has flourished in Indiana. There are 23 symphony orchestras in the state. The Arthur Jordan College of Music of Butler University in Indianapolis and Indiana University's School of Music in Bloomington are major music schools. From 1987 to 1991, federal and state funding for the arts in Indiana amounted to $17,302,012.

34 LIBRARIES AND MUSEUMS

In 1991 there were 53 county libraries, and every county received some form of library service. The largest book collections are at public libraries in Indianapolis, Fort Wayne, Gary, Evansville, South Bend, and Hammond. The total book stock of all Indiana public libraries was 18,138,785 volumes in 1991. The Indiana State Library maintains a major collection of documents about Indiana's history and a large genealogical collection.

Private libraries and museums include those maintained by historical societies in Indianapolis, Fort Wayne, and South Bend. Also of note are the General Lew Wallace Study museum in Crawfordsville and the Elwood Haynes Museum of early technology in Kokomo. In all, Indiana had 162 museums in 1994. Indiana's historic sites of most interest to visitors are the Lincoln Boyhood National Memorial near Gentryville, and the Benjamin Harrison Memorial Home and the James Whitcomb Riley Home, both in Indianapolis.

35 COMMUNICATIONS

About 91% of all households had telephone service in March 1993. The state's first radio station was licensed in 1922 at Purdue University, Lafayette. Indiana had 87 AM and 190 FM radio stations and 30 commercial and 9 educational television stations as of 1993. Powerful radio and television transmissions from Chicago and

Cincinnati also blanket the state. In 1993, 19 large cable systems served the state.

36 PRESS

In 1994, the state had 15 morning dailies and 56 evening dailies; Sunday papers numbered 21. In 1994, the Indianapolis morning *Star* had a daily circulation of 231,892 (Sunday circulation, 416,752); the Indianapolis evening *News* had a daily circulation of 95,598; and the Gary evening *Post-Tribune's* circulation averaged 72,992 daily and 85,721 on Sundays.

A number of national magazines are published in Indiana, including *Children's Digest* and *The Saturday Evening Post*. Indiana University Press is an important publisher of scholarly books.

37 TOURISM, TRAVEL, AND RECREATION

Tourism is of moderate economic importance to Indiana. Summer resorts are located in the north, along Lake Michigan and in Steuben and Kosciusko counties, where there are nearly 200 lakes. Popular tourist sites include the reconstructed village of New Harmony, site of famous communal living experiments in the early 19th century; the Indianapolis Motor Speedway and Museum; and the George Rogers Clark National Historic Park at Vincennes.

Among the natural attractions are the Indiana Dunes National Lakeshore on Lake Michigan; the state's largest waterfall, Cataract Falls, near Cloverdale; and the largest underground cavern, at Wyandotte. Indiana has 18 state parks, comprising 53,870 acres (21,800 hectares). The largest state park is Brown County (15,543 acres—6,290 hectares), near Nashville.

38 SPORTS

Indiana is represented in professional sports by the Indiana Pacers of the National Basketball Association and by the National Football League's Colts, who moved to Indianapolis from Baltimore in 1984. Indianapolis is also represented in baseball's Class AAA American Association. The state's biggest annual sport event is the Indianapolis 500, which has been held at the Indianapolis Motor Speedway on Memorial Day weekend almost every year since 1911. The state's most popular amateur sport is basketball.

Collegiate football in Indiana has a colorful tradition stretching back to at least 1913, when Knute Rockne of Notre Dame unleashed the forward pass as a potent football weapon. Notre Dame won the following string of bowl games: the Orange Bowl in 1975 and 1990, and the Cotton Bowl in 1971, 1978, 1979, 1993, and 1994. Indiana and Purdue Universities compete in the Big Ten.

39 FAMOUS INDIANANS

Indiana has contributed one US president and five vice-presidents to the nation. Benjamin Harrison (b.Ohio, 1833–1901), the 23d president, was a Republican who served one term (1889–93) and then returned to Indianapolis, where his home is now a national historic landmark. Three vice-presidents were Indiana residents: Thomas Hendricks (b.Ohio, 1819–85), who served only eight months under

The 1995 Indianapolis 500 Mile Race, high start.

President Cleveland and died in office; Schuyler Colfax (b.New York, 1823–85), who served under President Grant; and Charles Fairbanks (b.Ohio, 1852–1918), who served under Theodore Roosevelt. Two vice-presidents were native sons: Thomas Marshall of North Manchester (1854–1925), who served two four-year terms with President Wilson; and J(ames) Danforth Quayle of Indianapolis (b. 1947), who served with President George Bush during 1988–92.

A dozen native and adoptive Hoosiers have held cabinet posts, including postmasters general Will H. Hays (1879–1954), who resigned to become president of the Motion Picture Producers and Distributors (1922–45) and enforced its moral code in Hollywood films. Only one Hoosier, Sherman Minton (1890–1965), has served on the US Supreme Court. Ambrose Burnside (1824–81) and Lew Wallace (1827–1905) were Union generals during the Civil War. Wallace later wrote popular religious-historical novels.

Harold C. Urey (1893–1981) won the Nobel Prize in chemistry in 1934, and Wendell Stanley (1904–71) won it in 1946. The Nobel Prize in economics was awarded to Paul Samuelson (b. 1915) in 1970. Booth Tarkington (1869–1946) won the Pulitzer Prize for fiction in 1918 and 1921. A. B. Guthrie (b.1901) won it for fiction in 1950. Aviation pioneer

Wilbur Wright (1867–1912) was born in Millville. Alfred C. Kinsey (b.New Jersey, 1894–1956) investigated human sexual behavior and issued the famous "Kinsey Reports" in 1948 and 1953.

The best-known poet was James Whitcomb Riley (1849–1916). Juvenile writer Annie Fellows Johnston (1863–1931) produced the "Little Colonel" series. Other notable Indiana novelists include Theodore Dreiser (1871–1945), Jessamyn West (1907–84), and Kurt Vonnegut (b.1922). Well-known journalists were war correspondent Ernie Pyle (1900–45) and columnist Janet Flanner (1892–1978) who wrote as "Genet" at *The New Yorker*.

Among the noted painters Indiana has produced are William M. Chase (1851–1927), Marie Goth (1887–1975), and Floyd Hopper (b.1909). Composers of Indiana origin have worked mainly in popular music: Cole Porter (1893–1964) and Howard Hoagland "Hoagy" Carmichael

(1899–1981). Howard Hawks (1896–1977) was a renowned film director. Entertainers from Indiana include actor and dancer Clifton Webb (Webb Hollenbeck, 1896–1966); comedians Richard "Red" Skelton (b.1913) and David Letterman (b.1947); actress Carole Lombard (Jane Peters, 1908–42); and singer Michael Jackson (b.1958).

Hoosier sports heroes include Knute Rockne (b.Norway, 1888–1931), famed as a football player and coach at Notre Dame. Larry Bird (b.1956) was college basketball's player of the year at Indiana State University in 1978/79 and went on to play for the Boston Celtics of the NBA.

40 BIBLIOGRAPHY

Carter, Jared, and Darryl Jones. *Indiana*. Portland, Ore.: Graphic Arts Center Publishing Co., 1984.

Dorson, Ron. *The Indy Five Hundred*. New York: Norton, 1974.

Federal Writers' Project. *Indiana: A Guide to the Hoosier State*. Reprint. New York: Somerset, n.d. (orig. 1941).

Wilson, William E. *Indiana: A History*. Bloomington: Indiana University Press, 1966.

IOWA

ORIGIN OF STATE NAME: From a Siouan term meaning "beautiful land." Named for Iowa Indians of the Siouan family.

NICKNAME: The Hawkeye State.

CAPITAL: Des Moines.

ENTERED UNION: 28 December 1846 (29th).

SONG: "The Song of Iowa."

MOTTO: Our Liberties We Prize and Our Rights We Will Maintain.

FLAG: There are three vertical stripes of blue, white, and red; in the center a spreading eagle holds in its beak a blue ribbon with the state motto.

OFFICIAL SEAL: A sheaf and field of standing wheat and farm utensils represent agriculture; a lead furnace and a pile of pig lead are to the right. In the center stands a citizen-soldier holding a US flag with a liberty cap atop the staff in one hand and a rifle in the other. Behind him is the Mississippi River with the steamer *Iowa* and mountains; above him an eagle holds the state motto. Surrounding this scene are the words "The Great Seal of the State of Iowa" against a gold background.

BIRD: Eastern goldfinch.

FLOWER: Wild rose.

TREE: Oak.

STONE: Geode.

TIME: 6 AM CST = noon GMT.

1 LOCATION AND SIZE

Located in the western north-central US, Iowa is the smallest of the midwestern states situated west of the Mississippi River, and ranks 25th in size among the 50 states. The total area of Iowa is 56,275 square miles (145,752 square kilometers). The state extends 324 miles (521 kilometers) east-west. Its maximum extension north-south is 210 miles (338 kilometers). Its total boundary length is 1,151 miles (1,853 kilometers).

2 TOPOGRAPHY

The physical terrain of Iowa consists of a gently rolling plain. Iowa has the richest and deepest topsoil in the US. The state is drained by the Mississippi River and Missouri rivers and has 13 natural lakes.

3 CLIMATE

Iowa lies in the humid continental zone and generally has hot summers, cold winters, and wet springs. Temperatures vary widely during the year, with an annual average of 49°F (9°C). Des Moines, in the central part of the state, has a normal daily maximum temperature of 86°F (30°C) in July and a normal daily minimum of 10°F (–4°C) in January. The record low temperature for the state of Iowa is –47°F (–44°C). The record high is 118°F (48°C). Rainfall averages 32 inches (81 centimeters) annually, and snowfall, 30 inches (76 centimeters).

4 PLANTS AND ANIMALS

Although most of Iowa is under cultivation, such unusual wild specimens as bunchberry and bearberry can be found in the northeast. Other notable plants are pink lady's slipper and twinleaf.

Common Iowa mammals include red and gray foxes, raccoon, opossum, and woodchuck. Common birds include the cardinal, rose-breasted grosbeak, and eastern goldfinch (the state bird). Game fish include rainbow trout, smallmouth bass, and walleye. Among endangered species listed by the state are the red-backed vole, black bear, bobcat, and piping plover.

5 ENVIRONMENTAL PROTECTION

In the 1980s and 1990s, Iowans were particularly concerned with improving air quality, preventing chemical pollution, and preserving water supplies. Iowa produces 850 tons of solid waste annually. The state had 83 municipal landfills and two curbside recycling programs operating in the state in 1991. Iowa devoted 4.2% of its total budget to the environment in 1991 ($62.26 per person). In 1994, the state had 19 hazardous waste sites.

Iowa Population Profile

Estimated 1995 population:	2,703,000
Population change, 1980–90:	–4.7%
Leading ancestry group:	German
Second leading group:	Irish
Foreign born population:	1.6%
Hispanic origin†:	1.2%
Population by race:	
White:	96.6%
Black:	1.7%
Native American:	0.3%
Asian/Pacific Islander:	0.9%
Other:	0.5%

Population by Age Group

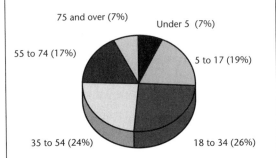

75 and over (7%)
Under 5 (7%)
55 to 74 (17%)
5 to 17 (19%)
35 to 54 (24%)
18 to 34 (26%)

Top Cities with Populations Over 25,000

City	Population	National rank	% change 1980–90
Des Moines	194,540	82	1.1
Cedar Rapids	111,659	172	–1.3
Davenport	97,508	208	–7.7
Sioux City	81,907	271	–1.8
Waterloo	67,124	356	–12.5
Iowa City	59,313	410	18.3
Dubuque	58,575	419	–7.7
Council Bluffs	54,884	458	–3.8
Ames	46,672	566	3.1
Cedar Falls	35,094	783	–5.5

Notes: †A person of Hispanic origin may be of any race. NA indicates that data are not available.
Sources: Economic and Statistics Administration, Bureau of the Census. *Statistical Abstract of the United States, 1994–95.* Washington, DC: Government Printing Office, 1995; Courtenay M. Slater and George E. Hall. *1995 County and City Extra: Annual Metro, City and County Data Book.* Lanham, MD: Bernan Press, 1995.

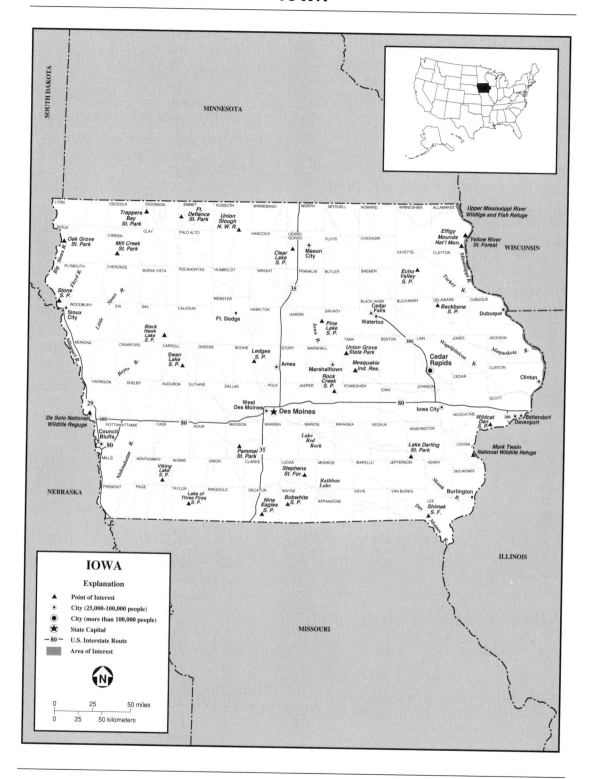

IOWA

Explanation

▲ Point of Interest
⊙ City (25,000-100,000 people)
◉ City (more than 100,000 people)
★ State Capital
– 80 – U.S. Interstate Route
▨ Area of Interest

0   25   50 miles
0   25   50 kilometers

6 POPULATION

Iowa is the 25th in size of the 50 states. It ranked 30th in state population at the 1990 census, with 2,776,755 residents. The estimated population for 1995 is 2,703,000. Population density was 49.7 persons per square mile (19 persons per square kilometer). In 1990, 60.6% of all Iowans lived in urban areas. Iowa is tied for second at 15.1% with Pennsylvania and behind only Florida in the concentration of population over 65. In 1992, the largest cities were: Des Moines, 194,540; Cedar Rapids, 111,659; Davenport, 97,508; and Sioux City, 81,907. In 1990, the Des Moines metropolitan area had 392,928 residents.

7 ETHNIC GROUPS

In 1990, there were 48,000 black Americans, 7,000 American Indians, and 33,000 people of Hispanic origin living in Iowa. Among Iowans of European descent there were 1,394,542 Germans; 536,720 English, Scottish, or Welsh; 527,428 Irish; and 152,084 Norwegians. The foreign-born population numbered 43,316 in 1990, and their main countries of origin included Germany, Mexico, Laos, Canada, Korea, and Vietnam.

8 LANGUAGES

Iowa English reflects the three major migration streams: Northern in that half of the state above Des Moines and North Midland in the southern half, with a slight South Midland trace in the extreme southeastern corner. In 1990, 96.1% of all Iowans aged five or more spoke only English at home. Other languages reported by Iowans, and the number speaking each at home, included German, 21,429; Spanish, 31,620; and French, 7,941.

9 RELIGIONS

In 1990 there were more than 1,154,034 Protestants, including 272,098 members of the United Methodist Church, 124,021 adherents of the Lutheran Church-Missouri Synod, and 50,771 adherents of the Disciples of Christ (Christian Church). Roman Catholic membership totaled 520,322 and the Jewish population was 6,701.

10 TRANSPORTATION

As of 1991, Iowa had 4,448 rail miles (7,157 kilometers) of railroad track. Amtrak operates the long-distance California Zephyr (Chicago–Oakland, California), with 51,914 Iowa riders in 1991/92. Iowa ranked 11th among the states in road mileage in 1993. The state had 103,490 miles (166,515 kilometers) of rural roads and 9,218 miles (14,832 kilometers) of urban roads, including 783 miles (1,260 kilometers) of interstate highways. There were 1,947,821 registered automobiles and 781,282 trucks and buses in the state.

Iowa is bordered by two great navigable rivers, the Mississippi and the Missouri. Freight is still transported by water as far east as Pennsylvania and west to Oklahoma. The busiest airfield is Des Moines Municipal Airport, which handled 12,796 departures and 677,739 boarded passengers in 1991.

Photo credit: Greater Des Moines Convention & Visitors Bureau.

Des Moines has the largest skywalk system per capita in the world.

11 HISTORY

The first permanent settlers of the land were the Woodland Indians, who built villages in the forested areas along the Mississippi River and introduced agriculture. Not until June 1673 did the first known white men, explorer Louis Jolliet and the Catholic priest Jacques Marquette, come to the territory. Iowa was part of the vast Louisiana Territory that extended from the Gulf of Mexico to the Canadian border and was ruled by the French until the title was transferred to Spain in 1762.

Napoleon took the territory back in 1800 and then promptly sold all of Louisiana Territory to the amazed American envoys who had come to Paris seeking only the purchase of New Orleans and the mouth of the Mississippi. After Iowa had thus come under US control in 1803, the Lewis and Clark expedition worked its way up the Missouri River to explore the newly purchased land.

Placed under the territorial jurisdiction of Michigan in 1834, and then two years later under the newly created Territory of Wisconsin, Iowa became a separate territory in 1838. The first territorial governor, Robert Lucas, began planning for statehood by drawing aggressive boundary lines that extended county boundaries and local government westward and northward. Under the Missouri Compromise,

Iowa came into the Union with Florida as its slaveholding counterpart. A serious dispute, concerning how large the state would be, delayed Iowa's admission into the Union until 28 December 1846.

State Development

The settlement of Iowa was rapidly accomplished. With one-fourth of the nation's fertile topsoil located within its borders, Iowa was a powerful magnet that drew farmers by the thousands from many areas. The settlers were overwhelmingly Protestant in religion and remarkably uniform in ethnic and cultural backgrounds. Fiercely proud of its claim to be the first free state created out of the Louisiana Purchase, Iowa was an important center of abolitionist sentiment throughout the 1850s. The Underground Railroad for fugitive slaves from the South ran across the southern portion of Iowa to the Mississippi River. When the Civil War came, Iowa overwhelmingly supported the Union cause.

The railroad had been lavishly welcomed by Iowans in the 1850s. By the 1870s, Iowa farmers were battling the railroad interests for effective regulatory legislation. The National Grange (an association of farmers) was powerful enough in Iowa to push through the so-called Granger laws regulating the railroads. Following World War I, conservatives regained control of the ruling Republican Party and remained in control until the 1960s. Then new liberal leadership was forced on the party after the disastrous 1964 presidential campaign of Barry Goldwater and effective opposition from a revitalized Democratic Party led by Harold Hughes.

After Hughes gave up the governorship in 1969 to become a US senator, he was succeeded in office by Robert Ray, a liberal Republican who dominated the state throughout the 1970s. Iowa's economy suffered in the 1980s from a combination of high debt and interest rates, numerous droughts, and low crop prices. Businesses departed or shrank their work forces. By the 1990s, however, the companies that had survived were in a much stronger position, and Iowa began enjoying a period of cautious prosperity. The state's unemployment rate in 1992 was 4.7 percent, lower than the national average.

In 1993, unusually heavy spring and summer rains produced record floods along the Mississippi River by mid-July. The entire state of Iowa was declared a disaster area. The floods forced 11,200 people to evacuate their homes and caused $2.2 billion in damages.

12 STATE GOVERNMENT

The state legislature, or general assembly, consists of a 50-member senate and a 100-member house of representatives. Each house may introduce or amend legislation, with a simple majority vote required for passage. The governor's veto of a bill may be overridden by a two-thirds majority in both houses. The state's elected executives are the governor, lieutenant governor, secretary of state, auditor, treasurer, attorney general, and secretary of agriculture.

13 POLITICAL PARTIES

For 70 years following the Civil War, a majority of Iowa voters supported the Republicans over the Democrats in nearly all state and national elections. During the Great Depression of the 1930s, Iowa briefly turned to the Democrats, supporting Franklin D. Roosevelt in two presidential elections. But from 1940 through 1992, the majority of Iowans voted Republican in 10 of 12 presidential elections. Republicans won 34 of the 42 gubernatorial elections from 1900 through 1990 and controlled both houses of the state legislature for 112 of the 130 years from 1855 to 1984.

In 1992, Iowa gave Democrat Bill Clinton 43% of the vote, while Republican George Bush received 37%, and Independent Ross Perot picked up 19%. Republicans had a 4–2 edge in the US House delegation, and Terry Branstad, a Republican, won election to a fourth term as governor in 1994. As of 1994, a Democrat and a Republican both served in the US Senate—Republican Charles Grassley, who won election to a third term in 1992, and Democrat Tom Harkin, who won re-election in 1990. After the November 1994 elections, there were 27 Democrats and 23 Republicans in the state senate, and 64 Republicans and 36 Democrats in the state house.

Iowa's presidential caucuses are held in January of presidential campaign years. This is earlier than any other state, thus giving Iowans a degree of influence in national politics.

Iowa Presidential Vote by Political Parties, 1948–92

YEAR	IOWA WINNER	DEMOCRAT	REPUBLICAN	PROGRESSIVE	PROHIBITION	SOCIALIST LABOR
1948	*Truman (D)	522,380	494,018	12,125	3,382	4,274
1952	*Eisenhower (R)	451,513	808,906	5,085	2,882	—
						CONSTITUTION
1956	*Eisenhower (R)	501,858	729,187	—	—	3,202
1960	Nixon (R)	550,565	722,381	—	—	—
1964	*Johnson (D)	733,030	449,148	—	1,902	—
				SOC. WORKERS	AMERICAN IND.	
1968	*Nixon (R)	476,699	619,106	3,377	66,422	—
					AMERICAN	PEACE AND FREEDOM
1972	*Nixon (R)	496,206	706,207	—	22,056	1,332
						LIBERTARIAN
1976	Ford (R)	619,931	632,863	—	3,040	1,452
				CITIZENS		
1980	*Reagan (R)	508,672	676,026	2,191	NA	12,324
1984	*Reagan (R)	605,620	703,088	—	—	—
1988	Dukakis (D)	670,557	545,355	755	540	2,494
				IND. (Perot)		
1992	*Clinton (D)	586,353	504,891	253,468	3,079	1,177

* Won US presidential election.

Photo credit: Greater Des Moines Convention & Visitors Bureau.

The five-domed state capitol in Des Moines has a 23-karat gold center dome.

14 LOCAL GOVERNMENT

The state's 99 counties are governed by boards of supervisors consisting of three to five members. County officials enforce state laws, collect taxes, supervise welfare activities, and manage roads and bridges. Local government was exercised by 953 municipal units in 1992. The mayor-council system functioned in the great majority of these municipalities. The power to tax is authorized by the general assembly.

15 JUDICIAL SYSTEM

The Iowa supreme court consists of nine justices appointed by the governor, who select one of their number as chief justice. The court exercises appeals jurisdiction in civil and criminal cases, supervises the trial courts, and establishes the rules of civil and appeals procedure. The supreme court transfers certain cases to the five-member court of appeals. Iowa's total crime rate in 1994 was 3,654.6 per 100,000 population. As of 1993 there were 4,898 prisoners in federal and state institutions

16 MIGRATION

Iowa was opened, organized, and settled by a generation of migrants from other states. After 1850 they were joined by immigrants from northern Europe. During and immediately after the Civil War, some former slaves fled the South for Iowa, and more blacks settled in Iowa cities after

1900. Many of the migrants who came to Iowa did not stay long. Some Iowans left to join the gold rush, and others settled lands in the West. Migration out of the state has continued to this day, as retired Iowans seeking warmer climates have moved to California and other southwestern states. From 1970 through 1990, Iowa's net loss through migration amounted to over 266,000.

An important migratory trend within the state has been from the farm to the city. Although Iowa has remained a major agricultural state, the urban population increased to over 60.6% of the total population by 1990.

17 ECONOMY

Iowa's economy is based on agriculture. Although the value of the state's manufactures exceeds the value of its farm production, manufacturing is basically farm-centered. The major industries are food processing and the manufacture of agriculture-related products, such as farm machinery.

Technological progress in agriculture and the growth of manufacturing industries have enabled Iowans to enjoy general prosperity since World War II. In the early 1980s, high interest rates and falling land prices created serious economic difficulties for farmers and contributed to the continuing decline of the farm population. By 1992, the state had recovered.

18 INCOME

With a personal income per capita (per person) of $20,176 in 1994, Iowa ranked 30th among the 50 states. Total personal income was $57.1 billion in 1994. Some 10.3% of the population was below the federal poverty level in 1993.

19 INDUSTRY

Because Iowa was primarily a farm state, the first industries were food processing and the manufacture of farm implements. These industries have retained a key role in the economy. In recent years, Iowa has added a variety of others—including pens, washing machines, and even mobile homes.

20 LABOR

Since 1950, Iowa has consistently ranked above the national average in employment of its work force. Iowa's unemployment rate of 3.7% for 1994 was well below the overall US rate of 6.1%. The civilian labor force in 1994 totaled 1,565,000. In 1993, there were nine national labor unions operating in the state. As of 1994, 13.2% of all workers were union members.

21 AGRICULTURE

Iowa recorded a gross farm income of $10 billion in 1994. More than half of all cash receipts from marketing came from the sale of livestock and meat products. In that year, Iowa ranked first nationwide in output of corn for grain and soybeans. In 1994, Iowa had 101,000 farms, with an average size of 325 acres (132 hectares) per farm.

Nearly all of Iowa's land is tillable, and about 88% of it is given to farmland. Corn is grown practically everywhere, and wheat is raised in the southern half of the state and in counties bordering the Mississippi and Missouri rivers. In 1994, agricultural production included corn for grain, 1.93 billion bushels; soybeans, 447.2 million bushels; oats, 26.7 million bushels; and hay, 5.8 million tons.

22 DOMESTICATED ANIMALS

Iowa produced about 26% of the nation's pork in 1994. In that year, hog production accounted for 25.4% of agricultural receipts; cattle production, 17.2%. Livestock in 1994 included 14,200,000 hogs and 4,250,000 cattle. Iowa dairy farms accounted for 4.9% of agricultural receipts in 1994. In that year, the state's poultry producers raised 19.5 million chickens.

23 FISHING

Fishing has little commercial importance in Iowa. Game fishing in the rivers and lakes is a popular sport.

24 FORESTRY

In 1990, Iowa had 2.1 million acres of forestland, representing 5.7% of the state's land area. The state's lumber industry produced over 100 million board feet of lumber in 1990.

25 MINING

The value of nonfuel mineral production in Iowa was estimated at $426 million in 1994. Crushed stone (mostly limestone-dolomite) continued as the state's leading mineral commodity, accounting for almost 47% of the estimated total nonfuel mineral value.

26 ENERGY AND POWER

Although Iowa's fossil fuel resources are extremely limited, the state's energy supply has been adequate for consumer needs. In 1992, Iowa consumed 330.6 million Btu per capita (per person). According to 1991 estimates, oil supplied about 33% of the state's energy requirements, natural gas, 25%; coal, 37%; hydropower, less than 1%; and nuclear energy, 4%. There was one nuclear power plant in 1993. The state's production of electricity totaled 31 billion kilowatt hours in 1993. Coal-fired plants supplied 86% of this electricity. The state's per capita (per person) energy expenditures in 1992 were $1,889.

27 COMMERCE

Iowa had 1992 wholesale sales of $29.4 billion; 1993 retail sales of $24.3 billion; and 1992 service establishment receipts of $8.8 billion. The most valuable categories of goods traded were agricultural raw materials, durable goods, groceries and related products, and farm supplies. Iowa's exports of goods in 1992 had an estimated value of $2.5 billion.

28 PUBLIC FINANCE

The public budget is prepared by the state comptroller with the governor's approval and is adopted or revised by the general assembly.

Iowa's estimated fiscal year 1994 budget included revenues of $3,931,200,000 and expenditures of $3,524,400,000. The state had an outstanding debt of $651 per capita (per person) in 1993, or $1.8 billion total.

[29] TAXATION

In 1994, Iowa taxed personal income, corporate income, retail sales, gasoline, cigarettes, alcoholic beverages, insurance premiums, inheritances, chain stores, and business franchises.

[30] HEALTH

In 1993, Iowa's 119 community hospitals admitted some 348,000 patients, and hospital expenses averaged $612 per inpatient day with an average cost per stay of $4,980. As of 1993, there were an estimated 4,500 nonfederal doctors and 26,000 nurses. Some 9.2% of Iowans did not have health insurance in 1993.

[31] HOUSING

Iowa ranks high in the number of housing units that are family-owned and occupied. According to a 1993 estimate based on the 1990 census, there were 1,168,000 housing units. In 1993, the state authorized the construction of 11,100 new privately owned housing units, valued at $897 million. The median monthly cost for owners with a mortgage in 1990 was $553, one of the lowest amounts in the nation. The monthly median cost of housing for renters in 1990 was $336. The median value of a home in 1990 was $45,900, lower than any state except Mississippi and South Dakota.

[32] EDUCATION

Iowa's progressive public school system has been an innovator in school curriculum development, teaching methods, educational administration, and school financing. In 1993, Iowa had a total of 499,000 pupils enrolled in the public school system, 349,000 in grades K-8, and 150,000 in grades 9–12. Per pupil expenditures averaged $5,185 in 1993 (29th in the nation).

In fall 1991, 171,024 students were enrolled in institutions of higher learning. Iowa had three state universities, with 67,957 students; 35 private colleges; and 23 vocational schools and area community colleges. Small liberal arts colleges and universities include Cornell College, Mt. Vernon; Drake University, Des Moines; Briar Cliff College, Sioux City; Grinnell College, Grinnell; and Iowa Wesleyan College, Mt. Pleasant.

[33] ARTS

There is an opera company in Indianola, and there are art galleries, little theater groups, symphony orchestras, and ballet companies in the major cities and college towns. The Des Moines Arts Center is a leading exhibition gallery for native painters and sculptors. There are regional theater groups in Des Moines, Davenport, and Sioux City. The Writers' Workshop at the University of Iowa (Iowa City) has an international reputation. One problem for the arts in Iowa is the continued migration of native artists to cultural centers in New York, California, and elsewhere. From 1987 to 1991, the State of Iowa generated $9,596,975 from federal and state sources to support its art programs.

[34] LIBRARIES AND MUSEUMS

Beginning with the founding in 1873 of the state's first tax-supported library at Independence, Iowa's public library system has

Des Moines skyline.

grown to include total book holdings of 11,234,348 volumes in 1992. Iowa had 124 museums and zoological parks in 1994. The Herbert Hoover National Historical Site, in West Branch, houses the birthplace and grave of the 31st US president and a library and museum with papers and memorabilia.

35 COMMUNICATIONS

In March 1993, about 1,069,000 housing units, or 96.1% of all occupied units, had telephones. In 1993 there were 216 radio stations, including 83 AM stations and 133 FM stations. In 1993, Iowa had a total of 19 commercial television stations and 9 educational stations. In that year, five large cable television systems served the state. A statewide fiberoptic telecommunications system links all 99 counties.

36 PRESS

Overall, Iowa had 38 dailies (26 evening, 10 morning, 2 all-day) and 10 Sunday papers in 1994. The *Des Moines Register* remained the leader, with a morning circulation of 206,204 and a Sunday circulation of 344,522 as of 1994. Also published in Iowa were 113 periodicals, among them *Better Homes and Gardens* (circulation, 8,002,585), and *Successful Farming* (491,749).

37 TOURISM, TRAVEL, AND RECREATION

The Mississippi and Missouri rivers offer popular water sports facilities for both out-of-state visitors and resident vacationers. Notable tourist attractions include the Effigy Mounds National Monument (near Marquette), which has hundreds of prehistoric Indian mounds and village sites. Tourist sites in the central part of the state include the state capitol and the Herbert Hoover National Historic Site (West Branch), with its Presidential Library and Museum. Iowa has about 85,000 acres (34,400 hectares) of lakes and reservoirs and 19,000 miles (30,600 kilometers) of fishing streams. There are 66 state parks and 7 state forests.

38 SPORTS

Iowa has no major league professional sports teams. High school and college basketball and football teams draw thousands of spectators, particularly to the state high school basketball tournament at Des Moines in March. In intercollegiate competition, the University of Iowa Hawkeyes belong to the Big Ten Conference. They have a legendary wrestling program that has won the NCAA Championship 18 times since 1969. Iowa has over 350 golf courses, eight major ski areas, and is the nation's leading state in pheasant hunting.

39 FAMOUS IOWANS

Iowa was the birthplace of Herbert Clark Hoover (1874–1964), the first US president born west of the Mississippi. Hoover was buried in West Branch, the town of his birth. Iowa has also produced one US vice-president, Henry A. Wallace (1888–1965), who served in that office during Franklin D. Roosevelt's third term (1941–45) and ran unsuccessfully as the Progressive Party's presidential candidate in 1948.

Appropriately, Iowans have dominated the post of secretary of agriculture in this century with figures who included Henry A. Wallace; his father, Henry C. Wallace (b.Illinois, 1866–1924); and James "Tama Jim" Wilson (b.Scotland, 1835–1920), who served in that post for 16 years and set a record for longevity in a single cabinet office. Harry L. Hopkins (1890–1946) was Franklin D. Roosevelt's closest adviser in all policy matters, foreign and domestic. Prominent US senators from Iowa have included William Boyd Allison (b.Ohio, 1829–1908), chairman of the powerful Senate Appropriations Committee for nearly 30 years.

Among Iowa's most influential governors were the first territorial governor, Robert Lucas (b.Virginia, 1781–1853); William Larrabee (b.Connecticut, 1832–1912); and, in recent times, Harold Hughes. Iowa has produced a large number of radical dissenters and social reformers. Abolitionists, strong in Iowa before the Civil War, included Josiah B. Grinnell (b.Vermont, 1821–91), and Asa Turner (b.Massachusetts, 1799–1885). William "Billy" Sunday (1862–1935) was an evangelist with a large following among rural Americans. John L. Lewis (1880–1969), head of the United Mine Workers, founded the Congress of Industrial Organizations (CIO).

Iowa can claim two winners of the Nobel Peace Prize: religious leader John R. Mott (b.New York, 1865–1955), and agronomist and plant geneticist Norman E. Borlaug (b.1914). Distinguished scientist George Washington Carver (b.Missouri 1864–1943) was an Iowa resident. George H. Gallup (1904–84), a public-opinion analyst, originated the Gallup Polls.

Iowa writers of note include Hamlin Garland (b.Wisconsin, 1860–1940) and Wallace Stegner (1909–93). Two Iowa playwrights, Susan Glaspell (1882–1948) and her husband, George Cram Cook (1873–1924), were instrumental in founding influential theater groups. Columnists Abigail Van Buren (Pauline Esther Friedman, b.1918) and her twin sister Ann Landers (Esther Pauline Friedman Lederer, b.1918) are from Sioux City. Iowans who have contributed to America's musical heritage include popular composers Meredith Willson (1902–84) and Peter "PDQ Bach" Schickele (b. 1935), jazz musician Leon "Bix" Beiderbecke (1903–31), bandleader Glenn Miller (1904–44), and opera singer Simon Estes (b. 1938). Iowa's artists of note include Grant Wood (1892–1942), whose *American Gothic* is one of America's best-known paintings.

Iowa's contributions to the field of popular entertainment include William F. "Buffalo Bill" Cody (1846–1917); circus promoter Charles Ringling (1863–1926) and his four brothers; and one of America's best-loved movie actors, John Wayne (Marion Michael Morrison, 1907–79). Johnny Carson (b. 1925), host of the *Tonight Show* for many years, was born in Corning. Iowa sports figures of note are baseball Hall of Famers Adrian C. "Cap" Anson (1851–1922) and Robert "Bob" Feller (b.1918), and football All-American Nile Kinnick (1918–44).

40 BIBLIOGRAPHY

Iowa Development Commission. *1985 Statistical Profile of Iowa*. Des Moines, 1985.

Sage, Leland. *A History of Iowa*. Ames: Iowa State University Press, 1974.

Wall, Joseph Frazier. *Iowa: A Bicentennial History*. New York: Norton, 1978.

KANSAS

State of Kansas

ORIGIN OF STATE NAME: Named for the Kansa (or Kaw) Indians, the "people of the south wind."

NICKNAME: The Sunflower State. (Also: the Wheat State; the Jayhawk State.)

CAPITAL: Topeka.

ENTERED UNION: 29 January 1861 (34th).

SONG: "Home on the Range."

MARCH: "The Kansas March."

MOTTO: *Ad astra per aspera* (To the stars through difficulties).

FLAG: The flag consists of a dark blue field with the state seal in the center; a sunflower on a bar of twisted gold and blue is above the seal; the word "Kansas" is below it.

OFFICIAL SEAL: A sun rising over mountains in the background symbolizes the east; commerce is represented by a river and a steamboat. In the foreground, agriculture, the basis of the state's prosperity, is represented by a settler's cabin and a man plowing a field. Beyond this is a wagon train heading west and a herd of buffalo fleeing from two Indians. Around the top is the state motto above a cluster of 34 stars; the circle is surrounded by the words "Great Seal of the State of Kansas, January 29, 1861."

ANIMAL: American buffalo.

BIRD: Western meadowlark.

FLOWER: Wild native sunflower.

TREE: Cottonwood.

INSECT: Honeybee.

TIME: 6 AM CST = noon GMT; 5 AM MST = noon GMT.

1 LOCATION AND SIZE

Located in the western north-central US, Kansas is the second-largest midwestern state (following Minnesota) and ranks 14th among the 50 states. The total area of Kansas is 82,277 square miles (213,097 square kilometers). The state has a maximum extension east-west of about 411 miles (661 kilometers) and an extreme north-south distance of about 208 miles (335 kilometers). Kansas has a total boundary length of 1,219 miles (1,962 kilometers).

2 TOPOGRAPHY

Three main land regions define the state: the eastern third, consisting of plains, hills, and lowlands; the central third, comprised of the Smoky Hills to the north and the Great Bend Prairie and Red Hills to the south; and the high plains to the west. More than 50,000 streams run through the state, and there are hundreds of artificial lakes. Major rivers include the Missouri, the Arkansas, and the Kansas.

3 CLIMATE

Kansas's continental climate is highly changeable. The average mean temperature is 55°F (13°C). The record high in the state is 121°F (149°C), and the record low is –40°F (–40°C). The normal annual precipitation ranges from slightly more than 40 inches (101.6 centimeters) in the southeast to as little as 16 inches (40.6 centimeters) in the west. Tornadoes are a regular fact of Kansas life.

4 PLANTS AND ANIMALS

Native grasses cover one-third of Kansas, which is much overgrazed. Bluestem—both big and little—grows in most parts of the state. One native conifer, eastern red cedar, is found generally throughout the state. Hackberry, black walnut, and sycamore grow in the east, while box elder and cottonwood predominate in western Kansas. The wild native sunflower, the state flower, is found throughout the state. Other characteristic wildflowers include coneflower and black-eyed Susan.

Kansas's native mammals include the common cottontail, black-tailed jackrabbit, and black-tailed prairie dog. The western meadowlark is the state bird. The black-footed ferret, gray bat, and bald eagle are threatened or endangered.

5 ENVIRONMENTAL PROTECTION

No environmental problem is more crucial to Kansas than water quality. A law passed in 1979 mandated each county with a

Kansas Population Profile

Estimated 1995 population:	2,515,320
Population change, 1980–90:	4.8%
Leading ancestry group:	German
Second leading group:	Irish
Foreign born population:	2.5%
Hispanic origin†:	3.8%
Population by race:	
White:	90.0%
Black:	5.8%
Native American:	0.9%
Asian/Pacific Islander:	1.3%
Other:	2.0%

Population by Age Group

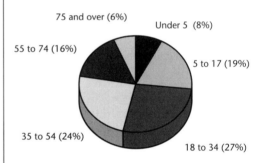

75 and over (6%)
Under 5 (8%)
55 to 74 (16%)
5 to 17 (19%)
35 to 54 (24%)
18 to 34 (27%)

Top Cities with Populations Over 25,000

City	Population	National rank	% change 1980–90
Wichita	311,746	51	8.9
Kansas City	146,507	117	–7.0
Topeka	120,257	151	4.0
Overland Park	119,260	153	36.7
Lawrence	67,824	348	24.4
Olathe	67,510	351	70.0
Salina	43,304	612	1.1
Leavenworth	40,782	667	14.4
Shawnee	39,508	687	28.2
Hutchinson	39,320	695	–2.4

Notes: †A person of Hispanic origin may be of any race. NA indicates that data are not available.
Sources: Economic and Statistics Administration, Bureau of the Census. *Statistical Abstract of the United States, 1994–95.* Washington, DC: Government Printing Office, 1995; Courtenay M. Slater and George E. Hall. *1995 County and City Extra: Annual Metro, City and County Data Book.* Lanham, MD: Bernan Press, 1995.

KANSAS

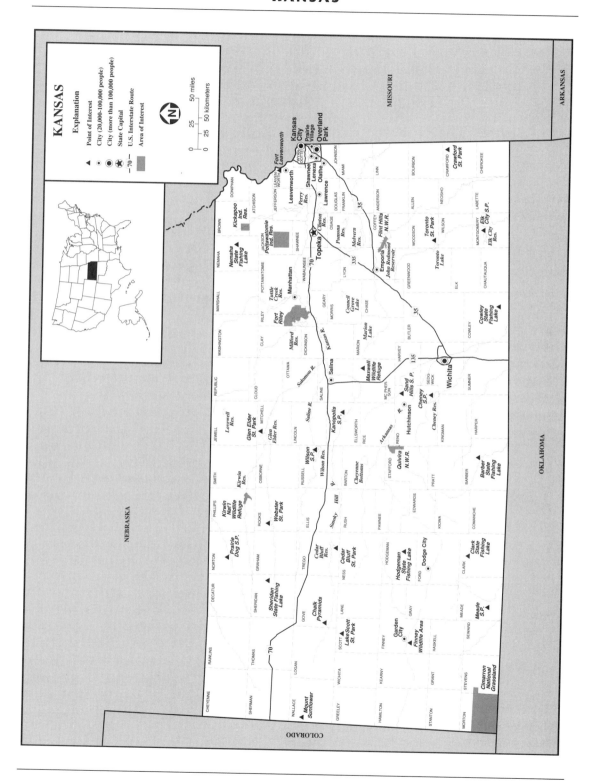

The American Buffalo, Kansas's state animal.

population of more than 30,000 to establish wastewater treatment plants by July 1983. About a third of the state's cropland soil has been damaged or destroyed.

Strip mining for coal, in southeast Kansas, is subject to a 1969 law requiring immediate leveling and seeding of the disturbed land. Kansas produces 2,400 tons a year of solid waste. The state had 115 municipal landfills and 10 curbside recycling programs operating in the state in 1991. As of 1993, there were 10 hazardous waste sites in Kansas.

6 POPULATION

With a population in 1990 of 2,477,574, Kansas ranked 32d among the states. The estimated population in 1995 is 2,515,320. The population density in 1990 was 30 persons per square mile (12 persons per square kilometer). About 69.1% of the population lived in urban areas and 30.9% in rural areas. Estimates for 1992 showed 311,746 residents in Wichita and 146,507 in Kansas City.

7 ETHNIC GROUPS

There were 22,000 Native Americans in Kansas as of 1990. Black Americans in Kansas numbered 143,000—more than 5% of the population—in 1990, when the state also had 94,000 residents of Hispanic origin. The 1990 census recorded 32,000 Asian-Pacific peoples, the largest group being 6,001 Vietnamese, followed by 5,406 Laotians, and 4,298 Cambodians.

8 LANGUAGES

Regional features of Kansas speech are almost entirely those of the Northern and North Midland dialects. Kansans typically play as children on a *teetertotter,* make *white bread* sandwiches, carry water in a *pail,* and may designate the time 2:45 as a quarter *to,* or *of,* or *till* three. The migration by southerners in the mid-19th century is evidenced in southeastern Kansas by such South Midland terms as *pullybone* (wishbone) and *light bread* (white bread). In 1990, 2,158,011 Kansans—94.3%— spoke only English at home. Kansans who spoke another language at home included Spanish, 62,059; German, 22,887; and French, 7,851.

9 RELIGIONS

The leading Protestant denominations in 1990 were United Methodist, 238,029; Southern Baptist Convention, 96,524; and Christian Church (Disciples of Christ), 58,314. Roman Catholics constitute the largest single religious group in the state, with 369,241 adherents in 1990. Kansas's estimated Jewish population that year was 9,151.

10 TRANSPORTATION

In the heartland of the nation, Kansas is at the crossroads of US road and railway systems. In 1992, the state had 5,704 miles (9,178 kilometers) of railroad track. An Amtrak passenger train crosses Kansas en route from Chicago to Los Angeles. The total number of riders through the state in

Photo credit: Kansas Division of Travel and Tourism.

Young member of the Kickapoo Tribe at the All Mid-American Indian Center.

1991/92 was 33,574. As of the end of 1993, the state had 133,256 miles (214,409 kilometers) of roads. There were 1,264,010 autos, 654,465 trucks, 53,073 motorcycles, and 3,754 buses registered in Kansas in 1993. The busiest airport, at Wichita, had 12,871 departing flights carrying 533,393 passengers. The chief river ports are Atchison, Leavenworth, and Kansas City.

11 HISTORY

Plains tribes—the Wichita, Pawnee, Kansa, and Osage—were living or hunting in

Kansas when the earliest Europeans arrived. Around 1800, they were joined on the Central Plains by the nomadic Cheyenne, Arapaho, Comanche, and Kiowa. The first European, explorer Francisco Coronado, entered Kansas in 1541. Between 1682 and 1739, French explorers established trading contacts with the Native Americans. France ceded its claims to the area to Spain in 1762 but received it back from Spain in 1800.

Most of Kansas was sold to the US by France as part of the Louisiana Purchase of 1803. (The extreme southwestern corner was gained after the Mexican War.) Early settlement of Kansas was sparse, limited to a few thousand Native Americans—including Shawnee, Delaware, Ojibwa, and Wyandot. These tribes were forcibly removed from their lands and relocated in what is now eastern Kansas.

The Santa Fe Trail was opened to wagon traffic in 1822, and for 50 years that route, two-thirds of which lay in Kansas, was of commercial importance to the West. During the 1840s and 1850s, thousands of migrants crossed northeastern Kansas on the California-Oregon Trail. Kansas Territory was created by the Kansas-Nebraska Act (30 May 1854). Almost immediately, disputes arose as to whether Kansas would enter the Union as a free or slave state. Both free-staters and pro-slavery settlers were brought in, and a succession of governors tried to mediate between the two groups.

Statehood

Kansas entered the Union on 29 January 1861 as a free state, and Topeka was named the capital. Although Kansas lay west of the major Civil War action, more than two-thirds of its adult males served in the Union Army and gave it the highest military death rate among the northern states. Following the Civil War, settlement expanded in Kansas, particularly in the central part of the state. White settlers encroached on the hunting grounds of the Plains tribes, and their settlements were attacked in retaliation. Most of the Native Americans were eventually removed to the Indian Territory in what is now Oklahoma.

By 1872, both the Union Pacific and the Santa Fe railroads had crossed Kansas, and other lines were under construction. Rail expansion brought more settlers, who established new communities. It also led to the great Texas cattle drives that meant prosperity to a number of Kansas towns—including Abilene, Ellsworth, Wichita, Caldwell, and Dodge City—from 1867 to 1885. This was when Bat Masterson, Wyatt Earp, and Wild Bill Hickok reigned in Dodge City and Abilene—the now romantic era of the Old West.

A strain of hard winter wheat that proved particularly well-suited to the state's soil was brought to Kansas in the 1870s by Russian Mennonites fleeing czarist rule, and Plains agriculture was transformed. Significant changes in agriculture, industry, transportation, and communications came after 1900. Mechanization became commonplace in farming,

Bullwhacker Days in Olathe. Bullwhackers were men who drove teams of oxen during Oregon Trail days.

and vast areas were opened to wheat production, particularly during World War I. The Progressive movement of the early 1900s focused attention on control of monopolies, public health, labor legislation, and more representative politics.

1930s–1990s

Kansas suffered through the Great Depression of the 1930s. The state's western region, part of the Dust Bowl, was hardest hit. Improved weather conditions and the demands of World War II revived Kansas agriculture in the 1940s. The World War II era also saw the development of industry, especially in transportation. Other heavy industry grew, and mineral production—oil, natural gas, salt, coal, and gypsum—expanded greatly.

Since World War II, Kansas has become increasingly urban. Agriculture has become highly commercialized, and there are dozens of large industries that process and market farm products and supply materials to crop producers. Livestock production, especially in closely controlled feedlots, is a major enterprise. Recent governors have worked to expand international exports of Kansas products, and by 1981/82, Kansas ranked seventh among the states in agricultural exports, with sales of more than $1.6 billion.

The late 1980s and early 1990s brought dramatic extremes of weather. A severe drought in 1988 drove up commodity prices and depleted grain stocks. From April through September of 1993, Kansas experienced the worst floods of the century. Some 13,500 people evacuated their homes, and the floods caused $574 million dollars worth of damage.

12 STATE GOVERNMENT

The Kansas legislature consists of a 40-member senate and a 125-member house of representatives. Officials elected statewide include the governor, lieutenant governor, secretary of state, attorney general, and treasurer. A bill becomes law when it has been approved by 21 senators and 63 representatives and signed by the governor. A veto can be overridden by one more than two-thirds of the members of both houses.

13 POLITICAL PARTIES

Although the Republicans remain the dominant force in state politics, the Democrats controlled several state offices in the mid–1990s. Democrats held the governorship for 18 of the 28 years between 1957 and 1985. The most recent Democratic governor was Joan Finney, elected in 1990. Republican Bill Graves was elected governor in 1994. Republicans have regularly controlled the legislature, however. In 1994, the state had 587,303 registered Republicans (43% of registered voters) and 424,478 registered Democrats (31%).

In 1988 and 1992, Kansans voted for George Bush in the presidential elections. In the 1992 election, Bush won 39% of the vote; Clinton received 34%; and Perot, 27%. Republican Robert Dole, first elected to the US Senate in 1968 and elected Senate majority leader in 1984, was reelected in 1992. He reclaimed the

Kansas Presidential Vote by Political Parties, 1948–92

YEAR	KANSAS WINNER	DEMOCRAT	REPUBLICAN	PROGRESSIVE	SOCIALIST	PROHIBITION
1948	Dewey (R)	351,902	423,039	4,603	2,807	6,468
1952	*Eisenhower (R)	273,296	616,302	6,038	530	6,038
1956	*Eisenhower (R)	296,317	566,878	—	—	3,048
1960	Nixon (R)	363,213	561,474	—	—	4,138
1964	*Johnson (D)	464,028	386,579	—	1,901	5,393
				AMERICAN IND.		
1968	*Nixon (R)	302,996	478,674	88,921	—	2,192
1972	*Nixon (R)	270,287	619,812	21,808	—	4,188
				LIBERTARIAN		
1976	Ford (R)	430,421	502,752	4,724	3,242	1,403
1980	*Reagan (R)	326,150	566,812	7,555	14,470	—
1984	*Reagan (R)	333,149	677,296	—	3,329	—
1988	*Bush (R)	422,636	554,049	3,806	12,553	—
				IND. (Perot)		
1992	Bush (R)	390,434	449,951	312,358	4,314	—

* Won US presidential election.

post of Senate majority leader when the Republicans gained control of the Senate in the elections of 1994. Kansas's other Republican senator, Nancy Landon Kassebaum, was reelected in 1990. Following the 1994 election, Republicans held all four US congressional seats. In the state legislature in 1994, there were 27 Republicans and 13 Democrats in the senate, and 66 Republicans and 59 Democrats in the state house.

14 LOCAL GOVERNMENT

As of 1992, Kansas had 105 counties, 627 incorporated cities, 1,355 townships, and 324 school districts. Each county government is headed by three elected county commissioners. Most cities are run by mayor-council or mayor-commission systems.

15 JUDICIAL SYSTEM

The supreme court, the highest court in the state, is composed of a chief justice and six other justices. An intermediate-level court of appeals consists of a chief judge and six other judges. In 1994 there were 31 district courts. Kansas's crime rate was 4,893.8 per 100,000 inhabitants in 1994. The state had a prison population of 5,935 in 1994.

16 MIGRATION

From 1980 to 1990, Kansas had a net loss of 63,411 from migration. As of 1990, 61.3% of all Kansans had been born within the state. Steady migration from farms to cities has been a feature of Kansas life throughout this century, with urban population surpassing farm population after World War II.

17 ECONOMY

Today, agricultural products and meat-packing industries are rivaled by the large aircraft industry centered in Wichita. Three Kansas companies, all located in Wichita, manufacture two-thirds of the world's general aviation aircraft. Kansas leads all states and trails only seven countries in wheat production. The Kansas City metropolitan area is a center of automobile production and printing. Metal fabrication, printing, and mineral products are the main industries in the nine southeastern counties.

18 INCOME

In 1994, Kansas's income per capita (per person) was $20,762 (24th in the US). In that year, total personal income was $53 billion. About 13.1% of all Kansans lived below the federal poverty level as of 1993.

19 INDUSTRY

Transportation equipment, machinery, food products, and petroleum and coal products accounted for 66% of the estimated value of shipments, which totaled $36.7 billion in 1991. Kansas is a world leader in aviation, claiming a large share of both US and world production and sales of commercial aircraft.

20 LABOR

Kansas has traditionally had a fairly low unemployment rate. In 1994, the civilian

Photo credit: Kansas Division of Travel and Tourism.

Wheat harvest. Kansas is one of the highest wheat-producing states in the US.

labor force was 1,331,000, with an unemployment rate of 5.3%. There were three national labor unions operating in the state in 1993. As of 1994, 10% of all workers were union members.

21 AGRICULTURE

Known as the Wheat State and the breadbasket of the nation, Kansas produces more wheat than any other state. It ranked sixth in total farm income in 1994, with cash receipts of over $7.6 billion. Between 1940 and 1994, the number of farms declined from 159,000 to 65,000, while the average size of farms more than doubled. The following table shows figures for several leading crops in 1994:

CROP	PRODUCTION (BUSHELS)	VALUE
Wheat	433,200,000	$1,473,000,000
Sorghum (grain)	231,200,000	474,000,000*
Corn (grain)	304,590,000	716,000,000
Soybeans	75,600,000	401,000,000

*Estimated

Other leading crops are alfalfa, hay, oats, barley, popcorn, rye, dry edible beans, corn and sorghums for silage, wild hay, red clover, and sugar beets.

22 DOMESTICATED ANIMALS

Cash receipts from livestock and animal products totaled $4.8 billion in 1994, when 6,900,000 and 2,300,000 hogs were slaughtered for commercial purposes. Cattle production in 1994 was valued at about $4.3 billion, or 56.4% of the state's total agricultural receipts (11.9% of all US cattle receipts).

The total value of milk in 1994 was $1,441,440,000. Twenty-five plants manufactured 12,038,000 pounds of butter, 38,926,000 pounds of American cheese, and 6,828,000 pounds of ice cream and ice milk.

23 FISHING

There is little commercial fishing in Kansas. Sport fishermen can find bass, crappie, catfish, perch, and walleye in the state's reservoirs and artificial lakes.

24 FORESTRY

Kansas was at one time so barren of trees that early settlers were offered 160 acres (65 hectares) free if they would plant trees on their land. Today much of Kansas is still treeless. Kansas has 1,400,000 acres (569,000 hectares) of forestland, 2.6% of the total state area.

25 MINING

The value of nonfuel mineral production in Kansas was estimated at $495 million in 1994. Kansas ranked fourth of the 14 states producing salt in 1992, with 2.1 million short tons, worth $94.1 million. Kansas also ranked first of four states producing grade-A helium (42 million cubic meters, valued at $83.6 million).

26 ENERGY AND POWER

In 1993, Kansas's electrical output was 36.4 billion kilowatt hours, of which 73.6% was coal-fired. In 1993, Kansas produced a total of 50,000,000 barrels of crude petroleum. There were proven reserves of 300,000,000 barrels at the end of 1991. Natural gas production was 686 billion cubic feet (19.4 billion cubic meters) in 1993. Three surface mines produced 363,000 tons of bituminous coal in 1992. There is one nuclear power plant that generates an estimated 21.7% of the state's electricity. In 1992, Kansas's per capita (per person) energy expenditures were $2,103.

27 COMMERCE

The state's wholesale sales totaled $34.9 billion in 1992; retail sales totaled $21.3 billion in 1993; and service establishment receipts were $9.6 billion in 1992. Kansas's agricultural and manufactured goods have a significant role in US foreign trade.

28 PUBLIC FINANCE

The total indebtedness of state government exceeded $935 million as of 1993, or about $369 per capita (per person).

The state general fund revenues for fiscal years 1994/95 (estimated) were $3,126,820,000; expenditures were $3,144,247,931.

29 TAXATION

Kansas ranked 29th in state taxes per capita (per person) in 1991, at $1,120.80. The state taxes the income of individuals and corporations. The state sales tax rate was 4.9% in 1995. Kansas also collects liquor and bingo taxes, cigarette and tobacco products taxes, inheritance taxes, and other types of tax. Property taxes are the largest source of income for local governments. In 1991, Kansans paid almost $9.8 billion in federal taxes.

30 HEALTH

Heart disease, the leading cause of death in the state, accounted for 33% of all deaths in 1992. Topeka, a major US center for psychiatric treatment, is home to the world-famous Menninger Clinic. In 1993, Kansas had 134 community hospitals with 11,300 beds. The average hospital cost per inpatient day in 1993 was $666, and the average cost per stay was $5,108. Kansas had 4,600 nonfederal physicians and 19,800 nurses as of 1993. Some 12.7% of state residents did not have health insurance in 1993.

31 HOUSING

By 1993, there were an estimated 1,070,000 housing units in Kansas. The median monthly cost in 1990 of housing for owners with a mortgage was $628. The median monthly rent was $372. The median value of a house was $52,200.

32 EDUCATION

Kansans are, by and large, better educated than most other Americans. In 1991, 25% of the Kansas population had completed four or more years of college. Enrollment in the state's 1,498 public schools in 1993/94 was 457,744: 126,984 students were in high school, 14,995 in junior high school, and 65,010 in middle school. There were about 16,380 elementary-school teachers and 13,902 secondary-school teachers. In 1993, the state spent a per pupil average of $5,490 (22d in the nation).

In 1993/94 there were 6 state universities, 19 two-year community colleges, 4 private two-year colleges, 17 church-affiliated universities and four-year colleges, and 16 vocational-technical schools. In 1991, 167,699 students were enrolled in institutions of higher education.

33 ARTS

The Kansas Arts Commission is a 12-member panel appointed by the governor. In 1984/85, it sponsored 360 touring arts programs. Wichita has a resident symphony orchestra. From 1987 to 1991, the state of Kansas generated $9,141,046 from federal and state sources to support its arts programs.

34 LIBRARIES AND MUSEUMS

The Dwight D. Eisenhower Library in Abilene houses the collection of papers and memorabilia from the 34th president. There is also a museum. The Menninger Foundation Museum and Archives in Topeka maintains various collections pertaining to psychiatry. Kansas had 338 public libraries in 1994, with 9,594,318 volumes and a circulation of over 17,300,000. Additionally there were 35 county and regional libraries, 10 bookmobiles, 28 college libraries, and 24 junior college libraries. Seven regional library systems serve state residents who have no local library service.

Almost 154 museums, historical societies, and art galleries were scattered across the state in 1994. Among the art museums are the Mulvane Art Center in Topeka, the Helen Foresman Spencer Museum of Art at the University of Kansas (Lawrence), and the Wichita Art Museum.

35 COMMUNICATIONS

About 96.5% of all households had telephone service in March 1993, about 2.3% higher than the US average. The state had 60 AM and 103 FM radio stations, 19 commercial television stations, and 4 public television stations in 1993. As of 1993, there were three large cable television systems.

36 PRESS

In 1994, Kansas had 46 daily newspapers and 17 Sunday papers. Leading newspapers and their daily circulations in 1994 were the *Wichita Eagle-Beacon* (122,324) and the *Topeka Capital-Journal* (67,119).

37 TOURISM, TRAVEL, AND RECREATION

During 1993, travel and tourism expenditures were estimated at $433 million. Kansas has 23 state parks, 24 federal reservoirs, and more than 100 privately owned campsites. During 1991, some 1,577,000 visitors used the state park system. There are two national historic sites, Fort Larned and Fort Scott, both 19th century frontier army bases.

Topeka features a number of tourist attractions, including the Kansas Museum of History and the Menninger Foundation. Dodge City offers a reproduction of Old Front Street as it was when the town was the "cowboy capital of the world." In Hanover stands the only remaining original and unaltered Pony Express station. A recreated "Little House on the Prairie," near the childhood home of author Laura Ingalls

Photo credit: Kansas Division of Travel and Tourism.

Bernard Warkentin House in Newton. Warkentin brought the hardy "Turkey Red" winter wheat to Kansas and 5,000 German-speaking Mennonites to help farm it.

Wilder, is 13 miles (21 kilometers) southwest of Independence. The Eisenhower Center in Abilene contains the 34th president's family home, library, and museum.

38 SPORTS

There are no major professional sports teams in Kansas. During spring, summer, and early fall, horses are raced at Eureka Downs. The University of Kansas and Kansas State both play collegiate football in the Big Twelve Conference.

39 FAMOUS KANSANS

Kansas claims only one US president and one US vice-president. Dwight D. Eisenhower (b.Texas, 1890–1969) was elected the 34th president in 1952 and was reelected in 1956. Charles Curtis (1860–1936) was vice-president during the Hoover administration.

Two Kansans have been associate justices of the US Supreme Court: David J. Brewer (1837–1910) and Charles E. Whittaker (1901–73). Prominent US senators include Robert Dole (b.1923), who was the Republican candidate for vice-president in 1976 and became Senate majority leader in 1984 and again in 1994; and Nancy Landon Kassebaum (b.1932), elected to the US Senate in 1978. Gary Hart, a senator and a presidential candidate in 1984 and 1988, was born in Ottawa, Kansas, on 28 November 1936. Other prominent Kansan political figures included Alfred M. Landon (1887–1984), a former governor who ran for US president on the Republican ticket in 1936; and Carrie Nation (1846–1911), the prohibition activist.

Leaders in medicine and science include the Menninger doctors—C. F. (1862–1953), William (1899–1966), and Karl (1893–1990)—who established the Menninger Foundation, a leading center for mental health; and Clyde Tombaugh (b.1906), who discovered the planet Pluto. Kansas also had several pioneers in aviation including Clyde Cessna (b.Iowa, 1880–1954) and Amelia Earhart (1898–1937). William Coleman (1870–1957) was an innovator in lighting, and Walter Chrysler (1875–1940) was a prominent automotive developer.

Most famous of Kansas writers was William Allen White (1868–1944), whose son William L. White (1900–73) also had a distinguished literary career. Damon Runyon (1884–1946) was a popular journalist and storyteller, Gordon Parks (b.1912) is a well-known photographer, and Mort Walker (Mortimer Walker Addison, b.1923) is a famous cartoonist. William Inge (1913–73) was a prize-winning playwright who contributed to the Broadway stage. Notable painters include John Noble (1874–1934) and John Steuart Curry (1897–1946). Jazz great Charlie "Bird" Parker (Charles Christopher Parker, Jr., 1920–55) was born in Kansas City. Stage and screen notables include Joseph "Buster" Keaton (1895–1966), Louise Brooks (1906–85), Edward Asner (b.1929), and Kirstie Alley (b.1955).

Glenn Cunningham (1909–88) and Jim Ryun (b.1947) both set running records for the mile. Also prominent in sports history were James Naismith (b.Ontario, Canada, 1861–1939), the inventor of basketball; and baseball pitcher Walter Johnson (1887–1946).

40 BIBLIOGRAPHY

Davis, Kenneth S. *Kansas: A Bicentennial History.* New York: Norton, 1976.

——. *Soldier of Democracy: A Biography of Dwight Eisenhower.* New York: Doubleday, 1945, 1952.

Howes, Charles C. *This Place Called Kansas.* Norman: University of Oklahoma Press, 1984.

KENTUCKY

Commonwealth of Kentucky

ORIGIN OF STATE NAME: Possibly derived from the Wyandot Indian word *Kah-ten-tah-teh* (land of tomorrow).

NICKNAME: The Bluegrass State.

CAPITAL: Frankfort.

ENTERED UNION: 1 June 1792 (15th).

SONG: "My Old Kentucky Home."

MOTTO: United We Stand, Divided We Fall.

FLAG: A simplified version of the state seal on a blue field.

OFFICIAL SEAL: In the center are two men exchanging greetings; above and below them is the state motto. On the periphery are two sprigs of goldenrod and the words "Commonwealth of Kentucky."

COLORS: Blue and gold.

BIRD: Cardinal.

WILD ANIMAL: Gray squirrel.

FISH: Bass.

FLOWER: Goldenrod.

INSECT: Viceroy butterfly.

TREE: Tulip poplar.

TIME: 7 AM EST = noon GMT; 6 AM CST = noon GMT.

1 LOCATION AND SIZE

Located in the eastern south-central US, the Commonwealth of Kentucky is the smallest of the eight south-central states and ranks 37th in size among the 50 states. The total area of Kentucky is 40,409 square miles (104,659 square kilometers). The state extends about 350 miles (563 kilometers) east-west; its maximum north-south extension is about 175 miles (282 kilometers). Its total boundary length is 1,290 miles (2,076 kilometers). Because of a double bend in the Mississippi River, about 10 square miles (26 square kilometers) of southwest Kentucky is separated from the rest of the state by a narrow strip of Missouri.

2 TOPOGRAPHY

The eastern quarter of the state is dominated by the Cumberland Plateau, which is on the western border of the Appalachian Mountains. The western coalfields are the most level part of the state. In the far west are the coastal plains of the Mississippi River. The highest point in Kentucky is Black Mountain in Harlan County, at 4,145 feet (1,263 meters).

The only large lakes in Kentucky are artificial. The biggest is Lake Cumberland at 79 square miles (205 square kilometers). Including the Ohio and Mississippi rivers on its borders and the tributaries of the Ohio, Kentucky claims at least 3,000 miles (4,800 kilometers) of navigable rivers. This is more than any other state except Alaska. The Cumberland Falls, 92 feet (28 meters) high and 100 feet (30 meters) wide, are located in Whitley County.

3 CLIMATE

Kentucky has a moderate, relatively humid climate, with abundant rainfall. The southern and lowland regions are slightly warmer than the uplands. In Louisville, the normal monthly mean temperature ranges from 33°F (1°C) in January to 76°F (24°C) in July. The record high for the state was 114°F (46°C) in 1930. The record low, –34°F (–37°C), was set in 1963. The normal annual precipitation is 43 inches (109 centimeters). Snowfall totals about 18 inches (46 centimeters) a year.

4 PLANTS AND ANIMALS

Kentucky's forests are mostly of the oak/hickory variety, with some beech/maple areas. Four species of magnolia are found, and the tulip poplar, eastern hemlock, and eastern white pine are also common. Kentucky's famed bluegrass is actually blue only in May, when dwarf iris and wild columbine are in bloom.

Game mammals include the raccoon, muskrat, and opossum. The eastern chipmunk and flying squirrel are common small mammals. At least 300 bird species have been recorded, including blackbirds, cardinals (the state bird), and robins. Eagles are winter visitors. The Indiana bat, cougar, and brown bear are among Kentucky's endangered species.

Kentucky Population Profile

Estimated 1995 population:	3,851,000
Population change, 1980–90:	0.7%
Leading ancestry group:	German
Second leading group:	Irish
Foreign born population:	0.9%
Hispanic origin†:	0.6%
Population by race:	
White:	92.0%
Black:	7.1%
Native American:	0.2%
Asian/Pacific Islander:	0.5%
Other:	0.2%

Population by Age Group

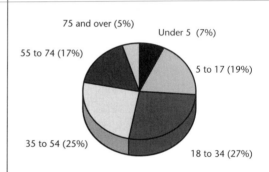

75 and over (5%)
Under 5 (7%)
55 to 74 (17%)
5 to 17 (19%)
35 to 54 (25%)
18 to 34 (27%)

Top Cities with Populations Over 25,000

City	Population	National rank	% change 1980–90
Louisville	271,038	59	–9.8
Lexington–Fayette	232,562	70	10.4
Owensboro	53,366	484	–1.7
Covington	42,490	630	–12.7
Bowling Green	42,017	641	0.5
Hopkinsville	30,887	907	9.1
Frankfort	27,192	1,022	0.0
Paducah	26,853	1,031	–7.0
Henderson	26,453	1,043	4.5

Notes: †A person of Hispanic origin may be of any race. NA indicates that data are not available.
Sources: Economic and Statistics Administration, Bureau of the Census. *Statistical Abstract of the United States, 1994–95.* Washington, DC: Government Printing Office, 1995; Courtenay M. Slater and George E. Hall. *1995 County and City Extra: Annual Metro, City and County Data Book.* Lanham, MD: Bernan Press, 1995.

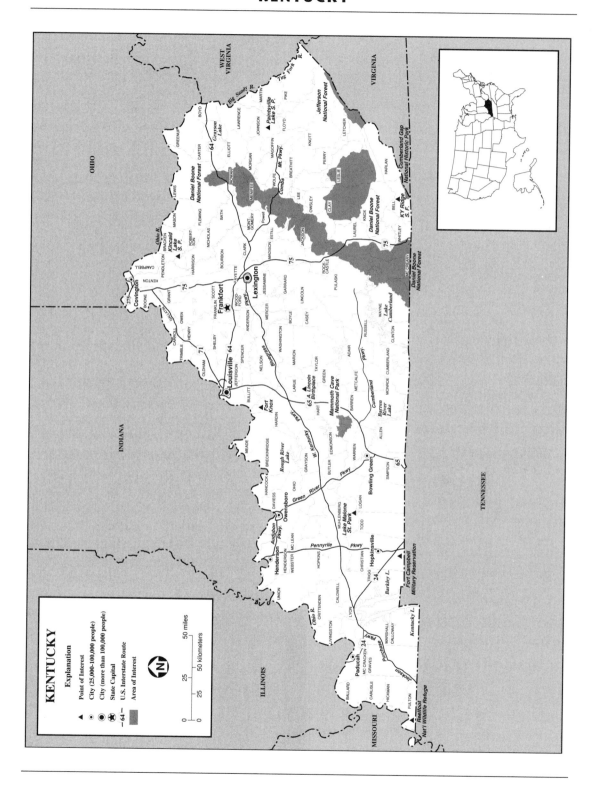

5 ENVIRONMENTAL PROTECTION

The most serious environmental concern in Kentucky is damage to land and water from strip-mining. The first comprehensive attempts at control did not begin until the passage in 1977 of the Federal Surface Mining Control and Reclamation Act. Flooding is a chronic problem in southeastern Kentucky, where strip-mining has worsened soil erosion. Kentucky produces 3,500 tons a year of solid waste. There were 34 municipal landfills and 10 curbside recycling programs operating in the state in 1991. Kentucky has 20 hazardous waste sites as of 1994. Leakage of radioactive materials had been discovered at Maxey Flats, a closed nuclear waste disposal facility in Fleming County.

6 POPULATION

Kentucky ranked 23d in population among the states in 1990 with a census population of 3,685,296. At the time of the 1990 census, Kentucky's population was 51% urban, far below the national norm of 75.2%. The estimated population for 1995 was 3,851,000; the projected population for 2000 is 3,989,000. The population density in 1990 was 92.8 persons per square mile (35.6 persons per square kilometer). Louisville, the state's largest city, had a 1992 population of about 271,038. Lexington-Fayette urban county was next with 232,562 residents in 1992. Owensboro, with 53,366 residents in 1992 was the state's third most populous city.

7 ETHNIC GROUPS

Since there was relatively little opportunity for industrial employment, Kentucky attracted small numbers of foreign immigrants in the 19th and 20th centuries. Among persons reporting a single ancestry in the 1990 census, a total of 552,802 claimed English descent, 798,001 German, 695,853 Irish, 222,428 African-American, and 92,588 French. Kentucky had a black population of 263,000 (7.1%) in 1990.

There were 208,938 Kentuckians reporting at least some Native American ancestry in 1990. The 1990 census also found 4,264 Koreans, 2,367 Asian Indians, 3,275 Japanese, 1,340 Vietnamese, and 3,137 Chinese. A total of 22,000 state residents were of Hispanic origin, with 6,823 reporting Mexican ancestry and 2,692 Puerto Rican ancestry.

8 LANGUAGES

Speech patterns in the state generally reflect the first settlers' Virginia and Kentucky backgrounds. South Midland features are best preserved in the mountains, but some common to Midland and Southern are widespread. In 1990, 97.5% of all residents five years old and older spoke only English at home. Other languages spoken at home included Spanish, German, Korean, and Chinese.

9 RELIGIONS

As of 1990 there were 1,847,667 known Protestants in Kentucky, of whom 962,945 belonged to the Southern Baptist Convention; 227,143 to the United Methodist Church; 66,798 to the Christian Church (Disciples of Christ); and 90,520

The green fields and white fences of Lexington's notable Thoroughbred farms.

to the Christian Churches and Churches of Christ. The Roman Catholic Church had 365,270 members at the beginning of 1990. There were an estimated 14,810 Jews in Kentucky in 1990.

10 TRANSPORTATION

As of December 1992, Kentucky had 2,929 rail miles (4,713 kilometers) of railroad track, including 2,342 rail miles (3,768 kilometers) of Class I track. In 1991/92, the total number of Amtrak riders came to 9,056. In 1993, Kentucky had 72,632 miles (116,865 kilometers) of public roads. There were 761 miles (1,224 kilometers) of interstate highway. In 1992, 1,938,635 automobiles, 1,034,290 trucks,

and 35,133 motorcycles were registered in the state.

Louisville, on the Ohio River, is the chief port. In 1991, traffic through the port totaled 8,351,515 tons. Paducah is the outlet port for traffic on the Tennessee River. Greater Cincinnati Airport, located in northern Kentucky west of Covington, served 4,314,474 passengers in 1991. Standiford Field in Louisville boarded 893,817 passengers in 1991.

11 HISTORY

No Native American nations resided in central and eastern Kentucky when these areas were first explored by British-American surveyors Thomas Walker and

Christopher Gist in 1750 and 1751. The dominant Shawnee and Cherokee tribes utilized the region as a hunting ground, returning to homes in the neighboring territories of Ohio and Tennessee. The first permanent colonial settlement in Kentucky was established at Harrodstown (now Harrodsburg) in 1774.

North Carolina speculator Richard Henderson, assisted by famed woodsman Daniel Boone, purchased a huge tract of land in central Kentucky from the Cherokee and established Fort Boonesborough. Henderson sought approval for creation of a 14th colony, but the plan was blocked by Virginians, who in 1776 incorporated the region as the County of Kentucky.

Kentucky became the principal gateway for migration into the Mississippi Valley. By the late 1780s, its settlements were growing, and it was obvious that Kentucky could not long remain under the control of Virginia. In June 1792, Kentucky entered the Union as the 15th state.

State Development

Kentucky became a center for breeding and racing fine thoroughbred horses, an industry that still thrives today. More important was the growing and processing of tobacco, which accounted for half the agricultural income of Kentucky farmers by 1860. Finally, whiskey began to be produced in vast quantities by the 1820s, culminating in the development of a fine, aged amber-red brew known throughout the world as bourbon, after Bourbon County.

During the Civil War, Kentuckians were forced to choose sides between the Union, led in the North by Kentucky native Abraham Lincoln, and the Confederacy, led in the South by Kentucky native Jefferson Davis. Although the state legislature finally opted for the Union side, approximately 40,000 men went south to Confederate service, while 100,000—including nearly 24,000 black soldiers—served in the Union army.

In the decades following the war, railroad construction increased threefold and exploitation of timber and coal reserves began in eastern Kentucky. By 1900, Kentucky ranked first among southern states in per capita (per person) income. However, wealth remained very unevenly distributed—a third of all Kentucky farmers were landless tenants. The gubernatorial election scandal of 1899, in which Republican William S. Taylor was charged with fraud and reform-minded Democrat William Goebel was assassinated, polarized the state. Outside investment plummeted, and Kentucky fell into a prolonged economic depression. By 1940, the state ranked last among the 48 states in per capita income and was burdened by an image of poverty and feuding clans. The Great Depression hit the state hard, though an end to Prohibition revived the inactive whiskey industry.

Post-World War II

Kentucky has changed greatly since World War II. Between 1945 and 1980, the number of farms decreased by 53%, while the number of manufacturing plants increased from 2,994 to 3,504 between 1967 and

1982. Although Kentucky remains one of the poorest states in the nation, positive change is evident even in relatively isolated rural communities—a result of better roads, education, television, and government programs.

In the early 1990s, public corruption became a major issue in Kentucky politics. In a sting operation code-named Boptrot, legislators were filmed by hidden cameras accepting payments from lobbyists. Fifteen state legislators, lobbyists, and public figures were convicted or charged with bribery, extortion, fraud, and racketeering. An investigation carried out at the same time charged the husband of former Governor Martha Layne Collins, Dr. William Collins, with collecting $1.7 million in bribes while his wife was in office.

12 STATE GOVERNMENT

The state legislature, called the general assembly, consists of the house of representatives, which has 100 members elected for two-year terms, and the senate, with 38 members elected for staggered four-year terms. Except for revenue-raising measures, which must be introduced in the house of representatives, either chamber may introduce or amend a bill. Most bills may be passed by majority votes equal to at least two-fifths of the membership of each house. A majority of the members of each house is required to override the governor's veto. The elected executive officers of Kentucky include the governor, lieutenant governor, secretary of state, attorney general, and treasurer. All serve four-year terms and may succeed themselves one time only.

Kentucky Presidential Vote by Political Parties, 1948–92

YEAR	KENTUCKY WINNER	DEMOCRAT	REPUBLICAN	DEMOCRAT	STATES' RIGHTS PROHIBITION	PROGRESSIVE	SOCIALIST
1948	*Truman (D)	466,756	341,210	10,411	1,245	1,567	1,284
1952	Stevenson (D)	495,729	495,029	—	1,161	—	—
1956	*Eisenhower (R)	476,453	572,192	—	2,145	—	—
1960	Nixon (R)	521,855	602,607	—	—	—	—
				STATES' RIGHTS			
1964	*Johnson (D)	669,659	372,977	3,469	—	—	
				AMERICAN IND.			SOC. WRKRS
1968	*Nixon (R)	397,541	462,411	193,098	—	—	2,843
					AMERICAN	PEOPLE'S	
1972	*Nixon (R)	371,159	676,446	—	17,627	1,118	—
1976	*Carter (D)	615,717	531,852	2,328	8,308	—	—
						LIBERTARIAN	CITIZENS
1980	*Reagan (R)	617,417	635,274	—	—	5,531	1,304
1984	*Reagan (R)	539,539	821,702	—	—	1,776	599
1988	*Bush (R)	580,368	734,281	4,994	1,256	2,118	—
				IND. (Perot)			
1992	*Clinton (D)	665,104	617,178	203,944	430	4,513	989

*Won US presidential election.

13 POLITICAL PARTIES

Regional divisions in party affiliation during the Civil War era, based upon sympathy with the South (Democrats) or with the Union (Republicans), have persisted in the state's voting patterns. In general, the poorer mountain areas tend to vote Republican, while the more affluent lowlanders in the Bluegrass and Pennyroyal areas tend to vote Democratic.

In 1994, Kentucky had 1,418,835 registered Democrats or 67% of the total number of registered voters. There were 615,732 registered Republicans, or 30%; and 86,072 independents, or 3%. In 1983, Martha Layne Collins, a Democrat, defeated Republican candidate Jim Bunning to become Kentucky's first woman governor. Paul E. Patton was elected governor in 1995. Bill Clinton defeated George Bush by a narrow margin in the 1992 US presidential campaign. After the November 1994 elections, Democrats held 21 seats in the state senate, and Republicans held 17. The Democrats continued to dominate the house of representatives, with 63 seats to the Republicans' 37. At the national level, Kentucky was represented by Democratic Senator Wendell H. Ford (reelected in 1980, 1986, and 1992) and by Republican Senator McConnell, reelected in 1990. In the US House of Representatives, there are two Democrats and four Republicans.

14 LOCAL GOVERNMENT

The chief governing body of Kentucky's counties is the fiscal court. Elected officials include magistrates, commissioners, and sheriffs. Cities are assigned by the general assembly to one of six classes on the basis of population. Kentucky has two first-class cities, Louisville and Lexington. There are 14 second-class cities and 22 third-class cities. The mayor or other chief executive officer in the top three classes must be elected. In the bottom classes, the executive may be either elected by the people or appointed by a city council or commission. Other units of local government in Kentucky include urban counties and special-purpose districts.

15 JUDICIAL SYSTEM

Judicial power in Kentucky is vested in a unified court of justice. The highest court is the supreme court, consisting of a chief justice and six associate justices. It has appeals jurisdiction and also bears responsibility for the budget and administration of the entire system. The court of appeals consists of 14 judges, 2 elected from each supreme court district.

Circuit courts, with original and appellate jurisdiction, are held in each county. There are 56 judicial circuits. Under the revised judicial system, district courts, which have limited and original jurisdiction, replaced various local and county courts. The total crime rate in 1994 was 3,498.6 crimes per 100,000. In 1993 there were 10,440 prisoners in state and federal prisons in Kentucky.

16 MIGRATION

Until the early 1970s there was a considerable out-migration of whites, especially from eastern Kentucky to industrial areas of Ohio, Indiana, and other nearby states. From 1980 to 1990, net loss to migration

Photo credit: Louisville and Jefferson County Convention & Visitors Bureau.

Hillerich & Bradsby, makers of the "Louisville Slugger" baseball bat.

came to about 22,000. As of 1990, 77.4% of the state's residents had been born in Kentucky.

17 ECONOMY

Although agriculture is still important in Kentucky, manufacturing has grown rapidly since World War II and was, by the mid-1980s, the most important area of the economy as a source of both employment and personal income. Kentucky leads the nation in the production of coal and whiskey, and ranks second in tobacco output. In contrast to the generally prosperous Bluegrass area and the growing industrial cities, eastern Kentucky, highly dependent on coal mining, is one of the poorest regions in the US.

18 INCOME

Kentucky has long been one of the poorest of the 50 states, and in 1994, per capita (per person) income was $17,753, for a rank of 42d. Total personal income rose to $67.9 billion in 1992. In the state as a whole, 20.4% of all Kentuckians were below the federal poverty line in 1993.

19 INDUSTRY

Kentucky ranked 20th among the 50 states with shipments of manufactured goods valued at $53.5 billion in 1991. In 1993, Kentucky was the leading producer of American whiskey. It also produced 9.5% of the nation's trucks in assembly plants at Louisville (480,522 units) as well as 256,638 automobiles at Bowling Green and Georgetown.

20 LABOR

According to federal statistics, Kentucky's civilian labor force in 1994 was about l,825,000. There was an unemployment rate of 5.4%.

Agriculture, forestry, and fishing employed 59,346 in 1990. Mining employment amounted to 29,900 in 1992; construction, 69,200; transportation and public utilities, 81,800; wholesale trade, 73,100; retail trade, 282,300; finance, insurance, and real estate, 62,500; services, 350,600; and government, 274,000. As of 1993 there were nine national labor unions in Kentucky. Union membership amounted to 11.5% of the labor force in 1994.

21 AGRICULTURE

With cash receipts totaling $3.2 billion, Kentucky ranked 22d among the 50 states in farm marketings in 1994. In 1994 there were approximately 89,000 farms in Kentucky. Kentucky farms in 1994 produced about 458,075,000 pounds of tobacco. Other leading field crops in 1994 (in bushels) included corn for grain, 156,160,000; soybeans, 42,940,000; wheat, 25,200,000; sorghum, 1,012,000; and barley, 1,016,000.

22 DOMESTICATED ANIMALS

The Bluegrass region, which offers excellent pasturage and drinking water, has become renowned as a center for horse breeding and racing. Kentucky has a horse population of over 225,000, including Thoroughbreds, quarter horses, American saddle horses, Arabians, and standardbreds. In 1994, the sale of horses accounted for 15.1% of Kentucky's agricultural receipts.

Cattle production was Kentucky's most profitable source of agricultural income in 1994, accounting for 20% of agricultural receipts. Dairy products made up 8.2% of farm receipts that year.

23 FISHING

Fishing is of little commercial importance in Kentucky. Federal hatcheries distributed 742,545 (226,850 pounds) of cold-water species fish and roe (fish eggs) within the state in 1992.

24 FORESTRY

In 1992 there were about 12,000,000 acres (4,856,000 hectares) of forested land in Kentucky—47% of the state's land area. In 1991, Kentucky produced 752 million board feet of lumber, nearly all of it in hardwoods. The Division of Forestry of the Department of Natural Resources operates two forest tree nurseries producing 10–12 million seedling trees a year. There are two national forests—the Daniel Boone and the Jefferson on Kentucky's eastern border—enclosing two national wilderness areas.

25 MINING

The value of nonfuel mineral production in Kentucky in 1994 of about $431 million was an all-time high, according to estimated data. Kentucky is the nation's third-leading coal producer.

26 ENERGY AND POWER

At the end of 1991, Kentucky had 34 electric generating plants. In 1993, 85 billion kilowatt hours of power were produced. In 1992, energy expenditures were $1,935 per capita (per person). Southern Kentucky shares in the power produced by the Tennessee Valley Authority, which supports a coal-fired steam electric plant in Kentucky at Paducah. In 1992, eastern Kentucky produced an estimated 119,803,000 tons of coal; western Kentucky, 41,352,000. Kentucky has more underground mines than any other state.

In 1993, Kentucky produced 6,000,000 barrels of crude petroleum and was estimated to have about 31,000,000 barrels of proven oil reserves. In 1993, Kentucky produced 87 billion cubic feet (2.5 billion cubic meters) of natural gas. As of 31 December 1991, the state was estimated to have proven reserves totaling 1.1 trillion cubic feet of natural gas. Kentucky has no nuclear plants.

27 COMMERCE

Wholesale sales in 1992 totaled $31.6 billion; retail sales in 1993 totaled $27.5 billion; service establishment receipts in 1992 were $11.7 billion. The KFC Corporation, which owns and franchises Kentucky Fried Chicken restaurants, has its headquarters in Louisville. Kentucky's exports to foreign countries in 1992 totaled $3.7 billion.

28 PUBLIC FINANCE

The Kentucky biennial state budget is prepared by the Governor's Office for Policy and Management late in each odd-numbered year and submitted by the Governor to the General Assembly for approval. The fiscal year runs from July 1 to June 30. As of 1993, the total state debt was more than $6.8 billion, or about $1,798 per capita (per person).

29 TAXATION

Kentucky collected more than $5 billion in state taxes in 1991. The state imposes personal and corporate income taxes and severance taxes on oil and coal, and also levies a 6% sales and use tax (excluding food and drugs), a gasoline tax, an inheritance tax, and other taxes. In 1992, Kentucky's total share of the federal income tax burden was $10.7 billion, 39th largest in the nation.

30 HEALTH

In 1992, Kentucky ranked higher than the national averages in death rates from heart diseases, cancer, cerebrovascular diseases, accidents, and suicide. Black lung (pneumoconiosis) has been recognized as a serious work-related illness among coal miners. In 1993, Kentucky's 106 community hospitals had 15,900 beds. As of 1993, there were 6,700 nonfederal physicians and 24,500 nurses in Kentucky. The average hospital expense per inpatient day was $703 in 1993, and the average cost per stay was $4,749. Some 12.5% of state residents did not have health insurance in 1993.

31 HOUSING

According to a 1993 estimate, Kentucky had 1,548,000 year-round housing units. In 1993, 15,907 new housing units worth over $1.1 billion were authorized. The median cost for an owner with a mortgage was $536 per month in 1990. Median rent was $319 per month.

32 EDUCATION

Kentucky has consistently ranked below the national average in per capita (per person) spending on education and in the educational attainments of its citizens. In 1990 only 68.7% of all adults (41st in the nation) had completed four years of high school; only 15.3% had completed four or more years of college, placing Kentucky well below the national average of 21.3%. The Kentucky Education Reform Act of 1990 addressed the problems of the state's education system. Expenditures on education averaged $4,942 per pupil (31st in nation) in 1993.

In 1993, 652,000 students attended public schools in Kentucky. In 1992/93, Kentucky's higher education included 26 colleges and universities, three junior colleges, and 14 community colleges. In the fall of 1992, total enrollment at these institutions was over 181,000 students. The University of Kentucky is the state's largest public institution.

33 ARTS

The Actors Theater of Louisville holds a yearly festival of new American plays. The city also has a resident ballet company. The Louisville Orchestra has recorded numerous works by contemporary composers. Bluegrass, a form of country music featuring fiddle and banjo and played at a rapid tempo, is named after the style pioneered by Kentuckian Bill Monroe and his Blue Grass Boys.

From 1987 to 1991, Kentucky generated $20,936,200 from federal and state sources in support of its arts programs.

34 LIBRARIES AND MUSEUMS

In 1991/92 there were 115 public libraries in Kentucky, with a total of 7,109,315 volumes. The regional library system of 14 districts included university libraries and the state library at Frankfort, as well as city and county libraries. The state has more than 98 museums. The Kentucky Historical Society in Frankfort maintains the State History Museum. Art museums include the University of Kentucky Art Museum and the Headley-Whitney Museum, both in Lexington.

Among Kentucky's horse-related museums is the Kentucky Derby Museum in Louisville. The John James Audubon Museum is located in Audubon State Park at Henderson. Leading historical sites include Abraham Lincoln's birthplace at Hodgenville and the Mary Todd Lincoln and Henry Clay homes in Lexington.

35 COMMUNICATIONS

Only 90.9% of all occupied housing units in the state had a telephone in March 1993. In 1993 there were 296 radio stations, 132 AM and 164 FM. That year there were 20 commercial and 16 public television broadcasting stations. As of

1993 there were six large cable television systems serving Kentucky.

36 PRESS

In 1994, Kentucky had 25 daily newspapers (including 5 morning, 19 evening, and 1 all-day daily), and 14 Sunday papers. The leading Kentucky newspapers with their 1994 daily circulations are the Louisville *Courier-Journal* (238,527); the Lexington *Herald-Leader* (121,129); and the Frankfort *State Journal* (9,962).

37 TOURISM, TRAVEL, AND RECREATION

One of the state's top tourist attractions is Mammoth Cave National Park, which contains an estimated 150 miles (241 kilometers) of underground passages. Other units of the national park system in Kentucky include Abraham Lincoln's birthplace in Hodgenville, and Cumberland Gap National Historical Park, which extends into Tennessee and Virginia. As of 1994, the state operated 15 resort parks and 19 recreational parks.

38 SPORTS

There are no major league professional sports teams in Kentucky. There is a minor league baseball team in Louisville, however. The annual Kentucky Derby at Churchill Downs, first run on 17 May 1875, has become the single most famous event in US Thoroughbred racing. Keeneland Race Course in Lexington is the site of the Blue Grass Stakes and other major Thoroughbred races.

Rivaling horse-racing as a spectator sport is collegiate basketball. The University of Kentucky Wildcats won the NCAA

Photo credit: Louisville and Jefferson County Convention & Visitors Bureau.

Churchill Downs in Louisville, home of the Kentucky Derby.

Division I basketball championship in 1947, 1948, 1951, 1958, and 1978; the University of Louisville Cardinals captured the NCAA crown in 1980 and 1986; and Kentucky Wesleyan, at Owensboro, was the NCAA Division II titleholder in 1966, 1968, 1969, 1973, 1987, and 1990.

39 FAMOUS KENTUCKIANS

Kentucky has been the birthplace of one US president, four US vice-presidents, the only president of the Confederacy, and several important jurists, statesmen, writers, artists, and sports figures. Abraham Lincoln,

(1809–65) the 16th president of the US, was born in Hodgenville. His wife, Mary Todd Lincoln (1818–82), was a native of Lexington. Kentucky-born US vice-presidents have all been Democrats. The best known were Adlai Stevenson (1835–1914), who served with Grover Cleveland, and Alben W. Barkley (1877–1956) who, before his election with President Harry S Truman in 1948, was a US senator and longtime Senate majority leader.

Frederick M. Vinson (1890–1953) was the only Kentuckian to serve as chief justice of the US. Noteworthy associate justices were John Marshall Harlan (1833–1911), famous for his dissent from the segregationist *Plessy v. Ferguson* decision (1896); and Louis B. Brandeis (1856–1941), the first Jew to serve on the Supreme Court and a champion of social reform.

A figure prominently associated with frontier Kentucky is the explorer and surveyor Daniel Boone (b.Pensylvania, 1734–1820). Other frontiersmen include Kit Carson (1809–68) and Roy Bean (1825?–1903).

Other personalities of significance include James G. Birney (1792–1857) and Cassius Marcellus Clay (1810–1903), both major antislavery spokesmen. Clay's daughter Laura (1849–1941) and Madeline Breckinridge (1872–1920) were important contributors to the women's suffrage movement. During the 1920s, Kentuckian John T. Scopes (1900–70) gained fame as the defendant in the "monkey trial" in Dayton, Tennessee. Scopes was charged with teaching Darwin's theory of evolution.

Thomas Hunt Morgan (1866–1945), honored for his work in heredity and genetics, and chemist William N. Lipscomb (b.Ohio, 1919) are Kentucky's lone Nobel Prize winners. Notable businessmen include "Colonel" Harland Sanders (b.Indiana, 1890–1980), founder of Kentucky Fried Chicken restaurants. Robert Penn Warren (1905–89), a novelist, poet laureate, and critic, won the Pulitzer Prize three times and was the first author to win the award in both the fiction and poetry categories.

Among Kentuckians well recognized in the performing arts are film innovator D. W. Griffith (David Lewelyn Wark Griffith, 1875–1948); Academy Award-winning actress Patricia Neal (b.1926); and country music singers Loretta Lynn (b.1932) and her sister Crystal Gayle (Brenda Gail Webb, b.1951). Kentucky's sports figures include basketball coach Adolph Rupp (b.Kansas, 1901–77); shortstop Harold ("Pee Wee") Reese (b.1919); football great Paul Hornung (b.1935); and world heavyweight boxing champions Jimmy Ellis (b.1940) and Muhammad Ali (Cassius Clay, b.1942).

40 BIBLIOGRAPHY

Channing, Steven A. *Kentucky: A Bicentennial History.* New York: Norton, 1977.

Goldstein, Joel. *Kentucky Government and Politics.* Bloomington, Ind.: Tichenor, 1984.

Hollingsworth, Kent. *The Kentucky Thoroughbred.* Lexington: University Press of Kentucky, 1976.

Rennick, Robert M. *Kentucky Place Names.* Lexington: University Press of Kentucky, 1984.

LOUISIANA

State of Louisiana

ORIGIN OF STATE NAME: Named in 1682 for France's King Louis XIV.

NICKNAME: The Pelican State.

CAPITAL: Baton Rouge.

ENTERED UNION: 30 April 1812 (18th).

SONGS: "Give Me Louisiana;" "You are My Sunshine."

MOTTO: Union, Justice and Confidence.

COLORS: Gold, white, and blue.

FLAG: On a blue field, fringed on three sides, a white pelican feeds her three young, symbolizing the state providing for its citizens; the state motto is inscribed on a white ribbon.

OFFICIAL SEAL: In the center, pelican and young are as depicted on the flag; the state motto encircles the scene, and the words "State of Louisiana" surround the whole.

BIRD: Eastern brown pelican.

FLOWER: Magnolia.

TREE: Bald cypress.

GEM: Agate.

FOSSIL: Petrified palmwood.

INSECT: Honeybee.

TIME: 6 AM CST = noon GMT.

1 LOCATION AND SIZE

Situated in the western south-central US, Louisiana ranks 31st in size among the 50 states. The total area of Louisiana is 48,523 square miles (125,675 square kilometers). The state extends 237 miles (381 kilometers) east-west; its maximum north-south extension is 280 miles (451 kilometers). Louisiana is shaped roughly like a boot, with the heel in the southwest corner and the toe at the extreme southeast. The state's total boundary length is 1,486 miles (2,391 kilometers).

2 TOPOGRAPHY

Louisiana lies wholly within the Gulf Coastal Plain. In the northern part of the state, east and west of a central alluvial plain, are the upland districts. The coastal-delta section, in the southernmost portion of the state, consists of the Mississippi Delta and the coastal lowlands. The highest elevation in the state is Driskill Mountain at 535 feet (163 meters), in Bienville Parish.

Louisiana has the most wetlands of all the states, including floodplains, coastal swamps, and marshes. The largest lake is

Lake Pontchartrain, with an area of more than 620 square miles (1,600 square kilometers). The most important rivers are the Mississippi, Red, Pearl, Atchafalaya, and Sabine. Louisiana has nearly 2,500 coastal islands covering some 2,000 square miles (5,000 square kilometers).

3 CLIMATE

Louisiana has a relatively constant semi-tropical climate. The temperature in New Orleans ranges from 52°F (11°C) in January to 82°F (28°C) in July. The all-time high temperature is 114°F (46°C), recorded in 1936. The all-time low, –16°F (–27°C), was set in 1899. New Orleans has an average annual rainfall of 60 inches (152 centimeters). Snow falls occasionally in the north, but rarely in the south. During the summer and fall, tropical storms and hurricanes frequently batter the state, especially along the coast.

4 PLANTS AND ANIMALS

Forests in Louisiana consist of four major types: shortleaf pine uplands; pine flats and hills; hardwood forests; and cypress and tupelo swamps. Important commercial trees also include beech, eastern red cedar, and black walnut. Among the state's wildflowers are the ground orchid and several hyacinths. Spanish moss grows profusely in the southern regions but is rare in the north.

Louisiana's varied habitats—tidal marshes, swamps, woodlands, and prairies—offer a diversity of animals. Deer, squirrel, and bear are hunted as game, while muskrat, mink, and skunk are commercially valuable furbearers. Prized game

Louisiana Population Profile

Estimated 1995 population:	4,359,000
Population change, 1980–90:	0.3%
Leading ancestry group:	African American
Second leading group:	French
Foreign born population:	2.1%
Hispanic origin†:	2.2%
Population by race:	
White:	67.3%
Black:	30.8%
Native American:	0.4%
Asian/Pacific Islander:	1.0%
Other:	0.5%

Population by Age Group

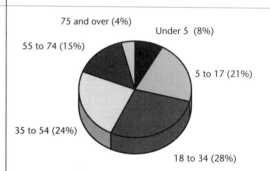

75 and over (4%)
Under 5 (8%)
55 to 74 (15%)
5 to 17 (21%)
35 to 54 (24%)
18 to 34 (28%)

Top Cities with Populations Over 25,000

City	Population	National rank	% change 1980–90
New Orleans	489,595	26	–10.9
Baton Rouge	224,704	72	0.1
Shreveport	196,645	79	–3.5
Lafayette	97,362	209	15.2
Kenner	73,737	311	8.5
Lake Charles	71,135	329	–6.2
Monroe	56,174	447	–4.7
Bossier City	52,874	492	3.7
Alexandria	48,950	543	–4.6
New Iberia	32,568	854	–2.9

Notes: †A person of Hispanic origin may be of any race. NA indicates that data are not available.
Sources: Economic and Statistics Administration, Bureau of the Census. *Statistical Abstract of the United States, 1994–95.* Washington, DC: Government Printing Office, 1995; Courtenay M. Slater and George E. Hall. *1995 County and City Extra: Annual Metro, City and County Data Book.* Lanham, MD: Bernan Press, 1995.

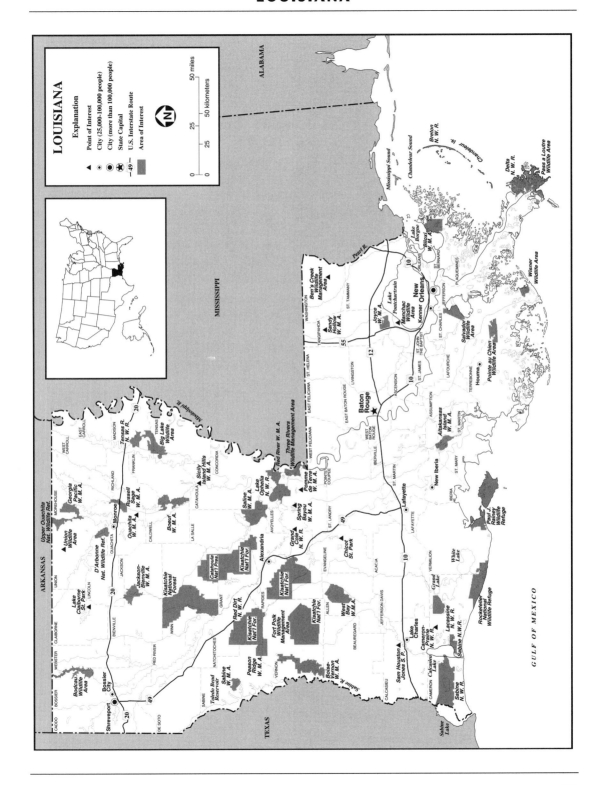

LOUISIANA

Explanation

▲ Point of Interest

◉ City (25,000-100,000 people)

⊙ City (more than 100,000 people)

✪ State Capital

–49– U.S. Interstate Route

▨ Area of Interest

50 miles

50 kilometers

ALABAMA

MISSISSIPPI

ARKANSAS

TEXAS

GULF OF MEXICO

Mississippi Sound

Chandeleur Sound

Chandeleur Is.

Breton N. W. R.

Delta N. W. R.

Pass a Loutre Wildlife Area

Wisner Wildlife Area

Lake Borgne

Biloxi W. M. A.

New Orleans

Kenner

Lake Pontchartrain

Salvador Wildlife Area

Pointe au Chien Wildlife Area

Houma

Pearl R.

Ben's Creek Wildlife Management Area

Sandy Hollow W.M.A.

Joyce W. M. A.

Manchac Wildlife Area

Baton Rouge

Atchafalaya Island W. M. A.

New Iberia

White Lake

Grand Lake

Rockefeller National Wildlife Refuge

Paul J. Rainey Wildlife Refuge

Lafayette

Chicot St. Park

Grand Cote N. W. R.

Three Rivers Wildlife Management Area

Pomme de Terre W. M. A.

Spring Bayou W. M. A.

Lake Ophelia N. W. R.

Sabine W. M. A.

Sicily Island Hills W. M. A.

Big Lake Wildlife Area

Red River W. M. A.

Tensas R. N. W. R.

Georgia Pacific W. M. A.

Russell Sage W. M. A.

Boeuf W. M. A.

Ouachita W. M. A.

Monroe

Union Wildlife Area

Upper Ouachita Nat. Wildlife Ref.

D'Arbonne Nat. Wildlife Refuge

Lake Claiborne St. Park

Bodcau Wildlife Area

Bossier City

Shreveport

Toledo Bend Reservoir

Sabine W. M. A.

Pesson Ridge W. M. A.

Boise-Vernon W. M. A.

Sam Houston Jones S.P.

Cameron-Prairie N.W.R.

Lake Charles

Calcasieu Lake

Sabine Lake

Sabine N. W. R.

Lacassine N. W. R.

Jackson-Bienville W. M. A.

Kisatchie Nat'l Forest

Catahoula Nat'l Press

Kisatchie Nat'l For.

Alexandria

Grand Cole N. W. R.

Red Dirt W. M. A.

Fort Polk Wildlife Management Area

Kisatchie Nat'l For.

Kisatchie Nat'l For.

West Bay W. M. A.

Mississippi R.

Sabine R.

10

12

55

49

20

20

20

10

10

10

49

CADDO

BOSSIER

WEBSTER

CLAIBORNE

UNION

MOREHOUSE

WEST CARROLL

EAST CARROLL

LINCOLN

JACKSON

BIENVILLE

RED RIVER

DE SOTO

SABINE

NATCHITOCHES

WINN

GRANT

RAPIDES

VERNON

BEAUREGARD

ALLEN

EVANGELINE

AVOYELLES

LA SALLE

CATAHOULA

CALDWELL

RICHLAND

OUACHITA

FRANKLIN

MADISON

TENSAS

CONCORDIA

POINTE COUPEE

WEST FELICIANA

EAST FELICIANA

ST. HELENA

TANGIPAHOA

WASHINGTON

ST. TAMMANY

LIVINGSTON

ASCENSION

ST. JAMES

ST. JOHN THE BAPTIST

ST. CHARLES

JEFFERSON

ORLEANS

ST. BERNARD

PLAQUEMINES

LAFOURCHE

TERREBONNE

ASSUMPTION

ST. MARTIN

IBERIA

ST. MARY

VERMILION

ACADIA

ST. LANDRY

LAFAYETTE

IBERVILLE

WEST BATON ROUGE

EAST BATON ROUGE

JEFFERSON DAVIS

CALCASIEU

CAMERON

Photo credit: Louisiana Office of Tourism.

Swamp of the Atchafalaya River. Louisiana has the most wetlands of all the states.

birds include quail, turkey, and various waterfowl, of which the mottled duck and wood duck are native. Coastal beaches are inhabited by sea turtles, and whales may be seen offshore. Freshwater fish include bass, crappie, and bream. Endangered animals include the American alligator, the Sei and sperm whales, and the eastern brown pelican (the state bird).

5 ENVIRONMENTAL PROTECTION

Louisiana's earliest and most pressing environmental problem was Mississippi River. In the 1920s, the US Congress funded construction of a system of flood-ways and spillways to divert water from the Mississippi when necessary. However, these flood control measures created another environmental problem, as salt water from the Gulf of Mexico has seeped into the wetlands. Louisiana's wetlands are more than wildlife refuges. They are central to the state's agriculture and fishing industries.

In 1984, Louisiana consolidated much of its environmental protection effort into a new state agency—The Department of Environmental Quality (DEQ). With approximately 100 major chemical and petrochemical manufacturing and refining facilities located in Louisiana, many DEQ programs deal with the regulation of hazardous waste generation, management and disposal, and chemical releases to the air and water. In 1994, there were 14 hazardous waste sites in Louisiana.

The two largest wildlife refuges in the state are the Rockefeller Wildlife Refuge in Cameron and Vermilion parishes, covering 84,000 acres (34,000 hectares). The other is the Marsh Island Refuge, 82,000 acres (33,000 hectares) of marshland in Iberia Parish.

6 POPULATION

In 1990 Louisiana's population was 4,219,973, placing it 21st among the 50 states. The estimated population for 1995 was 4,359.000. The US Census Bureau estimates that the state's population will be 4,141,000 in 2000. Louisiana's population density in 1990 was 97 persons per square mile (37 persons per square kilometer). About 75% of Louisianians lived in metropolitan areas in 1992. New Orleans is the largest city, with a 1992 population of 489,595, followed by Baton Rouge, 224,704; and Shreveport, 196,645.

7 ETHNIC GROUPS

Louisiana, especially the Delta region, is more ethnically diverse than other areas of the South. Two groups that have been highly identified with the culture of Louisiana are Creoles and Acadians (also called Cajuns). Both descend from early French immigrants to the state. The Cajuns trace their origins to rural Acadia (Nova Scotia), and the Creoles tend to be city people from France and, in some cases, from Nova Scotia, Spain, or the Caribbean island of Hispaniola. Acadians

still speak a French patois (dialect) and retain a distinctive culture and cuisine. In 1990, 432,549 residents claimed Acadian/ Cajun ancestry.

Blacks made up 30.8% of the population in 1990. Many of these, of mixed blood, are referred to locally as "colored Creoles," and have constituted a black elite in both urban and rural Louisiana. As of 1990, there were 18,541 Native Americans in Louisiana, along with 41,099 Asians and Pacific Islanders, including 14,696 Vietnamese.

8 LANGUAGES

Louisiana English is predominantly Southern. In 1990, 3,494,359 Louisiana residents—89.9% of the population—spoke only English at home. Other languages spoken at home (with number of speakers) included French, 261,678; Spanish, 72,173; and Vietnamese, 14,352. In 1990, about 495 Louisiana residents spoke a Native American language at home.

Unique to Louisiana is a large French-speaking area. West of New Orleans the French dialect called Acadian (Cajun) is used as the first language. From it, and from early colonial French, English has taken such words as *pirogue* (dugout canoe), *armoire* (wardrobe), and *lagniappe* (extra gift).

9 RELIGIONS

As of 1990, the Roman Catholic Church was the largest Christian denomination, with 1,369,154 church members. The leading Protestant denominations in 1990 were Southern Baptist, 757,639; United

Methodist, 172,676; Episcopal, 33,423; and Presbyterian, 27,105. In 1990, 15,625 Jews resided in Louisiana, about 70% of them in New Orleans. Voodoo, in some cases blended with Christian ritual, is more widespread in Louisiana than anywhere else in the US.

10 TRANSPORTATION

As of December 1992, Louisiana had a total railroad mileage of 2,936 route miles (4,724 kilometers), including 2,259 rail miles (3,635 kilometers) of Class 1 track. As of 1992, Amtrak provided passenger links with Los Angeles, Chicago, and New York and carried 192,804 passengers from seven stations through the state. At the end of 1993, Louisiana had a total of 59,599 miles (95,895 kilometers) of public roads, 77% of them rural. In 1993, 2,010,084 automobiles and 1,136,449 trucks were registered in the state.

Four of the nation's ten busiest ports are in Louisiana. New Orleans is a major center of domestic and international freight traffic. In volume of domestic and foreign cargo handled, it is the busiest port on the Gulf of Mexico and a leading port in the US. In 1992, the busiest air facility was New Orleans International Airport, which boarded 3,151,718 passengers and 13,801 tons of freight.

11 HISTORY

When European exploration and settlement of North America began, Louisiana was inhabited by a number of different Native American groups, including various tribes of the Caddo people, small Tunican-speaking groups, the Atakapa group, and the Chitimacha. The Spaniard Hernando de Soto was probably the first to penetrate the state's present boundaries, in 1541. Robert Cavelier, Sieur de la Salle reached the mouth of the Mississippi on 9 April 1682, named the land there Louisiana in honor of King Louis XIV, and claimed it for France. In 1714, Louis Juchereau de St. Denis established Natchitoches, the first permanent European settlement in Louisiana; Iberville's brother, the Sieur de Bienville, established New Orleans four years later.

Although Louisiana did not thrive economically under French rule, French culture was firmly implanted there and absorbed by non-French settlers, especially Germans from Switzerland and the Rhineland. In 1762, France ceded Louisiana to Spain. Governed by Spaniards, the colony was much more prosperous. New settlers—including Acadian refugees from Nova Scotia—added to the population. The territory grew to about 50,000 inhabitants by 1800, when Napoleon forced the Spanish government to return Louisiana to France. Three years later, Napoleon sold Louisiana to the US to keep it from falling into the hands of Great Britain.

President Thomas Jefferson concluded what was probably the best real estate deal in history, purchasing 800,000 square miles (2,100,000 square kilometers) for $15,000,000 and thus more than doubling the size of the US at a cost of about 3 cents per acre. The next year, that part of the purchase south of 33°N was separated from the remainder and designated the Territory of Orleans. When its population reached the level required for statehood in

1810, the people of the territory drew up a constitution, and Louisiana entered the Union on 30 April 1812.

State Development

American control of Louisiana was threatened soon afterward when British troops tried to take New Orleans in 1814 but were soundly defeated by a mixed contingent of forces under the command of Andrew Jackson. From 1815 to 1861, Louisiana was one of the most prosperous states in the South, producing sugar and cotton, and raising hogs and cattle. Wealthy planters, whose slaves made up almost half the population, dominated Louisiana politically and economically. When the secession crisis came in 1861, they led Louisiana into the Confederacy and, after four bloody years, to total defeat.

After the Civil War, Radical Republican governments elected by black voters ruled the state, but declining support from the North and fierce resistance from Louisiana whites brought the Reconstruction period to an end. Blacks and their few white allies lost control of state government and, in 1898, blacks were deprived almost entirely of their voting rights by a new state constitution drawn up primarily for that purpose. This constitution also significantly reduced the number of poorer whites who voted in Louisiana elections. Just as before the Civil War, large landowners—combined with New Orleans bankers, businessmen, and politicians— dominated state government, effectively blocking political and social reform.

Not until 1928, with the election of Huey P. Long as governor, did the winds of major change strike Louisiana. The years from 1928 through 1960 could well be called the Long Era. Three Longs dominated state politics for most of the period: Huey, who became governor but was assassinated in 1935; his brother Earl, who served as governor three times; and his son Russell, who became a powerful US senator. From a backward agricultural state, Louisiana evolved into one of the world's major petrochemical-manufacturing centers. What had been one of the most frugal states became one of the most liberal in welfare spending, care for the aged, highway building, and education. The state could afford these expanding programs because of ever-increasing revenues from oil and gas.

In the mid-1980s, the major problems confronting the state were racial and labor tensions, inadequate disposal sites for industrial wastes, and (despite important new discoveries) the depletion of oil and gas resources. In 1989, racial tensions took a new turn when white supremacist David Duke, running as a Republican, narrowly won a seat in the Louisiana state legislature. He then ran for the US Senate—with a showing of 44 percent among voters—and, in 1991, for governor. (He was defeated by former governor Edwin Edwards.) In opposing affirmative action, Duke appealed to whites' frustrations with the high unemployment brought on by the collapse of oil prices in the mid- and late 1980s, when the number of jobs in the state declined by 8%.

12 STATE GOVERNMENT

The state legislature consists of a 39-member senate and a 105-member house of representatives. All legislators are elected for four-year terms. Major elected executive officials include the governor and lieutenant governor (independently elected), secretary of state, attorney general, and treasurer, all elected for four-year terms.

To become law, a bill must receive majority votes in both the senate and the house and be signed by the governor; or be left unsigned but not vetoed by the governor; or be passed again by two-thirds votes of both houses over the governor's veto. Appropriation bills must originate in the house but may be amended by the senate. The governor has an item veto on appropriation bills. Constitutional amendments require approval by two-thirds of the elected members of each house and ratification by a majority of the people voting on it at the next general election.

13 POLITICAL PARTIES

The major political organizations are the Democratic Party and the Republican Party, each affiliated with the national party. However, differences in culture and economic interests have made Louisiana's politics extremely complex. After an extended period of Democratic dominance under the Long family, the 1960s and 1970s saw a resurgence of the Republican Party and the election in 1979 of David C. Treen, the state's first Republican governor since Reconstruction. However, Treen was succeeded by Democrats Edwin

Louisiana Presidential Vote by Political Parties, 1948–92

YEAR	LOUISIANA WINNER	DEMOCRAT	REPUBLICAN	STATES' RIGHTS DEMOCRAT	PROGRESSIVE	AMERICAN INDEPENDENT
1948	Thurmond (SRD)	136,344	72,657	204,290	3,035	—
1952	Stevenson (D)	345,027	306,925	—	—	—
				UNPLEDGED		
1956	*Eisenhower (R)	243,977	329,047	44,520	—	—
				NAT'L. STATES' RIGHTS		
1960	*Kennedy (D)	407,339	230,980	169,572	—	—
1964	Goldwater (R)	387,068	509,225	—	—	—
1968	Wallace (AI)	309,615	257,535	—	—	530,300
				AMERICAN	SOC. WORKERS	
1972	*Nixon (R)	298,142	686,852	44,127	12,169	—
				LIBERTARIAN	COMMUNIST	
1976	*Carter (D)	661,365	587,446	3,325	7,417	10,058
					CITIZENS	
1980	*Reagan (R)	708,453	792,853	8,240	1,584	10,333
1984	*Reagan (R)	651,586	1,037,299	1,876	9,502	—
					POPULIST	N ALLIANCE
1988	*Bush (R)	717,460	883,702	4,115	18,612	2,355
					IND. (Perot)	AMERICA FIRST
1992	*Clinton (D)	815,971	733,386	3,155	211,478	18,545

* Won US presidential election.

Edwards in 1983 and Charles Roemer in 1987, and Edwards again in 1991.

As of 1994 there were 1,169,653 registered Democrats, or 72% of the voters; 424,150 registered Republicans, or 19%; and 210,085 unaffiliated, or 9%. Both US senators—John Breaux and J. Bennett Johnston, Jr.—were Democrats in 1994. Louisiana's delegation of US representatives consisted of four Democrats and three Republicans. In 1994, 33 of the state senators were Democrats, and 6 were Republicans; 88 of the state representatives were Democrats while 16 were Republicans; and 1 was an Independent. In the 1992 presidential election, Louisianians gave Democrat Bill Clinton in the 46% of the vote, while George Bush received 41% and Ross Perot collected 12%.

Photo credit: Louisiana Office of Tourism.

The capitol building in Baton Rouge.

14 LOCAL GOVERNMENT

The church districts, called parishes, into which Louisiana was divided in the late 17th century remain the primary political divisions in the state, serving functions similar to those of counties in other states. In 1994 there were 64 parishes, many of them governed by police jury. Other parish officials are the sheriff, clerk of court, assessor, and coroner. As of 1992, Louisiana also had 301 municipal governments. Prominent local officials include the mayor, chief of police, and a council or board of aldermen.

15 JUDICIAL SYSTEM

The highest court in Louisiana is the supreme court, with appeals jurisdiction. There are five appeals circuits in the state, each divided into three districts. Each of the state's district courts serves at least one parish and has at least one district judge, elected for a six-year term. District courts have original jurisdiction in criminal and civil cases. City courts are the principal courts of limited jurisdiction. According to the FBI Crime Index in 1994, Louisiana had a crime index total of 6,671.1 per 100,000. As of 1993, 22,468 prisoners were in Louisiana's state and federal prisons—a ratio of 530 per 100,000.

16 MIGRATION

Beginning in World War II, large numbers of both black and white farm workers left

Louisiana and migrated north and west. During the 1960s, the state had a net out-migration of 15% of its black population, but the trend had slowed somewhat by 1975. Recent migration within the state has been from north to south, and from rural to urban areas, especially to Shreveport, Baton Rouge, and the suburbs of New Orleans. Overall, Louisiana suffered a net loss from migration of about 368,000 from 1940 to 1990. By 1990, 79% of all state residents were native-born, a proportion exceeded only by Pennsylvania.

17 ECONOMY

With the rise of the petrochemical industry, Louisiana's economy has regained much of the vitality it enjoyed before the Civil War. Today, Louisiana ranks second only to Texas in the value of its mineral products. Unfortunately, not all of Louisiana's citizens share in this newfound wealth. The state's unemployment rate has been higher than the national average, and the rate for women is especially high. Per capita (per person) income is still well below the national norm.

Louisiana is primarily an industrial state, but its industries are to a large degree based on its natural resources, principally oil, water, and timber. Industrial expansion suffered a severe blow in the early 1980s, when the price of oil dropped from $37 a barrel in 1981 to $15 a barrel in 1986. Energy-related industries, such as barge-building, machinery-manufacturing, and rig/platform production suffered. In an attempt to offset losses in employment, Louisiana planned to build several casinos.

18 INCOME

Louisiana's per capita (per person) income in 1994 was $17,615, for a rank of 44th in the US. Total personal income rose to $76 billion in 1994. Income, although increasing, is unequally distributed. In 1993, about 26.4% of all Louisianians were below the federal poverty level.

19 INDUSTRY

A huge and still-growing petrochemical industry has become a dominant force in the state's economy. Other expanding industries are wood products and, especially since World War II, shipbuilding. In 1992, the total value of shipments of manufactured goods was $60.9 billion. The largest employers among industry groups were chemicals and chemical products, transportation equipment, food and food products, and fabricated metal products, which together utilized 55% of the industrial work force.

20 LABOR

In 1994, Louisiana had a total civilian labor force of 1,939,000, or about 45% of the population. There was an unemployment rate of 8.0%. In 1994, 7.7% of all workers were union members. There were four national labor unions operating in the state in 1993.

21 AGRICULTURE

With a farm income of over $2 billion in 1994—65% from crops—Louisiana ranked 31st among the 50 states. Nearly every crop grown in North America could be raised somewhere in Louisiana. In the south are strawberries, oranges, and sweet potatoes;

in the southeast, sugarcane; and in the southwest, rice and soybeans. Soybeans are also raised in the cotton-growing area of the northeast. Oats, alfalfa, corn, potatoes, and peaches are among the other crops grown in the north.

As of 1994 there were an estimated 28,000 farms covering 7.8 million acres (3.2 million hectares). Louisiana long ranked first in the US in sugarcane production, but by the late 1970s, Florida had surpassed it. Cash receipts for the sugar crop in 1994 were about $225 million for 9,120,000 tons. Louisiana ranked third in the value of its rice production in 1994 with about $233 million for 2,944.8 million pounds.

22 DOMESTICATED ANIMALS

Livestock production in 1994 accounted for 35% of agricultural income. In 1994 there were 960,000 cattle and 45,000 hogs. The cattle output in 1994 accounted for 7.9% of Louisiana's agricultural receipts. Fur trapping has some local importance. In 1981, a month-long statewide alligator season was held for the first time in 18 years.

23 FISHING

In 1992, Louisiana was second only to Alaska in the size of its commercial fish landings, with over 1.0 billion pounds, and ranked second by value of catch at $294.9 million. The most important species caught in Louisiana are shrimp, menhaden, and oysters. In 1991, the menhaden catch was in excess of 1 billion pounds, and shrimp landings amounted to 95,088,000 pounds.

Louisiana produces most of the US crayfish harvest. By 1992, crayfish farms covered some 115,000 acres (46,540 hectares). The recent flooding of the midwest caused the water levels of the state's Atchafalaya Basin to rise, thus increasing the wild crayfish harvest and extending the season. Farm production of crayfish in 1991/92 was about 60 million pounds, with an estimated value of $33 million.

24 FORESTRY

As of 1991 there were 13,791,700 acres (5,581,425 hectares) of forestland in Louisiana, representing almost half the state's land area. The principal forest types are loblolly and shortleaf pine in the northwest, longleaf and slash pine in the south, and hardwood in a wide area along the Mississippi River. In 1993, forest landowner income from sales of timber was estimated at $491.3 million. Louisiana has one national forest, Kisatchie, with a gross area of 1,022,703 acres (413,875 hectares).

25 MINING

Louisiana's nonfuel mineral value totaled an estimated $328 million in 1994. The four leading mineral commodities, in terms of value, were salt, sulfur, and construction sand/gravel.

26 ENERGY AND POWER

In 1993, power plants in Louisiana generated a total of 59.4 billion kilowatt hours of power, and 1992 energy consumption was 3,558 trillion Btu, or 831.4 million Btu per capita (per person). Louisiana ranked third nationally in per capita energy consumption. The state's energy expenditures per capita (per person) were $2,893 in 1992. About 46% of the state's energy needs were supplied by natural gas, 42% by oil, and 12% by other sources. As of 1993, Louisiana had two nuclear power plants.

Oil and gas production has expanded greatly since World War II, but production reached its peak in the early 1970s and proven reserves are declining. Louisiana produced 139,000,000 barrels of crude oil during 1993. At the end of 1992, remaining proven reserves of oil in Louisiana amounted to 668 million barrels. Natural gas marketed production in 1993 was 5.2 trillion cubic feet.

27 COMMERCE

Louisiana had 1992 wholesale sales of $37.3 billion; 1993 retail sales of $31.4 billion; and 1992 service establishment receipts of $17.9 billion. In 1991, Louisiana ranked sixth among the 50 states in value of its goods exported abroad, with $16.2 billion.

28 PUBLIC FINANCE

The budget is prepared by the state executive budget director and submitted annually by the governor to the legislature for amendment and approval. Estimated revenues for fiscal year 1993 were $11,423 million; expenditures were $9,826 million. As of 1993, Louisiana had a total debt of $9.6 billion, or about $2,234 per capita (per person).

29 TAXATION

For most of the state's history, Louisianians paid little in taxes. Despite increases in taxation and expenditures since the late 1920s, when Huey Long introduced the graduated income tax, Louisiana's state tax burden per capita (per person), $1,013.5 in 1991, is still well below the national average. Income taxes yielded $1.1 billion in state revenues in 1991.

The state's 4% sales and use tax yielded nearly $1.3 billion to the state in 1991. State tax collections amounted to $4,334.4 million in 1994. The state also taxes gasoline sales, gifts and inheritances, soft drinks, alcoholic beverages, and tobacco products, among other items. Taxes on beer and chain stores contribute to local revenues, as does the property tax, although Louisiana relies less on this than do most other states.

30 HEALTH

Death rates from heart disease, cancer, suicide, cerebrovascular diseases, and accidents were above the US median. The only leprosarium on the US mainland is at Carville; however, most leprosy patients can be treated at home. In 1993, the 132 community hospitals in Louisiana had a total of 19,000 beds. The average hospital cost in 1993 was $875 per inpatient day, or $5,781 for an average cost per stay. There were 8,600 nonfederal physicians in 1993 and about 24,000 nurses. In 1993, about 24% of all state residents did not have health insurance.

31 HOUSING

According to a 1993 estimate there were 1,723,000 year-round housing units. In 1990, New Orleans had 264,146 housing units, 7.2% of which had been built during the previous decade. In 1993, some 11,226 new housing units worth $869 million were authorized in the state. The median value of a home in Louisiana was $58,500 in 1990. Owner-occupied monthly costs (including mortgage) had a median of $595 in 1990, when the median monthly rent was $352.

32 EDUCATION

As of 1990, only 68.7% of adult Louisianians had completed high school and 15.3% had completed four or more years of college. In fall 1993, total enrollment in Louisiana's public elementary and secondary schools was 899,545. A federal court order in 1966 brought about public school integration. By 1980, 36% of minority students in Louisiana were in schools with under 50% minority enrollment, and 25% were in schools with 99–100% minority enrollment. State expenditures on education averaged $4,330 per pupil in 1993 (43d in the nation).

As of 1990, in addition to 53 vocational-technical schools, there were 34 institutions of higher education in Louisiana, of which 22 were public and 12 private. The center of the state university system is Louisiana State University (LSU) in Baton Rouge, with a 1994/95 enrollment of 23,780. Tulane University in New Orleans is one of the most distinguished private universities in the South. Total state and local expenditures on public schools in 1993/94 exceeded $3.8 billion.

33 ARTS

New Orleans has long been one of the most important centers of artistic activity in the South. In the mid-1980s, Louisiana's principal theaters included the New Orleans Theater of the Performing Arts, Le Petit Theatre du Vieux Carre, and the Tulane Theater. The Free Southern Theatre is a black touring company based in New Orleans. Baton Rouge, Shreveport, Monroe, Lake Charles, and Hammond are among the cities with little theaters, and Baton Rouge, Lafayette, and Lake Charles have ballet companies. There are symphony orchestras in most of the larger cities, of which the Baton Rouge Symphony Orchestra is the best known.

It is probably in music that Louisiana has made its most distinctive contributions to culture. Jazz was born in New Orleans around 1900. Early jazz in the New Orleans style is called Dixieland. Traditional Dixieland may still be heard in New Orleans at Preservation Hall, Dixieland Hall, and the New Orleans Jazz Club. Equally distinctive is Cajun music, dominated by the sound of the fiddle and accordion. The French Acadian Music Festival, held in Abbeville, takes place in April.

Louisiana has an income tax checkoff for arts programs that allows taxpayers to designate part or all of their income tax refunds to be placed in a fund for the arts. From 1987 to 1991, Louisiana generated $10,519,195 in federal and state funds to support its arts programs.

[34] LIBRARIES AND MUSEUMS

Louisiana's 64 parishes were served by 62 public libraries in 1994. That year, the public library system held 9,669,544 volumes and had a total circulation of 19,184,972. The New Orleans Public Library features a special collection on jazz and folk music. As of 1994, Louisiana had 77 museums and historic sites and public gardens. Leading art museums are the New Orleans Museum of Art, the Lampe Gallery in New Orleans, and the R. W. Norton Art Gallery at Shreveport.

[35] COMMUNICATIONS

As of March 1993, 90.3% of Louisiana's 1,540,000 occupied housing units had telephones. As of 1993, the state had 216 radio broadcasting stations (93 AM and 123 FM) and 26 commercial and 8 educational television stations. That year, there were ten large cable television systems.

[36] PRESS

In 1994, Louisiana had a total of 10 morning dailies, 14 evening dailies, 1 all-day paper, and 19 Sunday papers. The principal dailies with their 1994 daily circulations are *The New Orleans Times-Picayune* (272,280) and *The Baton Rouge Advocate* (102,010). Two influential literary magazines originated in the state: the *Southern Review,* founded at LSU in the 1930s by Robert Penn Warren and Cleanth Brooks, and the *Tulane Drama Review.*

[37] TOURISM, TRAVEL, AND RECREATION

In 1994, the Louisiana tourist industry had an annual employment of 97,100. Domestic visitors spent an estimated $5.5 billion in the state that year. New Orleans is one of the major tourist attractions in the US. Known for its fine restaurants, serving such distinctive fare as gumbo, jambalaya, and crayfish, along with an elaborate French-inspired haute cuisine, New Orleans also offers jazz clubs, the graceful buildings of the French Quarter, and a lavish carnival called Mardi Gras ("Fat Tuesday"). Beginning on the Wednesday before Shrove Tuesday (preceding Lent), parades and balls, staged by private organizations called *krewes,* are held almost nightly.

Among the many other annual events that attract visitors to the state are the Natchitoches Christmas Festival, which includes 170,000 Christmas lights and spectacular fireworks displays. Louisiana's 34 state parks and recreation sites total 39,000 acres (15,800 hectares).

[38] SPORTS

Louisiana has one major league professional sports team: the Saints of the National Football League. Horse-racing is popular in the state. The principal tracks are the Louisiana Jockey Club at the Fair Grounds in New Orleans and Evangeline Downs at Lafayette. Gambling has long been widespread in Louisiana. The New Orleans Open Golf Tournament is held in April.

In 1935, Tulane University inaugurated the Sugar Bowl, an annual New Year's Day event and one of the most prestigious bowl games in college football. Louisiana State University last won the Sugar Bowl in 1968.

Canoeing and fishing in Chicot State Park, one of 34 state parks and recreation areas.

39 FAMOUS LOUISIANIANS

Zachary Taylor (b.Virginia, 1784–1850) is the only US president to whom Louisiana can lay claim. Taylor owned a large plantation north of Baton Rouge, which was his residence before his election to the presidency in 1848. Edward Douglass White (1845–1921) served as chief justice of the US Supreme Court.

Throughout the 20th century, the Longs have been the first family of Louisiana politics. Without question, the most important state officeholder in Louisiana history was Huey P. Long (1893–1935), elected to the governorship in 1928, who inaugurated a period of social and economic reform. In the process, he made himself very nearly an absolute dictator within Louisiana. Huey's brother Earl K. Long (1895–1960) served three times as governor. Huey's son, US Senator Russell B. Long (b.1918), was chairman of the Finance Committee from 1965 to 1980.

Also prominent in Louisiana history was Robert Cavelier, Sieur de la Salle (b.France, 1643–87), who was the first to claim the region for the French crown. Jean Étienne Boré (1741–1820) laid the foundation of the Louisiana sugar industry by developing a process for granulating sugar from cane; Norbert Rillieux (1806–94), a free black man, developed the much more efficient vacuum pan process of refining sugar.

Biochemist Andrew Victor Schally (b.Poland, 1926) shared the Nobel Prize for medicine in 1977 for his research on hormones. Among other distinguished Louisiana professionals have been historian T. Harry Williams (1909–79), who won the Pulitzer Prize for his biography of Huey Long; architect Henry Hobson Richardson (1838–86); and heart specialist Michael De Bakey (b.1908).

Louisiana's important writers include George Washington Cable (1844–1925), an early advocate of racial justice; Kate O'Flaherty Chopin (b.Missouri, 1851–1904); playwright and memoirist Lillian Hellman (1905–84); and novelists Walker Percy (b.Alabama 1916–90), Truman Capote (1924–84), Shirley Ann Grau (b.1929), and John Kennedy Toole (1937–69). The latter two were both winners of the Pulitzer Prize.

Louisianians in the arts include composer Louis Moreau Gottschalk (1829–69); jazz musicians Jelly Roll Morton (Ferdinand Joseph La Menthe, 1885–1941) and Louis "Satchmo" Armstrong (1900–71), gained nationwide popularity. Other prominent Louisianians in music are gospel singer Mahalia Jackson (1911–72); pianist-singer-songwriter Antoine "Fats" Domino (b.1928); and pop singer Jerry Lee Lewis (b.1935).

Louisiana baseball heroes include Hall of Famer Melvin Thomas "Mel" Ott (1909–58). Terry Bradshaw (b.1948) quarterbacked the Super Bowl champion Pittsburgh Steelers during the 1970s. Player-coach William F. "Bill" Russell (b.1934) led the Boston Celtics to 10 National Basketball Association championships between 1956 and 1969. Chess master Paul Morphy (1837–84) was born in New Orleans.

40 BIBLIOGRAPHY

Taylor, Joe Gray. *Louisiana: A Bicentennial History*. New York: Norton, 1976.

———. *Louisiana Reconstructed, 1863–77*. Baton Rouge: Louisiana State University Press, 1974.

Williams, T. Harry. *Huey Long*, New York: Random House, 1981.

Winters, John D. *The Civil War in Louisiana*. Baton Rouge: Louisiana State University Press, 1979.

MAINE

State of Maine

ORIGIN OF STATE NAME: Derived either from the French for a historical district of France, or from the early use of "main" to distinguish coast from islands.

NICKNAME: The Pine Tree State.

CAPITAL: Augusta.

ENTERED UNION: 15 March 1820 (23d).

SONG: "State of Maine Song."

MOTTO: *Dirigo* (I direct).

COAT OF ARMS: A farmer and sailor support a shield on which are depicted a pine tree, a moose, and water. Under the shield is the name of the state; above it are the state motto and the North Star.

FLAG: The coat of arms is on a blue field, with a yellow fringed border surrounding three sides.

OFFICIAL SEAL: Same as the coat of arms.

ANIMAL: Moose.

BIRD: Chickadee.

FISH: Landlocked salmon.

FLOWER: White pine Cone and Tassel.

TREE: Eastern white pine.

INSECT: Honeybee.

MINERAL: Tourmaline.

TIME: 7 AM EST = noon GMT.

1 LOCATION AND SIZE

Situated in the extreme northeastern corner of the US, Maine is the nation's most easterly state, the largest in New England, and 39th in size among the 50 states. The total area of Maine is 33,265 square miles (86,156 square kilometers). Maine extends 207 miles (333 kilometers) east-west; the maximum north-south extension is 322 miles (518 kilometers). Hundreds of islands dot Maine's coast. The largest is Mt. Desert Island. Others include Deer Isle, Vinalhaven, and Isle au Haut.

Maine's total boundary length is 883 miles (1,421 kilometers).

2 TOPOGRAPHY

Maine is divided into four main regions: coastal lowlands extending 10–20 miles (16–32 kilometers) inland; the piedmont, a transitional hilly belt; a mountain region, which marks the northern endpoint of the 2,000-mile (3,200-kilometer) Appalachian Trail; and Maine's uplands, a high, relatively flat plateau extending northward beyond the mountains. Maine has more than 2,200 lakes and ponds. The more than 5,000 rivers and streams include the Penobscot, Androscoggin, Kennebec, and Saco. Mt. Katahdin, at 5,268 feet (1,607 meters), is the highest point in the state.

3 CLIMATE

Maine has three climatic regions: the northern interior zone, comprising roughly the northern half of the state, between Quebec and New Brunswick; the southern interior zone; and the coastal zone. The northern zone is both drier and cooler in all four seasons than either of the other zones, while the coastal zone is more moderate in temperature year-round than the other two. Annual mean temperatures range from about 40°F (5°C) in the northern zone to 46°F (8°C) in the coastal zone. Record temperatures for the state are –48°F (–44°C) registered in 1925, and 105°F (41°C) in 1911. The mean annual precipitation ranges from 40.2 inches (102 centimeters) in the north to 45.7 inches (116 centimeters) on the coast.

4 PLANTS AND ANIMALS

Maine's forests are largely softwoods, comprising chiefly red and white spruces, eastern hemlock, and white and red pine. Important hardwoods include beech, white oak, and black willow. Maine is home to most of the flowers and shrubs common to the north temperate zone, including an important commercial resource, the low-bush blueberry. Maine has 17 rare orchid species (one, the small whorled pogonia, is on the federal endangered list).

Maine Population Profile

Estimated 1995 population:	1,295,000
Population change, 1980–90:	9.2%
Leading ancestry group:	English
Second leading group:	French
Foreign born population:	3.0%
Hispanic origin†:	0.6%
Population by race:	
White:	98.4%
Black:	0.4%
Native American:	0.5%
Asian/Pacific Islander:	0.5%
Other:	0.2%

Population by Age Group

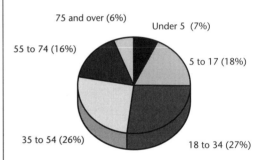

75 and over (6%)
Under 5 (7%)
55 to 74 (16%)
5 to 17 (18%)
35 to 54 (26%)
18 to 34 (27%)

Top Cities with Populations Over 25,000

City	Population	National rank	% change 1980–90
Portland	62,756	385	4.5
Lewiston	38,031	721	–1.8
Bangor	32,145	875	4.9

Notes: †A person of Hispanic origin may be of any race. NA indicates that data are not available.
Sources: Economic and Statistics Administration, Bureau of the Census. *Statistical Abstract of the United States, 1994–95.* Washington, DC: Government Printing Office, 1995; Courtenay M. Slater and George E. Hall. *1995 County and City Extra: Annual Metro, City and County Data Book.* Lanham, MD: Bernan Press, 1995.

MAINE

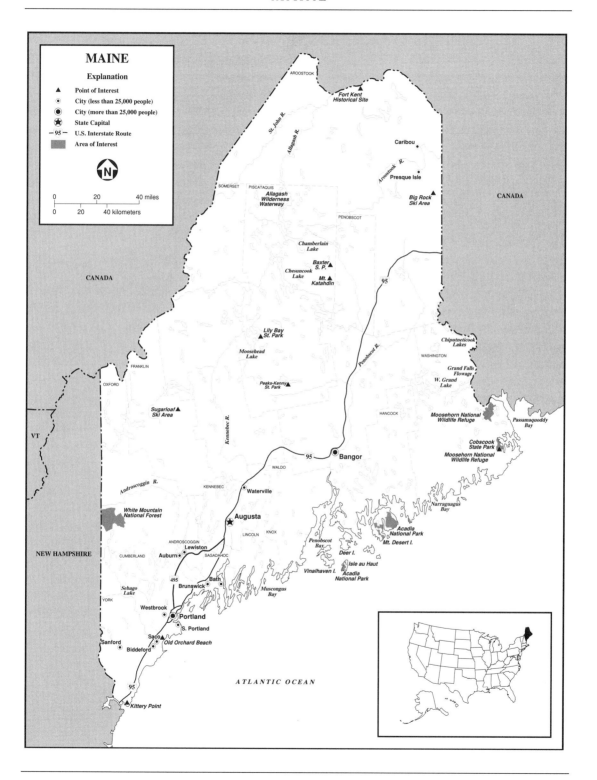

MAINE

Explanation

▲ Point of Interest

⊙ City (less than 25,000 people)

◉ City (more than 25,000 people)

★ State Capital

—95— U.S. Interstate Route

▨ Area of Interest

N

0   20   40 miles

0   20   40 kilometers

AROOSTOOK

St. John R.

Allagash R.

Fort Kent
Historical Site

Caribou

Aroostook R.

Presque Isle

SOMERSET

PISCATAQUIS

CANADA

*Allagash
Wilderness
Waterway*

PENOBSCOT

*Chamberlain
Lake*

Baxter
S. P. ▲

*Chesuncook
Lake*

Mt. ▲
Katahdin

95

CANADA

*Lily Bay
St. Park* ▲

*Moosehead
Lake*

Penobscot R.

WASHINGTON

*Chiputneticook
Lakes*

*Grand Falls
Flowage*
*W. Grand
Lake*

*Peaks-Kenny
St. Park* ▲

FRANKLIN

OXFORD

Sugarloaf ▲
Ski Area

Kennebec R.

HANCOCK

Moosehorn National
Wildlife Refuge

*Passamaquoddy
Bay*

VT

Cobscook
State Park ▲

Moosehorn National
Wildlife Refuge

95 ◉ Bangor

WALDO

Androscoggin R.

KENNEBEC

⊙ Waterville

White Mountain
National Forest

★ Augusta

LINCOLN KNOX

*Narraguagus
Bay*

*Penobscot
Bay*

*Acadia
National Park*

Deer I.

Mt. Desert I.

ANDROSCOGGIN
Lewiston ⊙

Auburn ⊙

SAGADAHOC

Vinalhaven I.

Isle au Haut

*Acadia
National Park*

NEW HAMPSHIRE

CUMBERLAND

495

Bath ⊙

Brunswick ⊙

*Muscongus
Bay*

*Sebago
Lake*

YORK

Westbrook ⊙

◉ Portland

⊙ S. Portland

Sanford ⊙

Saco ⊙ ▲

⊙ Old Orchard Beach

Biddeford ⊙

ATLANTIC OCEAN

95

▲ Kittery Point

79

Acadia National Park.

About 30,000 white-tailed deer are killed by hunters in Maine each year, but the herd does not appear to diminish. Other common forest animals include the bobcat, beaver, and snowshoe hare. Seals and porpoises are found in coastal waters, along with practically every variety of North Atlantic fish and shellfish, including the famous Maine lobster. Coastal waterfowl include the osprey, and herring and great black-backed gulls. Matinicus Rock is the only known North American nesting site of the common puffin, or sea parrot. Endangered species include the cougar, bald eagle, and shortnose sturgeon.

5 ENVIRONMENTAL PROTECTION

The Department of Environmental Protection administers laws regulating the selection of commercial and industrial sites, air and water quality, the prevention and cleanup of oil spills, the control of hazardous wastes, the licensing of oil terminals, the use of coastal wetlands, and mining. As of 1994, Maine had ten hazardous waste sites.

6 POPULATION

Maine's 1990 census population was 1,227,928 (38th among the 50 states). The 1995 population was estimated to be

1,295,000. The population density for 1990 was 40 persons per square mile (15 persons per square kilometer). More than half the population lives on less than one-seventh of the land within 25 miles (40 kilometers) of the Atlantic coast, and almost half the state is nearly uninhabited. The state's largest cities are Portland, with 62,756 people in 1992 (over 96,000 in the greater metropolitan area); Bangor, with 32,145; and Lewiston-Auburn, with 38,031.

7 ETHNIC GROUPS

Maine's population is primarily Yankee, of English and Scotch-Irish origins. The largest minority group consists of French-Canadians. Among those reporting at least one specific ancestry group in 1990, 372,042 claimed English ancestry; 223,653 French (not counting 123,857 who claimed Canadian or French-Canadian); and 217,226 Irish. As of 1990, Maine had 6,000 Native Americans, 5,000 blacks, 7,000 Asians and Pacific Islanders, and 7,000 residents of Hispanic origin.

8 LANGUAGES

Maine English is celebrated as typical Yankee speech. In 1990, 90.8% of Maine residents five years old or older reported speaking only English in the home. Some 81,012 residents spoke French, down from 95,181 in 1980. Native Algonkian place-names abound, including Saco, Kennebec, and Skowhegan.

9 RELIGIONS

Maine had 264,943 Roman Catholics in 1990 and an estimated 8,160 Jews. The leading Protestant denominations were United Methodist, with 36,164; United Church of Christ, 33,265; American Baptist USA, with 32,549; and Episcopal, 16,375.

10 TRANSPORTATION

Although Maine had no Class I railroads in 1992, seven regional and local railroads operated on 1,121 rail miles (1,804 kilometers) of track. About three-quarters of all communities depend entirely on highway trucking for the overland transportation of freight. In 1993, Maine had 22,510 miles (36,219 kilometers) of public roads. There were 1,027,942 registered motor vehicles in 1993. Maine has ten established seaports, with Portland and Searsport the main depots for overseas shipping. Portland International Jetport, the state's largest and most active airport, boarded 450,252 passengers in 1991.

11 HISTORY

Sometime around 1600, English expeditions began fishing the Gulf of Maine regularly. By 1630, however, there were permanent English settlements on several islands and at nearly a dozen spots along the coast. In 1652, the government of the Massachusetts Bay Colony began absorbing the small Maine settlements, and in 1691, Maine became a district of Massachusetts. During the first hundred years of settlement, Maine's economy was based on farming, fishing, trading, and exploitation of the forests.

The first naval encounter of the Revolutionary War occurred in Machias Bay, when, on 12 June 1775, angry colonials captured the British armed schooner *Margaretta*. An expedition through the Maine woods in the fall of 1775 intended to drive the British out of Quebec, but this failed. Another disaster was a 1779 expedition in which Massachusetts forces, failing to dislodge British troops at Castine, abandoned many of its own ships near the Penobscot River. Popular pressure for separation from Massachusetts mounted after the War of 1812. Admission of Maine to the Union as a free state was joined with the admission of Missouri as a slave state in the Missouri Compromise of 1820.

Textile mills and shoe factories came to Maine between 1830 and 1860. After the Civil War, the revolution in papermaking that substituted wood pulp for rags brought a vigorous new industry to the state. By 1900, Maine was one of the leading papermaking states in the US, and the industry continues to dominate the state today. The rise of tourism and the conflict between economic development and environmental protection have been central in the postwar period.

In the 1980s, the state government paid $81.5 million to the Penobscot and Passamaquoddy tribes. This settled a suit claiming that a 1794 treaty under which the Passamaquoddy handed over most of its land—amounting to the northern two-thirds of Maine—was illegal and had never been ratified by Congress.

12 STATE GOVERNMENT

The legislature, consisting of a senate of 31 to 35 members and a 151-member house of representatives, convenes every two years in joint session to elect the secretary of state, attorney general, and state treasurer. The governor is the only official elected statewide. The governor's veto may be overridden by a two-thirds vote of members present and voting in each legislative chamber.

13 POLITICAL PARTIES

The Republican Party dominated Maine politics for 100 years after its formation in the 1850s. The rise of Democrat Edmund S. Muskie, elected governor in 1954 and 1956 and to the first of four terms in the US Senate in 1960, signaled a change. Muskie appealed personally to many traditionally Republican voters, but his party's revival was also the result of demographic changes, especially an increase in the proportion of French-Canadian voters. In 1994 there were 272,089 registered Democrats, or 33% of the total number of registered voters; 246,277 registered Republicans, or 30%; and 306,292 unaffiliated registered voters, or 37%.

In the November 1994 elections, Independent Angus King became the governor. With his win, Maine became the only state in the nation with an Independent governor. Republican William S. Cohen won election to a third term in the Senate in 1990, and Republican Olympia Snowe, in 1994, won the seat vacated by the retiring Democrat George J. Mitchell. The two US House of Representatives seats were held by one Democrat and one Republican. Republicans also made gains in the state legislature in the November 1994 elections. In the state house of representatives the Democrats saw their advantage drop from 33 seats to 3 while the state senate became unevenly divided.

Maine Presidential Vote by Major Political Parties, 1948–1992

YEAR	MAINE WINNER	DEMOCRAT	REPUBLICAN
1948	Dewey (R)	111,916	150,234
1952	*Eisenhower (R)	118,806	232,353
1956	*Eisenhower (R)	102,468	249,238
1960	*Eisenhower (R)	102,468	249,238
1960	Nixon (R)	181,159	240,608
1964	*Johnson (D)	262,264	118,701
1968	Humphrey (D)	217,312	169,254
1972	*Nixon (R)	160,584	256,458
1976	Ford (R)	232,279	236,320
1980	*Reagan (R)	220,974	238,522
1984	*Reagan (R)	214,515	336,500
1988	*Bush (R)	243,569	307,131
1992**	*Clinton (D)	263,420	206,504

*Won US presidential election.
**Independent candidate Ross Perot received 206,820 votes.

14 LOCAL GOVERNMENT

The principal units of local government in 1992 were the 22 cities and 468 towns. In all, there were 806 local government units. As is customary in New England, the basic instrument of town government is the annual town meeting, with an elective board of selectmen supervising town affairs between meetings. Some of the larger towns employ full-time town managers. There is no local government in roughly half the state. Maine's 16 counties function primarily as judicial districts.

15 JUDICIAL SYSTEM

The highest state court is the supreme judicial court, which has statewide appeals jurisdiction in all civil and criminal matters. The 16-member superior court has original jurisdiction in cases involving trial by jury and also hears some appeals. The district courts hear non-felony criminal cases and small claims and juvenile cases. Maine's crime rate in 1994 was 3,272.7 per 100,000 persons. There were 1,469 state and federal prisoners in 1993.

16 MIGRATION

Although net losses from migration have continued through most of this century, there was a net gain of about 80,000 from 1970 to 1990. As of 1990, some 68.5% of all state residents had been born in Maine.

17 ECONOMY

Maine's greatest economic strengths are its forests and waters, yielding wood products, waterpower, fisheries, and ocean commerce. Today, the largest industry by far is paper manufacturing, for which both forests and waterpower are essential. Maine's greatest current economic weakness is its limited access to the national transportation network that links major production and manufacturing centers with large metropolitan markets. On the other hand, this relative isolation, combined with the state's traditional natural assets, has contributed to Maine's attractiveness as a place for tourism and recreation.

18 INCOME

Personal income in 1994 was $19,482 per capita (per person), 35th in the US and the lowest in New England. Total personal income in the same year was $24.2 billion. Some 15.4% of the population lived below the federal poverty level in 1993.

19 INDUSTRY

Manufacturing in Maine has always been related to the forests. From the 17th century through much of the 19th, the staples of Maine industry were shipbuilding and lumber. Today they are papermaking and wood products, but footwear, textiles and apparel, shipbuilding, and electronic components and accessories are also important items.

Maine has the largest paper-production capacity of any state in the nation. There are large papermills and pulpmills in more than a dozen towns and cities. Wood-related industries—paper, lumber, wood products—accounted for 43% of the value of manufacturers shipments in 1991.

20 LABOR

Maine's civilian labor force totaled 613,000 in 1994. The unemployment rate in 1994 was 7.4%. The number of unemployed was 45,000. Labor union membership among Maine's workers in 1994 amounted to 15.6%. There were eight national labor unions operating in Maine in 1993.

21 AGRICULTURE

Maine's gross farm income in 1994 was $482.7 million (42d in the US). There were 7,600 farms in 1994, with an estimated 1,300,000 acres (526,000 hectares) of land. Potatoes, grown primarily in Aroostook County, are by far the most important crop. Maine was the eighth-largest potato-growing state in the US in 1994, producing 1,725 million pounds, which accounted for 23.2% of state agricultural receipts that year. Other crops included commercial apples, 57,000,000 pounds; oats, 1,820,000 bushels; and hay, 406,000 tons. Maine is also a leading producer of blueberries.

22 DOMESTICATED ANIMALS

Livestock and livestock products accounted for 57% of Maine's income from farm marketings in 1994. In 1994, egg production yielded about $108 million in gross income. There were 113,000 cattle on Maine farms at the end of 1994, when production was worth about $24 million. The dairy output was valued at about $89 million.

23 FISHING

Fishing has been important to the economy of Maine since its settlement. In 1992, 201.2 million pounds of finfish and shellfish worth $163.3 million were landed at Maine ports. The most valuable Maine fishery product is the lobster. Flounder, halibut, scallops, and shrimp are also caught. In 1992, federal hatcheries distributed over 2.5 million (173,580 pounds) coldwater-species fish and roe (fish eggs) within the state, made up of mostly Atlantic salmon. Receipts from fish farming amounted to about $42 million in 1994.

24 FORESTRY

Maine's 17.6 million acres of forest in 1990 contained an estimated 3.6 billion trees and covered 89% of the state's land area, the largest percentage of any state in the US. Principal commercial hardwoods include ash, hard maple, white and yellow birch, beech, and oak. Commercially significant softwoods include white pine,

Photo credit: Susan D. Rock.

Fishing boats at anchor in Bar Harbor.

hemlock, cedar, spruce, and fir. Timber operations in 1991 produced 652 million board feet of softwood lumber, 301 million board feet of hardwood lumber, and 3.8 million cords of pulpwood.

25 MINING

The value of nonfuel mineral production in Maine in 1994 was estimated to be $58 million. Leading mineral commodities were construction sand and gravel (valued at $18,600,000), crushed stone, (valued at $10,800,000), and cement. Other mineral commodities produced included clay, peat, dimension stone, and gem stones.

26 ENERGY AND POWER

In recent decades, waterpower has been surpassed in importance by oil-fired steam plants and, most recently, by nuclear power. As of 1993, Maine had one nuclear power plant. In 1991, the Maine Yankee Atomic Power Company station in Wiscasset generated 66% of the state's electric power. Oil-fired steam units accounted for 13% and hydroelectric units for 19%. Electric power production in 1993 totaled 8.1 billion kilowatt hours. All fuel oil and coal must be imported. Energy expenditures were $2,077 per capita (per person) in 1992.

27 COMMERCE

Maine had 1992 wholesale sales of $6.5 billion; 1993 retail sales of almost $12 billion; and 1992 service establishment receipts of $4.2 billion. The value of Maine's exports amounted to $902 million of goods in 1992.

28 PUBLIC FINANCE

Maine's biennial budget is prepared by the Bureau of the Budget and submitted by the Governor to the Legislature for consideration. The revenues for the fiscal year ending 30 June 1993, were $3,367.4 million; expenditures were $3,378.9 million. The state had a total debt of nearly $3 billion as of 1993, or about $2,419 per capita (per person).

29 TAXATION

The leading source of tax revenue as of 1993 was a sales and use tax of 6%. Maine imposes personal and corporate income taxes. Other state levies include taxes on utilities, inheritance and estate taxes, liquor and cigarette taxes, and a tax on gasoline, fuel, and motor carriers. Federal expenditures traditionally outstrip the state's federal tax burden by a large amount.

30 HEALTH

The death rate of 902.5 per 100,000 in 1992 was slightly higher than the US norm, reflecting a higher than average population in the upper age levels. The pulmonary disease death rate of 50.8 per 100,000 population was above the national rate. In 1993, Maine had 39 community hospitals, with 4,400 beds. Licensed medical personnel included 2,400 nonfederal physicians and 10,600 nurses in 1993. The average per-inpatient expense for hospital care in 1993 was $738 per day, or $5,543 for an average cost per stay. About 11% of state residents did not have health insurance in 1993.

31 HOUSING

There were an estimated 603,000 housing units in Maine in 1993. About one-seventh of all Maine homes are for seasonal rather than year-round use. The median home value in Maine was $87,400 in 1990. Maine had the lowest median owner (including mortgage) and renter costs in New England in 1990, at $664 and $419 per month, respectively.

32 EDUCATION

Maine has a long and vigorous tradition of education at all levels, both public and private. In 1990, 81% of the adult population had completed high school, but only 14.4% had completed college, the lowest rate in New England. In fall 1993, Maine's public school enrollment was about 218,000. Expenditures on education averaged $6,162 per pupil in 1993.

Since 1968, the state's system of state colleges and universities has been incorporated into a single University of Maine, which in fall 1991 had 33,123 undergraduate, graduate, and professional students. Of the state's 16 private colleges and professional schools, Bowdoin College in Brunswick, Colby College in Waterville, and Bates College in Lewiston are the best known.

33 ARTS

Maine has long held an attraction for painters and artists, Winslow Homer and Andrew Wyeth among them. The state abounds in summer theaters, the oldest and most famous of which is at Ogunquit. The Portland Symphony is Maine's leading orchestra; another ensemble is in Bangor. From 1987 to 1991, the State of Maine generated a total of $8,047,433 from federal and state sources to support its arts programs.

34 LIBRARIES AND MUSEUMS

In 1991, Maine public libraries had 4,734,820 volumes and a combined circulation of 7,379,171. Leading academic libraries in 1991 were those of Maine State at Augusta, the University of Maine at Orono, Bowdoin College at Brunswick, and the University of Southern Maine at Portland. Maine has at least 113 museums and historic sites. The privately supported Maine Historical Society in Portland maintains a research library and the Wadsworth Longfellow House, the boyhood home of Henry Wadsworth Longfellow. The largest of several maritime museums is in Bath.

35 COMMUNICATIONS

In March 1993, 96.9% of the 490,000 occupied housing units had telephones. Maine had 101 commercial radio stations (31 AM, 70 FM) in 1993, along with 19 commercial and 11 noncommercial educational television stations. Educational television stations broadcast from Augusta, Biddeford, Calais, Orono, and Presque Isle. In 1993, three large cable television systems served the state.

Photo credit: Maine Office of Tourism.

A statue of Paul Bunyon in Bangor—the lumber capital of the world in the 1880s.

36 PRESS

Maine had eight daily newspapers in 1994. The most widely read newspapers were the *Bangor Daily News* (mornings, 76,290; weekend, 92,640) and the *Portland Press Herald* (mornings, 75,000). Maine's only Sunday newspaper is the *Maine Sunday Telegram* (145,000).

37 TOURISM, TRAVEL, AND RECREATION

Calling itself "Vacationland," the state of Maine is a year-round resort destination.

Expenditures by tourists were estimated at over $1.4 billion in 1993. Most out-of-state visitors continue to come in the summer, when the southern coast offers sandy beaches, icy surf, and several small harbors for sailing and saltwater fishing. Northeastward, the scenery becomes more rugged and spectacular, and sailing and hiking are the primary activities. White-water canoeing lures the adventurous along the Allagash Wilderness Waterway in northern Maine. Maine has always attracted hunters, especially during the fall deer season. Wintertime recreation facilities include nearly 60 ski areas and countless opportunities for cross-country skiing.

In 1992 there were 28 state parks and beaches. Acadia National Park, a popular attraction, drew 2,400,000 visitors in 1992. There are four other federal parks, forests, and wildlife areas, and seven national wildlife refuges. The state fair is at Bangor.

38 SPORTS

Maine has no major league professional sports team. The Portland Pirates (a minor league team) of the American Hockey League play on their home ice at the Cumberland County Civic Center in Portland. The Portland Seadogs, a minor league baseball team, is affiliated with the Florida Marlins. Harness-racing is held at Scarborough Downs and other tracks and fairgrounds throughout the state.

39 FAMOUS MAINERS

The highest federal officeholders born in Maine were Hannibal Hamlin (1809–91), the nation's first Republican vice-president, under Abraham Lincoln; and Nelson A. Rockefeller (1908–79), governor of New York State from 1959 to 1973 and US vice-president under Gerald Ford. Margaret Chase Smith (1897–1995) served longer in the US Senate—24 years—than any other woman.

Maine claims a large number of well-known reformers and humanitarians: Dorothea Lynde Dix (1802–87), who led the movement for hospitals for the insane; Elijah Parish Lovejoy (1802–37), an abolitionist killed while defending his printing press from a proslavery mob in St. Louis, Missouri; and Harriet Beecher Stowe (b.Connecticut, 1811–96), whose novel *Uncle Tom's Cabin* (1852) was written in Maine.

Other important writers include poet Henry Wadsworth Longfellow (1807–82); Sarah Orne Jewett (1849–1909), novelist and short-story writer; and Kate Douglas Wiggin (1856–1923), author of *Rebecca of Sunnybrook Farm*. Edwin Arlington Robinson (1869–1935) and Edna St. Vincent Millay (1892–1950) were both Pulitzer Prize-winning poets. E. B. (Elwyn Brooks) White (1899–1985), *New Yorker* essayist and author of the children's classic *Charlotte's Web*, maintained a home in Maine, which inspired much of his writing. Winslow Homer (b.Massachusetts, 1836–1910) had a summer home at Prouts Neck, where he painted many of his seascapes.

40 BIBLIOGRAPHY

Alampi, Gary, ed. *Gale State Rankings Reporter.* Detroit: Gale Research Inc., 1994

Clark, Charles E. *Maine: A Bicentennial History.* New York: Norton, 1977.

MARYLAND

State of Maryland

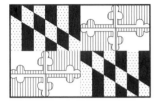

ORIGIN OF STATE NAME: Named for Henrietta Maria, queen consort of King Charles I of England.

NICKNAME: The Old Line State; Free State.

CAPITAL: Annapolis.

ENTERED UNION: 28 April 1788 (7th).

SONG: "Maryland, My Maryland."

MOTTO: *Fatti maschii, parole femine* (Manly deeds, womanly words).

FLAG: Bears the quartered arms of the Calvert and Crossland families (the paternal and maternal families of the founders of Maryland).

OFFICIAL SEAL: REVERSE: A shield bearing the arms of the Calverts and Crosslands is surmounted by an earl's coronet and a helmet and supported by a farmer and fisherman. The state motto (originally that of the Calverts) appears on a scroll below. The circle is surrounded by the Latin legend *Scuto bonæ voluntatis tuæ coronasti nos,* meaning "With the shield of thy favor hast thou compassed us"; and "1632," the date of Maryland's first charter. OBVERSE: Lord Baltimore is seen as a knight in armor on a charger. The surrounding inscription, in Latin, means "Cecilius, Absolute Lord of Maryland and Avalon New Foundland, Baron of Baltimore."

BIRD: Baltimore oriole.

FISH: Rockfish.

FLOWER: Black-eyed Susan.

TREE: White oak.

DOG: Chesapeake Bay retriever.

CRUSTACEAN: Blue crab.

INSECT: Baltimore checkerspot butterfly.

SPORT: Jousting.

TIME: 7 AM EST = noon GMT.

1 LOCATION AND SIZE

Located on the eastern seaboard of the US in the South Atlantic region, Maryland ranks 42d in size among the 50 states. Maryland's total area is 10,460 square miles (27,092 square kilometers). The state extends 199 miles (320 kilometers) east-west and 126 miles (203 kilometers) north-south. The total boundary length of Maryland is 842 miles (1,355 kilometers).

Important islands in Chesapeake Bay, off Maryland's Eastern Shore (part of the Delmarva Peninsula), include Kent, Bloodsworth, South Marsh, and Smith.

2 TOPOGRAPHY

Three distinct regions characterize Maryland's terrain. The first and major area is the coastal plain, nearly cut in half by Chesapeake Bay. The Piedmont Plateau to the west is a broad, rolling upland with several deep gorges. Farther west is the Appalachian Mountain region, containing the state's highest hills. Backbone Mountain in westernmost Maryland is the state's highest point, at 3,360 feet (1,024 meters). A few small islands lie in Chesapeake Bay, Maryland's dominant waterway. The state has 23 rivers and bays. Principal rivers include the Potomac, the Patapsco, the Patuxent, and the Susquehanna.

3 CLIMATE

Despite its small size, Maryland has a diverse climate. Temperatures vary from an annual average of 48°F (9°C) in the extreme western uplands to 59°F (15°C) in the southeast, where the climate is moderated by Chesapeake Bay and the Atlantic Ocean. The mean temperature for Baltimore ranges from 33°F (1°C) in January to 77°F (25°C) in July. The record high temperature for the state is 109°F (43°C), set on 10 July 1936; the record low is −40°F (−40°C), set on 13 January 1912.

Precipitation ranges from 36 inches (91 centimeters) annually in the Cumberland area to about 49 inches (124 centimeters) in the southeast. As much as 100 inches (254 centimeters) of snow falls in western Garrett County, while 8–10 inches (20–25 centimeters) is average for the Eastern Shore.

4 PLANTS AND ANIMALS

Maryland's three life zones—coastal plain, piedmont, and Appalachian—mingle wildlife characteristics of both North and South. Most of the state lies within a hardwood belt in which red and white oaks,

Maryland Population Profile

Estimated 1995 population:	5,078,000
Population change, 1980–90:	13.4%
Leading ancestry group:	German
Second leading group:	African American
Foreign born population:	6.6%
Hispanic origin†:	2.6%
Population by race:	
White:	71.0%
Black:	24.9%
Native American:	0.3%
Asian/Pacific Islander:	2.9%
Other:	0.9%

Population by Age Group

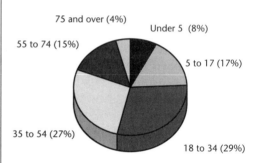

75 and over (4%)
Under 5 (8%)
55 to 74 (15%)
5 to 17 (17%)
35 to 54 (27%)
18 to 34 (29%)

Top Cities with Populations Over 25,000

City	Population	National rank	% change 1980–90
Baltimore	726,096	14	−6.5
Rockville	45,165	584	2.3
Frederick	43,386	611	42.9
Gaithersburg	41,413	652	49.6
Bowie	40,281	676	11.6
Hagerstown	37,572	727	3.8
Annapolis	34,070	812	4.6

Notes: †A person of Hispanic origin may be of any race. NA indicates that data are not available.
Sources: Economic and Statistics Administration, Bureau of the Census. *Statistical Abstract of the United States, 1994–95.* Washington, DC: Government Printing Office, 1995; Courtenay M. Slater and George E. Hall. *1995 County and City Extra: Annual Metro, City and County Data Book.* Lanham, MD: Bernan Press, 1995.

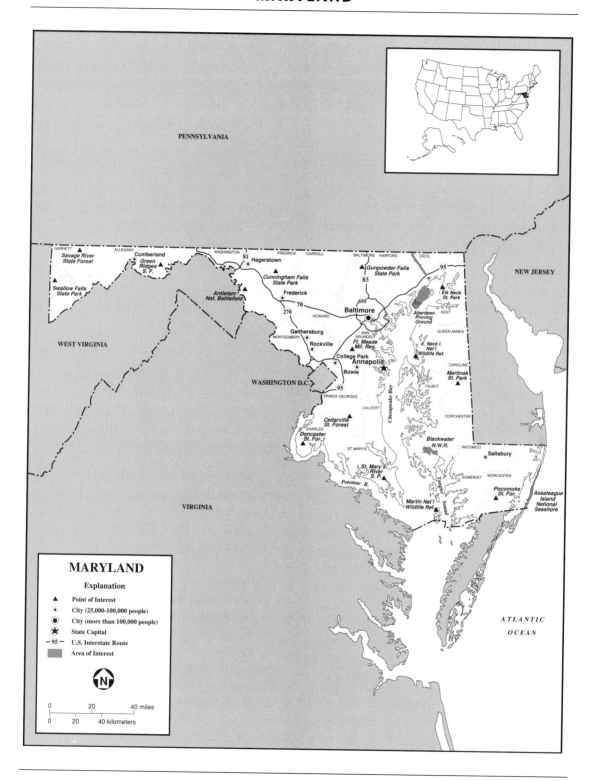

PENNSYLVANIA

NEW JERSEY

WEST VIRGINIA

GARRETT
Savage River
State Forest

ALLEGANY
Cumberland
Green
Ridges
S. F.

WASHINGTON
81
Hagerstown

FREDRICK

CARROLL

BALTIMORE   HARFORD

CECIL
95

Swallow Falls
State Park

Cunningham Falls
State Park

Gunpowder Falls
State Park

Elk Neck
St. Park

Antietam
Nat. Battlefield

Frederick

70

83

695

KENT

Baltimore

Aberdeen
Proving
Ground

270

HOWARD

WASHINGTON D.C.

Gaithersburg

Rockville

ANN
ARUNDEL
Ft. Meade
Mil. Res.

College Park

Annapolis

Bowie

QUEEN ANNES

E. Neck I.
Nat'l
Wildlife Ref.

CAROLINE

Martinak
St. Park

95

PRINCE GEORGES

TALBOT

CALVERT

Chesapeake Bay

DORCHESTER

Cedarville
St. Forest

CHARLES
Doncaster
St. For.

ST MARYS

Blackwater
N.W.R.

WICOMICO

Salisbury

St. Mary's
River
S. P.

SOMERSET   WORCESTER

VIRGINIA

Potomac R.

Pocomoke
St. For.

Assateague
Island
National
Seashore

Martin Nat'l
Wildlife Ref.

ATLANTIC
OCEAN

MARYLAND

Explanation

▲ Point of Interest

⊙ City (25,000-100,000 people)

◉ City (more than 100,000 people)

★ State Capital

— 95 — U.S. Interstate Route

Area of Interest

N

| 0 | 20 | 40 miles |
| 0 | 20 | 40 kilometers |

yellow poplar, and beech, among others, are represented. Shortleaf and loblolly pines are the leading softwoods. Honeysuckle, Virginia creeper, and wild raspberry are also common. Wooded hillsides are rich with such wildflowers as trailing arbutus, early blue violet, and wild rose.

The white-tailed (Virginia) deer, eastern cottontail, and raccoon, among others, are native to Maryland, although urbanization has sharply reduced their habitat. Common small mammals are the woodchuck, eastern chipmunk, and gray squirrel. Birds include the cardinal, chestnut-sided warbler, and rose-breasted grosbeak. Among saltwater species, shellfish—especially oysters, clams, and crabs—have the greatest economic importance. The Indiana bat, eastern cougar, and Maryland darter are among the species listed as endangered in the state.

5 ENVIRONMENTAL PROTECTION

The Maryland Department of the Environment (MDE) serves as the state's primary environmental protection agency. Besides protecting and restoring the quality of Maryland's land, air, and water, MDE regulations also control the storage, transportation, and disposal of hazardous wastes and ensure long-term, environmentally sound solid-waste recycling and disposal capabilities. As of 1992, Maryland had 30 municipal landfills and, in 1994, 13 hazardous waste sites.

MDE leads the state's efforts to restore the Chesapeake Bay and protect it from the effects of stormwater run-off and both airborne and waterborne pollutants.

Additionally, Maryland's Department of Natural Resources manages water allocation, fish and wildlife, state parks and forests, land reclamation, and open space.

6 POPULATION

The enormous expansion of the federal government and exodus of people from Washington, D.C., to the surrounding suburbs contributed to the rapid growth of Maryland. As of 1990, it was the 19th most populous state, with 4,781,468 people. The estimated 1995 population was 5,078,000 and it is projected that the population will reach 5,608,000 by 2000. The population density in 1990 was 489 persons per square mile (188 persons per square kilometer).

Almost all the growth since World War II has occurred in the four suburban counties around Washington, D.C., and Baltimore. Metropolitan Baltimore, embracing Carroll, Howard, Harford, Anne Arundel, and Baltimore counties, expanded from 2,244,700 to 2,382,000 inhabitants between 1984 and 1990. The city of Baltimore, on the other hand, declined from 763,570 to 736,000 during the same period. Baltimore is the state's only major city.

7 ETHNIC GROUPS

Black Americans, numbering 1,190,000 in 1990, constitute the largest racial minority in Maryland. Hispanic Americans, mostly from Puerto Rico and Central America, numbered 125,000 in 1990. The Asian population was relatively large: 29,471 Koreans, 26,479 Chinese, 21,086 Filipinos, 10,067 Japanese, and 7,809 Vietnamese.

Foreign-born residents numbered 313,494 in 1990, many having immigrated to Maryland in the 1970s. The leading countries of origin in 1990 were Korea, India, El Salvador, Germany, and the Philippines. A significant proportion of the German, Polish, and Russian immigrants were Jewish refugees arriving just before and after World War II. Maryland's Native American population is small—only 13,000 in 1990.

8 LANGUAGES

The state's diverse terrain has contributed to unusual diversity in its basic speech. Proximity to Virginia and access to southeastern and central Pennsylvania helped to create a language mixture that now is dominantly Midland and yet reflects earlier ties to Southern English. In 1990, 4,030,234 residents, or 91.1% of the population five years old or older, spoke only English at home. Other languages spoken at home, with the number of speakers, included Spanish, 122,871; French, 39,484; and German, 26,454.

9 RELIGIONS

Maryland was founded as a haven for Roman Catholics, and they remain the state's leading religious group. As of 1990 there were 832,763 Roman Catholics in Maryland. Members of the major Protestant denominations included United Methodist Church, 310,008; Southern Baptist Convention, 131,627; Lutheran Church—Missouri Synod, 31,393; and Episcopal Church, 82,714. In 1990 there were an estimated 210,965 Jews.

10 TRANSPORTATION

As of 1992, total rail miles of track in Maryland amounted to 874 miles (1,406 kilometers), including 685 miles (1,102 kilometers) of Class I track. Amtrak operated about 30 trains through the state in 1991/92, carrying 1,510,405 passengers from six stations. The Maryland Mass Transit Administration inaugurated Baltimore's first subway line on 21 November 1983. In 1984, the Washington, D.C., mass transit system was extended to the Maryland suburbs.

As of 1993 there were 29,313 miles (47,165 kilometers) of roadway and 3,559,558 motor vehicles registered in Maryland. The Port of Baltimore, the nation's 16th busiest, handled 23,349,660 tons of foreign cargo, and 14,394,950 tons of domestic cargo in 1991. In the same year, Baltimore–Washington International Airport, the major air terminal in the state, handled 66,885 aircraft departures with 4,249,906 passengers.

11 HISTORY

The Indian tribes living in the region that was to become Maryland were Algonkian-speakers, including the Accomac, Susquehannock, and Piscataway. Although the Algonkian tribes hunted for much of their food, many (including the Susquehannock) also had permanent settlements where they cultivated corn (maize) and other crops. European penetration of the Chesapeake region began early in the 16th century, with the expeditions of Giovanni da Verrazano of Florence and the Spaniard Lucas Vázquez de Ayllón. Captain John Smith was the first English explorer

Photo credit: Maryland Tourism.

Fort McHenry (on Baltimore's waterfront), birthplace of the national anthem.

of Chesapeake Bay (1608) and produced a map of the area that was used for years.

Twenty years later, George Calvert received from King Charles I a land grant that embraced not only present-day Maryland but also the present State of Delaware, a large part of Pennsylvania, and the valley between the north and south branches of the Potomac River. When he died in 1632, the title passed to his son Cecilius Calvert, second Baron Baltimore, who named the region Maryland after Charles I's queen, Henrietta Maria. Calvert established the first settlement two years later as a refuge for persecuted Roman Catholics.

In 1689, with Protestants in power both in England and Maryland, the British crown took control of the province away from the Catholic Calverts, and in 1692, the Church of England became Maryland's established religion. The Fourth Baron Baltimore regained full hereditary rights—but only because he had embraced the Protestant faith. Rule by the Calvert family through their legitimate heirs continued until the eve of the American Revolution.

Statehood

After some initial hesitancy, Maryland cast its lot with the Revolution and sent approximately 20,000 soldiers to fight in the war. On 28 April 1788, it became the seventh state to ratify the federal Constitution. By the early 19th century, Baltimore, founded in 1729, was already the state's major center of commerce and industry. The city and harbor were the site of extended military operations during the War of 1812. It was during the bombardment of Ft. McHenry in 1814 that Francis Scott Key, detained on the British frigate, composed "The Star-Spangled Banner," which became the US national anthem in March 1931.

After the War of 1812, Maryland history was marked by the continued growth of Baltimore and increasing division over immigration, slavery, and secession, which the Maryland house of delegates rejected in 1861. Throughout the Civil War, Maryland was largely occupied by Union troops because of its strategic location. Marylanders fought on both sides during the war, and one major battle took place on Maryland soil—the Battle of Antietam (1862), during which a Union army thwarted a Confederate thrust toward the north, but at an enormous cost to both sides.

The state's economic activity increased during Reconstruction, as Maryland, and especially Baltimore, played a major role in rebuilding the South. Maryland's economic base gradually shifted from agriculture to industry, with shipbuilding, steelmaking, and the manufacture of clothing and shoes leading the way. The decades between the Civil War and World War I were also notable for the philanthropic activities of such wealthy businessmen as John Hopkins and George Peabody, who endowed some of the state's most prestigious cultural and educational institutions. Democrat Albert C. Ritchie won election to the governorship in 1919 and served in that office until 1935, stressing local issues, states' rights, and opposition to prohibition.

The decades since World War II have been marked by significant population growth. The state has witnessed the passage of open housing and equal opportunity laws to protect Maryland's black citizens. It has also been rocked by political scandal in recent years. Perhaps the most significant occurrence has been the redevelopment of Baltimore, which, though still the hub of the state's economy, had fallen into decay. Much of Baltimore's downtown area and harbor were revitalized by urban renewal projects in the late 1970s and 1980s. Although Maryland's economy declined less than those of other states during the recession of the late 1980s and early 1990s, the state has suffered from reductions in the defense and technology industries.

12 STATE GOVERNMENT

The general assembly, Maryland's legislative body, consists of two branches: a 47-member senate and a 141-member house of delegates. All legislators serve four-year terms. Executives elected statewide are the governor and lieutenant governor (who run jointly), the comptroller of the Treasury, and the attorney general. All serve four-year terms.

Bills passed by majority vote of both houses of the assembly become law when signed by the governor, or if left unsigned for 6 days while the legislature is in session or for 30 days if the legislature has adjourned. The only exception is the budget bill, which becomes effective immediately upon legislative passage. Gubernatorial vetoes may be overridden by three-fifths votes in both houses.

[13] POLITICAL PARTIES

As of 1994, there were 2,463,010 registered voters, of whom 61% were Democrats; 29% Republicans; and 10% independents and members of minor parties. Maryland was one of the few states carried by President Jimmy Carter in the November 1980 presidential election, but four years later the state went for President Ronald Reagan in the national Republican landslide. In 1992, Maryland gave 50% of its vote to Democrat Bill Clinton, 36% to Republican George Bush, and 14% to Independent Ross Perot.

Revelations of corruption afflicted both major parties during the 1970s. In 1973,

Republican Spiro T. Agnew, then vice-president of the US, was accused of taking bribes while he was Baltimore County executive and then governor. Agnew resigned from the vice-presidency on 10 October 1973. His gubernatorial successor, Democrat Marvin Mandel, was convicted of mail fraud and racketeering in 1977. He served 20 months of a 36-month prison sentence before receiving a presidential pardon in 1981.

In 1994, the governor's race was one of the closest in Maryland history. Democrat Parris N. Glendening, three-term Prince George's county executive, defeated Ellen R. Sauerbrey, Republican leader of the Maryland House, by a mere 5,993 votes. The two senators from Maryland, Paul S. Sarbanes and Barbara Mikulski, both Democrats, were reelected in 1994 and 1992, respectively.

Maryland Presidential Vote by Political Parties, 1948–92

YEAR	MARYLAND WINNER	DEMOCRAT	REPUBLICAN	PROGRESSIVE	DEMOCRAT	STATE'S RIGHTS SOCIALIST
1948	Dewey (R)	286,521	294,814	9,983	2,467	2,941
1952	*Eisenhower (R)	395,337	499,424	7,313	—	—
1956	*Eisenhower (R)	372,613	559,738	—	—	—
1960	*Kennedy (D)	565,808	489,538	—	—	—
1964	*Johnson (D)	730,912	385,495	—	—	—
1968	Humphrey (D)	538,310	517,995	AMERICAN IND. 178,734	—	—
1972	*Nixon (R)	505,781	829,305	AMERICAN 18,726	—	—
1976	*Carter (D)	759,612	672,661	—	—	—
1980	Carter (D)	726,161	680,606	—	LIBERTARIAN 14,192	—
1984	*Reagan (R)	787,935	879,918	—	5,721	—
1988	*Bush (R)	826,304	876,167	5,115	6,748	—
1992	*Clinton (D)	988,571	707,094	2,786	4,715	IND. (Perot) 281,414

* Won US presidential election.

As of the November 1994 elections, Maryland's congressional delegation consisted of four Democrats and four Republicans. There were 38 Democrats and 9 Republicans in the state senate and 116 Democrats and 25 Republicans in the state house.

14 LOCAL GOVERNMENT

As of 1992 there were 23 counties, 152 incorporated cities and towns, and 155 municipal governments in Maryland. Eight counties had charter governments, with (in most cases) elected executives and county councils, and 15 had elected boards of county commissioners.

Baltimore is the only city in Maryland not contained within a county. It provides the same services as a county, and shares in state aid according to the same allocation formulas. The city (not to be confused with Baltimore County, which surrounds the city of Baltimore but has its county seat at Towson) is governed by a mayor and a nine-member city council. Other cities and towns are each governed by a mayor and a council, town commissioners, or council and a manager, depending on the local charter.

15 JUDICIAL SYSTEM

The court of appeals, the state's highest court, comprises a chief judge and six associate judges. Most criminal appeals are decided by the court of special appeals, consisting of a chief judge and 12 associate judges. District courts handle all traffic cases, civil cases involving amounts less than $2,500, and criminal cases if the penalty is less than three years imprisonment or the fine is less than $2,500. Appeals are taken to one of eight judicial circuit courts. According to the FBI Crime Index for 1994, Maryland had a violent crime rate of 948 per 100,000 population and a property crime rate of 5,174.6. There were 20,264 prisoners in state and federal prisons in 1993.

16 MIGRATION

During the 19th century, Baltimore ranked second only to New York as a port of entry for European immigrants. After the Civil War, many blacks migrated to Baltimore, both from rural Maryland and from southern states.

Since World War II, both the metropolitan area of Baltimore and the Maryland part of the metropolitan Washington, D.C., area have experienced rapid growth, while their inner cities have lost population. Overall, Maryland experienced a net loss from migration of about 36,000 between 1970 and 1980, much of it to Pennsylvania, Virginia, and Florida. The out-migration stopped during the 1980s, however, with a net gain of over 200,000 from 1980 to 1990. By 1990, just under 50% of all Maryland residents had been born in the state.

17 ECONOMY

Although manufacturing output continues to rise, the biggest growth areas in Maryland's economy are government, construction, trade, and services. Manufacturing, which has shifted towards high technology, information, and health-related products, lost 39,000 jobs between 1981 and 1991. With the expansion of federal employment in the Washington metropolitan area between 1961 and 1980, many US government workers settled in suburban Maryland, primarily Prince George's and Montgomery counties. Construction and services in those areas expanded accordingly. Between 1982 and 1992, the number of jobs grew 24% in Maryland, somewhat above the national average of 21% for that period.

18 INCOME

As of 1994, Maryland ranked fifth nationwide in per capita (per person) income with $24,847. Total personal income was $124.4 billion in 1994. An estimated 479,000 Marylanders—9.7% of the population—were below the federal poverty level in 1993.

19 INDUSTRY

Baltimore is an important manufacturer of automobiles and parts, steel, and instruments. Value of shipments by manufacturers in 1992 was $31 billion. About a third of all manufacturing activity takes place in the city of Baltimore, followed by Baltimore County, Montgomery County, and Prince George's County. Leading Maryland corporations include Martin Marietta of Bethesda (aerospace), Crown Central Petroleum of Baltimore, Black & Decker Manufacturing of Towson (tools), and McCormick of Sparks (spices).

20 LABOR

Maryland's civilian labor force in 1994 numbered 2,691,000, with an unemployment rate of 5.1%. In 1993, there were nine national labor unions. As of 1994, 16% of all workers were union members.

21 AGRICULTURE

Maryland ranked 36th among the 50 states in agricultural income in 1994, with estimated receipts of $1,344 million, about 41% of that in crops. The state had some 15,000 farms covering 2,000,000 acres (809,400 hectares) in 1993. In 1991, Maryland produced an estimated 12,750,000 pounds of tobacco (11th in the US). Corn and cereal grains are grown mainly in southern Maryland. Production in 1994 included 46,020,000 bushels of corn for grain, 19,800,000 bushels of soybeans, and 12,100,000 bushels of wheat. Greenhouse and nursery products contributed 17.5% to agricultural receipts in 1994.

22 DOMESTICATED ANIMALS

About 59% of Maryland's farm income derives from livestock and livestock products. The Eastern Shore is an important dairy and poultry region. Cattle are raised in north-central and western Maryland, while the central region is notable for horse-breeding.

Maryland ranked eighth among the 50 states in broiler production in 1994, with 1,311 million pounds. Also produced during 1994 were 3 million pounds of turkeys. Dairy products made up 13.3% of agricultural receipts in 1994. Maryland farms and ranches had 91,000 milk cows, 315,000 cattle, and 120,000 hogs by 1994.

Photo credit: Maryland Tourism.

The "Pride of Baltimore II" under sail in Annapolis.

23 FISHING

A leading source of oysters, clams, and crabs, Maryland had a total commercial catch in 1992 of 57,067,000 pounds, valued at $36,424,000. Leading shellfish items were crabs (50% of the total value) and clams (27%). Bigeye and yellowfin tuna together were the most important finfish, followed by menhaden, dogfish shark, swordfish, and sea bass.

24 FORESTRY

Maryland's 2,700,000 acres (1,100,000 hectares) of forestland cover 43% of the state's land area. Hardwoods predominate, with red and white oaks and yellow poplar among the leading hardwood varieties.

25 MINING

The value of nonfuel mineral production in Maryland in 1994 was about $324 million. In 1992, output of sand and gravel and crushed stone totaled about 35 million tons (valued at $243,000,000).

26 ENERGY AND POWER

In 1993, production of electricity was 43.5 billion kilowatt hours. About 59% of the state's electricity was produced by coal-fired plants. Coal reserves in 1992 were estimated at 749.9 million tons of bituminous coal. The 1992 output of 17 coal mines totaled 3.3 million tons. There were two nuclear power plants in Maryland as of 1993. Energy expenditures in 1992 were $1,670 per capita (per person).

27 COMMERCE

Maryland had 1992 wholesale sales of $52.9 billion; 1993 retail sales of $40.2 billion; and 1992 service establishment receipts of $29.8 billion. Foreign exports of Maryland products totaled $3.9 billion in 1992.

28 PUBLIC FINANCE

The outstanding state debt exceeded $8.7 billion as of 1993, or $1,761 per capita (per person). The estimated revenues for the fiscal year 1994/95 were $13,345.4 million; expenditures were $13,360.2 million.

29 TAXATION

Among the taxes levied by the state in 1994 were an individual income tax; a corporate income tax; a 5% sales and use tax; a state property tax; and motor vehicle use, franchise, cigarette, and alcoholic beverage taxes. All county and some local governments levy property taxes. The counties also tax personal income. Marylanders paid $32.9 billion in federal income taxes in 1992.

30 HEALTH

The death rates for heart disease, cancer, and cerebrovascular diseases were all below or nearly equal to the US average for these categories. In 1993, Maryland had 50 community hospitals, with 13,000 beds. The average expense for hospital care in 1993 was $889 per inpatient day,

or $5,632 for an average cost of stay. The medical school at Johns Hopkins University in Baltimore has superbly equipped research facilities. Federal health centers located in Bethesda include the National Institutes of Health and the National Naval Medical Center. Maryland had 16,500 nonfederal physicians and about 38,200 nurses as of 1993. Some 13.5% of state residents did not have health insurance that year.

31 HOUSING

Maryland has sought to preserve many of its historic houses, especially in Annapolis, which has several ornate mansions. Block upon block of two-story brick row houses fill the older parts of Baltimore, and stone cottages built to withstand rough winters are still found in the western counties. There were an estimated 1,982,000 year-round housing units in Maryland in 1993. In 1990, the median value of a home was $116,500. During 1993, 29,956 new housing units were authorized. The median monthly cost for housing for owners with a mortgage in 1990 was $919, and $235 for owners without a mortgage. The median monthly rent throughout the state was $548 in 1990.

32 EDUCATION

As of 1992, 81% of all Marylanders had completed high school, and 25% had at least four years of college. There are 791 elementary and 202 secondary schools serving the state. Enrollment in 1993 for grades K–12 was 769,000 in public schools. Expenditures on education averaged $6,447 per pupil (11th in the nation) in 1993.

As of 1990 there were 30 four-year and 22 two-year accredited colleges and universities in the state. The total enrollment for public four-year institutions was 86,104 in 1990. There are four state colleges and two state universities (Towson and Morgan); other institutions include the University of Baltimore, the University of Maryland (College Park), and Mount St. Mary's College (Emmitsburg). By far the largest is the University of Maryland. The leading private institution in Maryland is The Johns Hopkins University in Baltimore. The State Board for Community Colleges oversees 17 community and 2 regional two-year schools. There are 3 private two-year colleges in the state.

33 ARTS

Though close to the arts centers of Washington, D.C., Maryland has its own cultural attractions. Center Stage in Baltimore is the designated state theater of Maryland, and the Olney Theatre in Montgomery County is the official state summer theater. Both the Maryland Ballet Company and Maryland Dance Theater are nationally known.

The state's leading orchestra is the Baltimore Symphony. Baltimore is also the home of the Baltimore Opera Company, and its jazz clubs were the launching pads for such musical notables as Eubie Blake, Ella Fitzgerald, and Cab Calloway. The Peabody Institute of Johns Hopkins University in Baltimore is one of the nation's most distinguished music schools. The State of Maryland generated $8,047,433 from federal and state sources from 1987 to 1991. In 1992, the State Arts Council supported theater productions by "Shakespeare on Wheels."

34 LIBRARIES AND MUSEUMS

Maryland's public libraries held 14,012,912 volumes in 1992 and had a combined circulation of 47,131,587. The center of the state library network is the Enoch Pratt Free Library in the city of Baltimore. Founded in 1886, it has 30 branches, 2,544,286 volumes, and a circulation of 2,554,286 in 1992. Each county also has its own library system. The largest academic libraries are those of Johns Hopkins University in Baltimore and the University of Maryland at College Park. Maryland is also the site of several federal libraries, including the National Agricultural Library, the National Library of Medicine, and the National Oceanic and Atmospheric Administration Library.

Of the approximately 123 museums and historic sites in the state, major institutions include the US Naval Academy Museum in Annapolis and Baltimore's Museum of Art and Maritime Museum. The latter's Peale Museum is the oldest museum building in the US. Important historic sites include Ft. McHenry National Monument and Shrine in Baltimore (inspiration for "The Star-Spangled Banner") and Antietam National Battlefield Site near Sharpsburg.

35 COMMUNICATIONS

In March 1993, 95.8% of Maryland's 1,871,000 occupied housing units had telephones. The state had 52 AM and 65

488,506). The *Washington Post* is also widely read in Maryland.

37 TOURISM, TRAVEL, AND RECREATION

Although not a major tourist center, Maryland attracted 7,828,000 visitors to its parks, historical sites, and national seashore (Assateague Island) in 1991. Income from tourism totaled about $6 billion in 1990. Among the state's attractions is Annapolis, the state capital and site of the US Naval Academy. On Baltimore's waterfront are monuments to Francis Scott Key and Edgar Allan Poe, historic Ft. McHenry, and many restaurants serving the city's famed crab cakes and other seafood specialties. Ocean City is the state's major seaside resort, and there are many resort towns along Chesapeake Bay. There are 15 state parks with camping facilities and 10 recreation areas.

38 SPORTS

Maryland has one major league professional sports team: the Baltimore Orioles of Major League Baseball. The Baltimore Colts of the National Football League moved to Indianapolis in 1984. The Baltimore Stallions of the Canadian Football League won the Grey Cup in 1995 but were scheduled to move after that season. The Washington Bullets of the National Basketball Association play in Landover but are considered a team of the District of Columbia. Horse-racing is a popular state pastime. The major tracks are Pimlico (Baltimore), Bowie, and Laurel. Several steeplechase events, including the prestigious Maryland Hunt Cup, are held annually.

Photo credit: Maryland Tourism.

Calvert Marine Museum, Solomons.

FM radio stations in 1993. Maryland Public Broadcasting operates six noncommercial television stations—in Annapolis, Baltimore, Frederick, Hagerstown, Oakland, and Salisbury. There were 14 large cable television systems in Maryland as of 1993.

36 PRESS

As of 1994, Maryland had 4 morning and 5 afternoon dailies, 1 all-day daily, and 9 Sunday papers, as well as 7 semiweekly newspapers and 88 weeklies. The most influential newspaper published in Baltimore is the *Sun* (daily, 391,952; Sunday,

In collegiate basketball, the University of Maryland won the National Invitation Tournament in 1972, and Morgan State took the NCAA Division II title in 1974. Other popular sports are lacrosse and jousting.

39 FAMOUS MARYLANDERS

Maryland has produced no US presidents; its lone vice-president was Spiro Theodore Agnew (b.1918), who served as governor of Maryland before being elected as Richard Nixon's vice-president in 1968. Reelected with Nixon in 1972, Agnew resigned the vice-presidency in October 1973 after a federal indictment had been filed against him. Roger Brooke Taney (1777–1864) was US chief justice when the Supreme Court heard the *Dred Scott* case in 1856, ruling that Congress could not exclude slavery from any territory.

As counsel for the National Association for the Advancement of Colored People, Thurgood Marshall (1908–93) argued the landmark *Brown v. Board of Education* school desegregation case before the Supreme Court in 1954. President Lyndon Johnson appointed him to the Court 13 years later. Other major officeholders born in Maryland include Albert C. Ritchie (1876–1936), governor from 1919 to 1935; Benjamin Civiletti (b.New York, 1935), attorney general under Jimmy Carter; and William D. Schaefer (b.1921), mayor of Baltimore during 1971–86, and governor during 1987–95.

Lawyer and poet Francis Scott Key (1779–1843) wrote "The Star-Spangled Banner"—now the national anthem—in 1814. The prominent abolitionists Frederick Douglass (Frederick Augustus Washington Bailey, 1817?–95) and Harriet Tubman (1820?–1913) were born in Maryland. Elizabeth Ann Bayley Seton (b.New York, 1774–1821), canonized by the Roman Catholic Church in 1975, was the first native-born American saint. Stephen Decatur (1779–1820), a prominent naval officer, has been credited with the toast "Our country, right or wrong!"

Prominent Maryland business leaders include George Peabody (b.Massachusetts, 1795–1869), founder of the world-famous Peabody Conservatory of Music (now the Peabody Institute of Johns Hopkins University); and Enoch Pratt (b.Masachusetts, (1808–96) who endowed the Enoch Pratt Free Library in Baltimore. Benjamin Banneker (1731–1806), a free black, assisted in surveying the new District of Columbia and published almanacs from 1792 to 1797. Ottmar Mergenthaler (b.Germany, 1854–99), who made his home in Baltimore, invented the linotype machine.

Financier-philanthropist Johns Hopkins (1795–1873) was a Marylander, and educators Daniel Coit Gilman (b.Connecticut, 1831–1908) and William Osler (b.Canada, 1849–1919), also a famed physician, were prominent in the establishment of the university and medical school named in Hopkins's honor. Peyton Rous (1879–1970) won the 1966 Nobel Prize for physiology-medicine.

Maryland's best-known modern writer was H(enry) L(ouis) Mencken (1880–1956), a Baltimore newspaper reporter who was also a gifted social commentator, political wit, and student of the American language. Edgar Allan Poe (b.Massachusetts, 1809–49), known for his poems and eerie short stories, died in Baltimore. Novelist-reformer Upton Sinclair (1878–1968) was born there, as was Emily Price Post (1873–1960), who wrote about social etiquette. Other writers associated with Maryland include James M. Cain (1892–1976); Leon Uris (b.1924); John Barth (b.1930); and Tom Clancy (Thomas L. Clancy, Jr., b.1947). Painters John Hesselius (b.Pennsylvania, 1728–78) and Charles Willson Peale (1741–1827) are also linked with the state.

Most notable among Maryland actors are Edwin Booth (1833–93) and his brother John Wilkes Booth (1838–65), notorious as the assassin of President Abraham Lincoln. Other famous actors include Francis X. Bushman (1883–1966), Catherine Calvert (1891–1971), and David Hasselhoff (b.1947). Maryland was the birthplace of several jazz musicians, including James Hubert "Eubie" Blake (1883–1983), William Henry "Chick" Webb (1907–39), and Billie Holiday (1915–59).

Probably the greatest baseball player of all time, George Herman "Babe" Ruth (1895–1948), was born in Baltimore. Other prominent ballplayers include Robert Moses "Lefty" Grove (1900–75); James Emory "Jimmy" Foxx (1907–67); Al Kaline (b.1934); and Cal Ripken, Jr. (Calvin Edwin Ripken, Jr., b.1960). Former lightweight boxing champion Joe Gans (1874–1910) was a Maryland native.

40 BIBLIOGRAPHY

Alampi, Gary, ed. *Gale State Rankings Reporter.* Detroit: Gale Research Inc., 1994.

Bode, Carl. *Maryland: A Bicentennial History.* New York: Norton, 1978.

Cohen, Richard M., and Jules Witcover. *A Heartbeat Away: The Investigation and Resignation of Vice President Spiro T. Agnew.* New York: Viking, 1974.

Walsh, Richard, and William Lloyd Fox, eds. *Maryland: A History.* Baltimore: Maryland Hall of Records, 1983.

MASSACHUSETTS

Commonwealth of Massachusetts

ORIGIN OF STATE NAME: Derived from the name of the Massachusett Indian tribe that lived on Massachusetts Bay; the name is thought to mean "at or about the Great Hill."

NICKNAME: The Bay State.

CAPITAL: Boston.

ENTERED UNION: 6 February 1788 (6th).

SONG: "All Hail to Massachusetts."

FOLK SONG: "Massachusetts."

POEM: "Blue Hills of Massachusetts."

MOTTO: *Ense petit placidam sub libertate quietem* (By the sword we seek peace, but peace only under liberty).

COAT OF ARMS: On a blue shield, an Indian depicted in gold holds in his right hand a bow, in his left an arrow pointing downward. Above the bow is a five-pointed silver star. The crest shows a bent right arm holding a broadsword. Around the shield beneath the crest is a banner with the state motto in green.

FLAG: The coat of arms on a white field.

OFFICIAL SEAL: Same as the coat of arms, with the inscription *Sigillum Reipublicæ Massachusettensis* (Seal of the Republic of Massachusetts).

HEROINE: Deborah Samson.

BIRD: Chickadee.

HORSE: Morgan horse.

DOG: Boston terrier.

MARINE MAMMAL: Right whale.

FISH: Cod.

FLOWER: Mayflower (ground laurel).

TREE: American elm.

GEM: Rhodonite.

MINERAL: Babingtonite.

ROCK: Roxbury pudding stone.

HISTORICAL ROCK: Plymouth Rock.

EXPLORER ROCK: Dighton Rock.

BUILDING AND MONUMENT STONE: Granite.

FOSSIL: Theropod dinosaur tracks.

BEVERAGE: Cranberry juice.

INSECT: Ladybug.

TIME: 7 AM EST = noon GMT.

1 LOCATION AND SIZE

Located in the northeastern US, Massachusetts is the fourth largest of the six New England states. It ranks 45th in size among the 50 states. The total area of Massachusetts is 8,284 square miles (21,456 square kilometers). Massachusetts extends about 190 miles (306 kilometers)

east-west; the maximum north-south extension is about 110 miles (177 kilometers). Two important islands lie south of the state's fishhook-shaped Cape Cod peninsula: Martha's Vineyard and Nantucket. The Elizabeth Islands, southwest of Cape Cod and northwest of Martha's Vineyard, consist of 16 small islands separating Buzzards Bay from Vineyard Sound. The total boundary length of Massachusetts is 515 miles (829 kilometers).

2 TOPOGRAPHY

The northern shoreline of the state is characterized by rugged high slopes, but at the southern end, along Cape Cod, the ground is flatter and covered with grassy heaths. East of the Connecticut River Valley are the eastern uplands, a ridge of heavily forested hills that is an extension of the White Mountains of New Hampshire. The Connecticut River Valley, characterized by red sandstone, curved ridges, and meadows, is the main feature of west-central Massachusetts. Found in western Massachusetts are the Taconic Range and Berkshire Hills (which extend southward from the Green Mountains of Vermont). Mt. Greylock is the highest point in the state, at 3,491 feet (1,064 meters).

There are more than 4,230 miles (6,808 kilometers) of rivers in the state. The principal ones include the Connecticut River (the longest) and the Charles, which flow into Boston harbor, and the Taunton, the Housatonic, and the Merrimack. Over 1,100 lakes dot the state. Martha's Vineyard and Nantucket Island are hilly. The Elizabeth Islands are characterized by broad, grassy plains.

Massachusetts Population Profile

Estimated 1995 population:	5,976,000
Population change, 1980–90:	4.9%
Leading ancestry group:	Irish
Second leading group:	English
Foreign born population:	9.5%
Hispanic origin†:	4.8%
Population by race:	
White:	89.8%
Black:	5.0%
Native American:	0.2%
Asian/Pacific Islander:	2.4%
Other:	2.6%

Population by Age Group

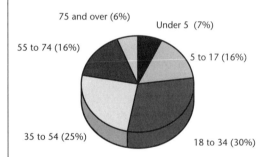

75 and over (6%)
Under 5 (7%)
55 to 74 (16%)
5 to 17 (16%)
35 to 54 (25%)
18 to 34 (30%)

Top Cities with Populations Over 25,000

City	Population	National rank	% change 1980–90
Boston	551,675	20	2.0
Worcester	163,414	107	4.9
Springfield	153,466	114	3.1
Lowell	99,873	200	11.9
New Bedford	96,892	211	1.5
Cambridge	93,554	223	0.5
Fall River	91,066	231	0.1
Brockton	89,191	235	–2.5
Quincy	84,457	259	0.3
Newton	82,126	270	–1.2

Notes: †A person of Hispanic origin may be of any race. NA indicates that data are not available.
Sources: Economic and Statistics Administration, Bureau of the Census. *Statistical Abstract of the United States, 1994–95.* Washington, DC: Government Printing Office, 1995; Courtenay M. Slater and George E. Hall. *1995 County and City Extra: Annual Metro, City and County Data Book.* Lanham, MD: Bernan Press, 1995.

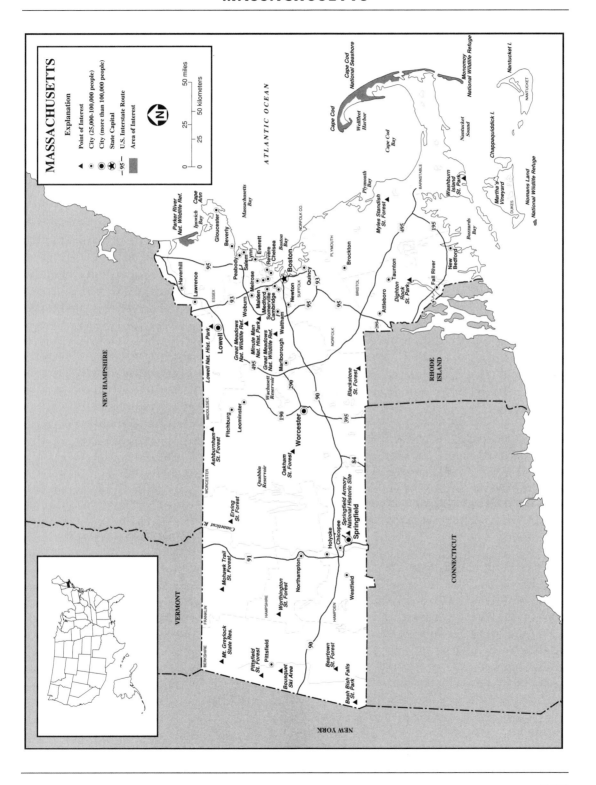

MASSACHUSETTS

Explanation

▲ Point of Interest
⊙ City (25,000-100,000 people)
◉ City (more than 100,000 people)
★ State Capital
—95— U.S. Interstate Route
▨ Area of Interest

50 miles
50 kilometers

N

ATLANTIC OCEAN

Cape Cod National Seashore
Cape Cod
Wellfleet Harbor
Cape Cod Bay
Monomoy National Wildlife Refuge
Nantucket I.
Nantucket
Nantucket Sound
Chappaquiddick I.
Martha's Vineyard
Nomans Land National Wildlife Refuge
DUKES

Massachusetts Bay
Plymouth Bay
Washburn Island St. Park
Buzzards Bay
New Bedford
Fall River
BARNSTABLE

Parker River Nat. Wildlife Ref.
Ipswich Bay
Cape Ann
Gloucester
Beverly
Peabody
Salem
Lynn
Revere
Chelsea
Everett
Boston
Medford
Somerville
Cambridge
Malden
Woburn
Melrose
Waltham
Newton
Quincy
Marlborough
NORFOLK CO.
PLYMOUTH
Brockton
Myles Standish St. Forest
495
195
BRISTOL
Taunton
Dighton Rock St. Park
Attleboro
NORFOLK
295
SUFFOLK
93
95
95

NEW HAMPSHIRE

Haverhill
Lawrence
95
ESSEX
93
MIDDLESEX
Lowell
Lowell Nat. Hist. Park
Minute Man Nat. Hist. Park
Great Meadows Nat. Wildlife Ref.
Great Meadows Nat. Wildlife Ref.
495
Wachusett Reservoir
290
90
Blackstone St. Forest

RHODE ISLAND

Ashburnham St. Forest
WORCESTER
Fitchburg
Leominster
190
Worcester
395
Oakham St. Forest
Quabbin Reservoir
Erving St. Forest
84
Springfield Armory National Historic Site
Springfield
Chicopee
Holyoke
Connecticut R.
91

CONNECTICUT

VERMONT
FRANKLIN
BERKSHIRE
Mohawk Trail St. Forest
Mt. Greylock State Res.
Pittsfield St. Forest
Pittsfield
Bousquet Ski Area
Bash Bish Falls St. Park
HAMPSHIRE
Worthington St. Forest
Northampton
Westfield
HAMPDEN
90
Beartown St. Forest

NEW YORK

3 CLIMATE

Although Massachusetts is a relatively small state, there are significant climatic differences between its eastern and western sections. The entire state has cold winters and moderately warm summers. The Berkshires in the west have both the coldest winters and the coolest summers. Normal temperatures for Pittsfield in the Berkshires are 22°F (–6°C) in January and 68°F (20°C) in July. The interior lowlands are several degrees warmer in both winter and summer. The coastal sections are the warmest areas of the state. Normal temperatures for Boston are 30°F (–1°C) in January and 74°F (23°C) in July. The record high temperature in the state was 107°F (42°C) in 1975; the record low was –35°F (–37°C) in 1981. Precipitation ranges from 39 to 46 inches (99 to 117 centimeters) annually. The average snowfall for Boston is 42 inches (107 centimeters), with the range in the Berkshires considerably higher.

4 PLANTS AND ANIMALS

Maple, birch, beech, and other species cover the Massachusetts uplands. Common shrubs include rhodora, mountain laurel, and shadbush. Various ferns grow throughout the state. Typical wild flowers include several varieties of orchid, lily, and goldenrod.

Common native mammals include the white-tailed deer, river otter, mink, and porcupine. Among the Bay State's 336 resident bird species are the mallard, ring-necked pheasant, downy woodpecker, and song sparrow. Native inland fish include brook trout, chain pickerel, and yellow perch. Common reptiles are the snapping turtle and northern water snake. The Cape Cod coasts are rich in a variety of shellfish, including clams, mussels, shrimps, and oysters. Among endangered mammals are the sperm, blue, and humpback whales.

5 ENVIRONMENTAL PROTECTION

In 1988, 10% of the flounder caught in Boston Harbor had liver tumors caused by toxic chemicals. With disposal of treated sewage sludge in Boston Harbor halted in 1991 and with improved sewage treatment, the harbor today is markedly cleaner. In 1993, no flounder tested had tumors.

With adoption of Massachusetts acid rain legislation in 1985, sulfur dioxide output from Massachusetts sources has been cut by 17%. Additional decreases, particularly from out-of-state power plants, are expected to further cut sulfur dioxide emissions in half by the year 2000. The state's solid waste recycling and composting rate stands at 28% in 1994. Its goal for the year 2000 is 46%. In 1994, about 49% of solid waste was incinerated. Active landfills dropped in number from 220 in 1988 to 119 in 1994. There were 30 hazardous waste sites in that year.

Wildlife management has restored populations of wild turkeys, white-tailed deer, Atlantic salmon, and other species. Since about 1900, the Commonwealth has protected 515,765 acres (208,730 hectares) through acquisitions or restrictions. All environment-related programs

Photo credit: Susan D. Rock.

The state house in Boston.

are administered by the Executive Office of Environmental Affairs (EOEA).

6 POPULATION

Massachusetts's population, according to the 1990 federal census, was 6,016,425 (13th in the US). A population of 5,950,000 is projected for 2000. The state's birthrate is well below the US average, and a net out-migration of 301,000 people between 1970 and 1983 was the largest drop of all New England states. Between 1990 and 1994, the state lost another 184,000 residents due to out-migration. In 1990, about 84.3% of the state was urban and 15.7% rural. A density of 767 persons per square mile (295

persons per square kilometer) in 1990 made Massachusetts the third most densely populated state.

The state's biggest city is Boston, which ranked 20th among the largest US cities with a population of 551,675 in 1992. Other large cities (with their 1992 populations) are Worcester, 163,414; Springfield, 153,466; and Lowell, 99,873. More than 70% of all state residents live in the Greater Boston area, which in 1990 had a metropolitan population of 4,172,000 (seventh largest in the US).

7 ETHNIC GROUPS

Early industrialization helped make Massachusetts a magnet for many European migrants, particularly the Irish. As late as 1990 more than half of the population identified with at least one single ancestry group, the largest being the Irish (26% of the population), English (15%), Italian (14%), French (10%), Portuguese (5%), and Polish (6%). In that year, 9.5% of the state's population was foreign-born.

The 20th century has seen an influx of working-class blacks from southern states, and a sizable class of black professionals has developed. In 1990 there were 300,000 black Americans in Massachusetts, or 5% of the population. Blacks constituted more than 25% of Boston's population. The state also had 288,000 people of Hispanic ancestry, predominantly Puerto Rican and Dominican.

Greater Boston has a small, well-organized Chinatown. In the suburbs reside many business and professional Chinese, as well as those connected with the region's numerous educational institutions. Statewide, there were 47,245 Chinese in 1990, 12,878 Koreans, 10,662 Japanese, and 13,101 Vietnamese. Although small tribal settlements persist on Cape Cod, Massachusetts had only 12,000 Native Americans in 1990. Cape Cod also has settlements of Portuguese fishermen, as has New Bedford.

8 LANGUAGES

On the whole, Massachusetts English is classed as Northern, but early migration up the Connecticut River created special variations within the eastern half of the state. A few place-names—such as Massachusetts itself, Chicopee, and Naukeag— are borrowed from the Algonkian-speaking Native American tribes. In 1990, 84.8% of the population five years of age or older spoke only English at home. Principal other languages spoken at home, and number of speakers, were Spanish, 228,458; Portuguese, 133,373; French, 124,973; Italian, 81,987; and Chinese, 43,248.

9 RELIGIONS

As of 1990, there were 2,961,259 Roman Catholics in Massachusetts, more than half the total population. The largest Protestant denominations were: United Church of Christ, 135,983 members; Episcopal, 122,190; American Baptist (USA), 66,156; United Methodist, 71,858; Unitarian, 35,787; Lutheran Church-Missouri Synod, 7,053; and Congregationalist, 9,931. Most of the state's estimated 107,116 Jewish population in 1990 lived in Boston.

Although small, the Church of Christ, Scientist is significant to Massachusetts's history. Its first house of worship was founded in 1879 in Boston by Mary Baker Eddy, who, four years earlier, had published the Christian Science textbook, *Science and Health with Key to the Scriptures*. In Boston, the church continues to publish an influential newspaper, the *Christian Science Monitor*.

10 TRANSPORTATION

As of 1991, eleven railroads transported freight through Massachusetts. Boston is the northern terminus of Amtrak's Northeast Corridor, linking New England with Washington, D.C., via New York City and Philadelphia. At the end of 1992, the state had 986 rail miles (1,345 kilometers) of track. In 1991/92, Amtrak operated about 19 trains through the state, with a total of 1,283,548 riders.

The Boston subway, which began operation in 1897, is the oldest subway system in the US. Boston also is one of the few cities in the US with an operating trolley system. About 40% of all Bostonians commute to work by public transportation, the second-highest percentage in the nation, following New York City.

In 1993, 30,563 miles (49,176 kilometers) of public roadways crisscrossed the state. The interstate highway network in Massachusetts totaled 565 miles (909 kilometers) in 1993. Some $2.2 billion was spent by all units of government for highways in 1992. In 1993, 3,873,497 motor vehicles were registered in the state, of which 3,326,871 were automobiles, 499,887 were trucks, and 10,739 were buses. There also were 68,466 motorcycles.

Because it is the major American city closest to Europe, Boston is an important shipping center for both domestic and foreign cargo. In 1991, 18,562,490 tons of cargo passed through the Port of Boston. Other important ports are Fall River and Salem. There were 77 airports and 106 heliports in the state as of 31 December 1991. Logan International, near Boston, was the 14th-busiest airport in the nation in 1991. In that year, it handled 109,090 departing aircraft, boarded 8,862,052 passengers, and processed 122,162 tons of freight and 29,806 tons of mail.

11 HISTORY

When English settlers arrived in present-day Massachusetts, they encountered five main Algonkian tribes: the Nauset, a fishing people on Cape Cod; the Wampanoag in the southeast; the Massachusetts in the northeast; the Nipmuc in the central hills; and the Pocumtuc in the west. In the wake of John and Sebastian Cabot's voyages (1497 and following), fishermen from England, France, Portugal, and Spain began fishing off the Massachusetts coast. Within 50 years, fur trading with the Native Americans was established.

Permanent English settlement, which would ultimately destroy the Algonkian peoples, began in 1620 when a small band of Puritans left their temporary haven at Leiden in the Netherlands to start a colony in the northern part of Virginia lands, near the Hudson River. Their ship, the *Mayflower,* was blown off course by an Atlantic storm, and they landed on Cape Cod before settling in an abandoned Wampanoag village they called Plymouth. Ten years later, a much larger Puritan group settled the Massachusetts Bay Colony, to the north in Salem. Between 1630 and 1640, about 20,000 English people, chiefly Puritans, settled in Massachusetts with offshoots moving to Connecticut and Rhode Island.

Farming soon overtook fishing and fur trading in economic importance. After the trade in beaver skins was exhausted, the remaining Native American tribes were devastated in King Philip's War (1675–76). Shipbuilding and Atlantic commerce brought added prosperity to the Massachusetts Bay Colony. In 1692, Massachusetts and the colony of Plymouth were merged under a new charter.

During the 18th century, settlement spread across the entire colony. Boston, the capital, attained a population of 15,000 by 1730. Colonial government provided more advantages than drawbacks for commerce, and supply contracts during the French and Indian War enriched the colony's economy. But the postwar recession after 1763 was accompanied by a new imperial policy that put pressure on Massachusetts as well as other colonies. From 1765, when Bostonians violently protested the Stamp Act, Massachusetts was in the forefront of the resistance.

By December 1773, when East India Company tea was dumped into Boston harbor to prevent its taxation, most of the colony was committed to resistance. When Parliament retaliated for the Tea Party by closing the port of Boston in 1774, Massachusetts was ready to rebel. Battle began at Lexington and Concord on 19 April 1775. By this time, Massachusetts had the backing of the Continental Congress. For Massachusetts, the battlefield experience of the Revolution was largely confined to 1775, after which the fighting shifted southward.

Statehood

Massachusetts entered the Union on 6 February 1788. Federalist policies—supporting a strong central government—were dominant, and they were supported by the Whigs in the 1830s and the Republicans from the late 1850s. This political alignment reflected the importance to the state of national commercial and industrial development, as Massachusetts lacked the resources for strong agricultural development.

At Waltham, Lowell, and Lawrence the first large-scale factories in the US were erected. Massachusetts became a leader in industries including textiles, metalworking, shoes and leather goods, and shipbuilding. By the 1850s, steam engines and clipper ships were both Bay State products. The industrial development of Massachusetts was accompanied by a literary and intellectual flowering centered in Concord, the home of Ralph Waldo Emerson, Henry David Thoreau, and a cluster of others who became known as transcendentalists. Abolitionism found some of its chief leaders in Massachusetts.

Post–Civil War

In the years following the Civil War, Massachusetts emerged as an urban industrial state. Its population, fed by immigrants from England, Scotland, Germany, and especially Ireland, grew rapidly in the middle decades of the century. Later, between 1880 and 1920, another wave of immigrants came from French Canada, Italy, Russia, Poland, Scandinavia, Portugal, Greece, and Syria. Still later, between 1950 and 1970, black southerners and Puerto Ricans settled in the cities.

The Massachusetts economy, relatively stagnant between 1920 and 1950, revived in the second half of the 20th century through a combination of university talent, investment, a skilled work force, and political clout. As the old industries and the mill cities declined, new high-technology manufacturing developed in Boston's suburbs, led by electronics and defense-related industries. White-collar employment and middle-class suburbs flourished, though run-down mill towns and Yankee dairy farms and orchards still dotted the landscape.

In the 1970s and early 1980s, a revolution in information technology and increased defense spending fueled a high-technology boom which centered on new manufacturing firms outside Boston along Route 128. Unemployment dropped from 12% in 1978 to 4% in 1987. However, with the beginnings of a nationwide recession in 1989, the Massachusetts economy declined dramatically, losing 14% of its total jobs in three years. Massachusetts's economic woes were increased by the collapse in the late 1980s of risky real estate

ventures. By 1992, a number of indications suggested that recovery, slow in coming, had begun to take hold.

12 STATE GOVERNMENT

The Massachusetts constitution of 15 June 1780 is, according to the state, the oldest written constitution in the world still in effect. The legislature of Massachusetts, known as the General Court, is composed of a 40-member senate and 160-member house of representatives, all of whom are elected every two years.

The governor and lieutenant governor are elected jointly every four years. The governor appoints all state and local judges, as well as the heads of the ten executive offices. Other elected officials include the attorney general, secretary of the commonwealth, and treasurer. Massachusetts also has an eight-member executive council with the power to review the

Massachusetts Presidential Vote by Political Party, 1948–92

YEAR	MASSACHUSETTS WINNER	DEMOCRAT	REPUBLICAN	SOCIALIST LABOR	PROGRESSIVE
1948	*Truman (D)	1,151,788	909,370	5,535	38,157
1952	*Eisenhower (R)	1,083,525	1,292,325	1,957	4,636
1956	*Eisenhower (R)	948,190	1,393,197	5,573	—
1960	*Kennedy (D)	1,487,174	976,750	3,892	—
1964	*Johnson (D)	1,786,422	549,727	4,755	—
					AMERICAN IND.
1968	Humphrey (D)	1,469,218	766,844	6,180	87,088
				SOC. WORKERS	AMERICAN
1972	McGovern (D)	1,332,540	1,112,078	10,600	2,877
1976	*Carter (D)	1,429,475	1,030,276	8,138	7,555
				LIBERTARIAN	
1980	*Reagan (R)	1,048,562	1,054,213	21,311	—
1984	*Reagan	1,239,600	1,310,936	—	—
					NEW ALLIANCE
1988	Dukakis (D)	1,401,415	1,194,635	24,251	9,561
					IND. (Perot)
1992	*Clinton (D)	1,318,639	805,039	9,021	630,731

*Won US presidential election.

governor's judicial appointments and pardons, and to authorize expenditures from the state treasury.

To win passage, a bill must gain a majority vote of both houses of the legislature. After a bill is passed, the governor has ten days in which to sign it, return it for reconsideration (usually with amendments), veto it, or refuse to sign it ("pocket veto"). A veto may be overridden by a two-thirds majority in both houses.

13 POLITICAL PARTIES

Democrats have, for the most part, dominated state politics in Massachusetts since 1928, when the state voted for Democratic presidential candidate Alfred E. Smith—the first time the Democrats won a majority in a Massachusetts presidential election. In 1960, John F. Kennedy, who had been a popular US senator from Massachusetts, became the first Roman Catholic president in US history. Since then the state has voted for all Democratic presidential candidates except Jimmy Carter in 1980 and Walter Mondale in 1984. In 1972, it was the only state carried by Democrat George McGovern. Massachusetts chose its native son, Democratic Governor Michael Dukakis, for president in 1988 and voted again for a Democrat in 1992, electing Bill Clinton.

As of 1994, there were 1,346,097 registered Democrats, or 40% of the total number of registered voters; 447,181 Republicans, or 13%; and 1,558,640 independents, or 47%. As of 1994, the governorship was held by a Republican, William Weld, and the US Senate seats were held by Democrats, Edward ("Ted")

Kennedy and John Kerry. The US House delegation in 1992 consisted of eight Democrats and two Republicans. The Massachusetts state senate had 31 Democrats and 9 Republicans, while the state house of representatives had 125 Democrats and 34 Republicans.

14 LOCAL GOVERNMENT

As of 1992, Massachusetts had 13 counties, 39 cities, and 312 towns. In all 13 counties except Suffolk County, executive authority was vested in three county commissioners. All Massachusetts cities are governed by mayors and city councils. Towns are governed by selectmen, who are usually elected to either one or two-year terms. Town meetings—a carryover from the colonial period—still take place regularly. By state law, to be designated a city, a place must have at least 12,000 residents. Towns with more than 6,000 inhabitants may hold representative town meetings that are limited to elected officials.

15 JUDICIAL SYSTEM

The supreme judicial court, composed of a chief justice and six other justices, is the highest court in the state. It has appeals jurisdiction in matters of law and also advises the governor and legislature on legal questions. The superior courts, actually the highest level of trial court, have a chief justice and 55 other justices. These courts hear law, equity, civil, and criminal cases, and make the final determination in matters of fact. The appeals court, consisting of a chief justice and nine other justices, hears appeals of decisions by district and municipal courts.

Photo credit: Susan D. Rock.

A view of Boston from across the Charles River.

Other court systems in the state include the land court, probate and family court, housing court, and juvenile court. Massachusetts's total crime rate per 100,000 inhabitants was 4,441 in 1994. As of 1993 there were 11,100 prisoners in state and federal correctional institutions.

16 MIGRATION

From 1970 to 1990, Massachusetts lost nearly 400,000 residents in net migration to other states, but experienced an overall net increase from migration of 59,000 due to migration from abroad. As of 1990, 68.7% of all state residents had been born in Massachusetts. The only significant migration from other areas of the US to

Massachusetts has been the influx of southern blacks since World War II. According to census estimates, Massachusetts gained 84,000 blacks between 1940 and 1975; in 1990, it had a black population of about 300,000 persons, mostly in the Boston area.

17 ECONOMY

From its beginnings as a farming and seafaring colony, Massachusetts became one of the most industrialized states in the country in the late 19th century and, more recently, a leader in the manufacture of high-technology products. Fueled in part by a dramatic increase in the Pentagon's budget that focused on sophisticated weaponry, as well as by significant advances in information technology, high-technology companies rose up around the outskirts of Boston in the 1970s. Wholesale and retail trade, transportation, and public utilities also prospered.

In the late 1980s, the boom ended. The minicomputer industry failed to innovate at the same pace as its competitors as the market became increasingly crowded, and defense contractors suffered from cuts in military spending. Between 1988 and 1991, jobs in both high-technology and non-high technology manufacturing declined by 17%. In addition, the early 1980s had also seen the rise of real estate ventures which collapsed at the end of the decade when the market became saturated. Unemployment rose to 9% in 1991. Since then, the economy has begun to make a slow recovery.

18 INCOME

In 1994, Massachusetts ranked fourth among the 50 states in per capita (per person) income, with $25,609 in current dollars. Total personal income for the state was $154.7 billion in 1994. Some 10.7% of all Bay Staters had incomes below the federal poverty line.

19 INDUSTRY

Massachusetts is an important manufacturing center. Significant concentrations of industrial machinery employment are in Attleboro, Wilmington, Worcester, and the Springfield area. Much of the manufacturing industry is located along Route 128. This is a superhighway that circles Boston, from Gloucester in the north to Quincy in the south, and is unique in its concentration of high-technology enterprises.

Massachusetts's future as a manufacturing center depends on its continued pre-eminence in the production of computers, optical equipment, and other sophisticated instruments. Nine of Massachusetts's 15 *Fortune 500* companies were engaged in the production of computer equipment, electronic components, or instruments. Among the major computer manufacturers in the state are Digital Equipment Corporation in Maynard, and Data General in Westboro.

20 LABOR

In 1994, the state's labor force numbered 3,179,000 persons. The unemployment rate for all workers in 1994 was 6%. As recently as 1977, the unemployment rate had been 13%, one of the highest in the US. As of mid-1993, there were 14 national labor unions operating in the state. About 15.9% of all workers in the state were members of labor unions in 1994.

21 AGRICULTURE

As of 1994, there were 6,000 farms in Massachusetts, covering 500,000 acres (200,000 hectares). Farming was mostly limited to the western Massachusetts counties of Hampshire, Franklin, and Berkshire, and southern Bristol County. Total agricultural income for 1994 was estimated at $458,731,000 (45th of the 50 states), of which crops provided 74%. Although the state is not a major farming area, it is the largest producer of cranberries in the US. Cranberry production for

1994 was 190 million pounds, nearly half of the US total. Output totals for other crops in 1991 were as follows: corn for silage, 488,000 tons; hay, 217,000 tons; and tobacco, 803,000 pounds.

22 DOMESTICATED ANIMALS

Massachusetts is not a major producer of livestock. Receipts from livestock and related products totaled $117,300,000 in 1994. As of 1994, the state had 68,000 cattle, 19,000 hogs, and 11,500 sheep. In 1994, dairy products and chicken eggs accounted for 14.2% and 3.6% of the state's agricultural receipts, respectively.

23 FISHING

The fishing ports of Gloucester and New Bedford were among the busiest in the US in 1992. The value of the commercial catch—$280,589,000—was the highest among the New England states and the third highest in the US at 274,269,000 pounds. The state's long shoreline and many rivers make sport-fishing a popular pastime for both deepsea and freshwater fishers.

24 FORESTRY

Forestry is a minor industry in the state. Forested lands cover about 3,203,000 acres (1,296,000 hectares). Red oak and white ash are found in the west. Specialty products include maple syrup and Christmas trees. Massachusetts has the sixth-largest state park system in the nation, with 38 state parks and 74 state forests totaling some 273,000 acres (110,000 hectares). There are no national forests in Massachusetts.

Photo credit: Susan D. Rock.

A seafood vendor at Haymarket.

25 MINING

The value of nonfuel mineral production in Massachusetts in 1994 was estimated at $157 million. Crushed stone and construction sand and gravel are the state's two leading mineral commodities. In 1992 there were 11.1 million short tons of crushed stone and 13.4 million short tons of sand and gravel produced, worth $82.3 million and $53.3 million, respectively. Other mineral commodities produced included common clay, lime, and peat, $11,636,000; industrial sand, $401,000; and dimension stone, $9,292,000. Industrial minerals processed or manufactured in the state included abrasives, graphite, gypsum, perlite, and vermiculite.

26 ENERGY AND POWER

Massachusetts is highly dependent on oil for electric generation and home heating, and energy costs in the state are among the highest in the US. During the early 1980s, as much as 81% of the state's electric power output was generated from oil. In 1993, about 28.2 billion kilowatt hours of electric power were produced. Approximately 34% of this electricity was for residential use, 41% commercial, 22% industrial, and 3% for other purposes. Massachusetts has no proven oil or coal reserves. There is one nuclear power plant. State energy expenditures in 1992 were $1,810 per capita (per person).

The state consumes but does not produce natural gas. In 1991 about 259 trillion Btu of natural gas were delivered. Altogether there were 23 hydroelectric generators which produced 22 trillion Btu in 1991.

27 COMMERCE

Massachusetts's machinery and electrical goods industries are important components of the state's wholesale trade, along with motor vehicle and automotive equipment, and paper and paper products. State wholesale sales totaled $86.7 billion in 1992; retail sales were $48.5 billion in 1993; and service establishments receipts were $43.7 billion in 1992. Foreign exports of Massachusetts products totaled $10.4 billion in 1992 (tenth in the US).

28 PUBLIC FINANCE

The total debt of state and local governments as of 1993 was more than $25.4 billion, or $4,223 per capita (per person).

The estimated revenues for the 1991/92 fiscal year were $22,646,907,000; expenses were $23,263,765,000.

29 TAXATION

Massachusetts's tax burden on a per capita (per person) basis as of 1991 was $1,615 (fourth among the states). Total tax revenues received in 1991 were the tenth highest in the country at $9.7 billion. As of 1994, the state levied a flat tax rate of 5.95% on income. The corporate income tax rate was 9.5%. There is also a sales tax, estate taxes, a cigarette tax, a gasoline tax, and a motor vehicle excise tax of $25 for every $1,000 of valuation. Bay Staters paid income taxes totaling $13.8 billion.

30 HEALTH

In 1990, Massachusetts ranked third (after New Jersey and Rhode Island) in the proportion of breast cancer deaths per 100,000 women, at 31.2. The death rate from cancer in 1992 was above the US average. The Division of Drug Rehabilitation administers drug treatment from a statewide network of hospital agencies and self-help groups. The state also runs a lead-poisoning prevention program.

Massachusetts had 99 community hospitals, with 21,100 beds in 1993. Among the best-known institutions are Massachusetts General Hospital, a leading research and treatment center, and the Massachusetts Eye and Ear Infirmary, a Boston clinic. In 1993 there were 21,700 nonfederal active physicians and about 63,800 nurses. Prominent medical schools located in the state include Harvard Medical

School and Tufts University School of Medicine. The average cost per inpatient day for hospital care was $1,036 in 1993, or $6,843 for an average cost per stay. Some 11.7% of state residents did not have health insurance in 1993.

31 HOUSING

Massachusetts's housing stock, much older than the US average, reflects the state's colonial heritage and its ties to English architectural traditions. Two major styles are common: colonial, typified by a wood frame, two stories, center hall entry, and center chimney; and Cape Cod, one-story houses built by fishermen, with shingled roofs, clapboard fronts, and unpainted shingled sides. Many new houses are also built in these styles.

As of 1993, there were an estimated 2,513,000 housing units in the state. In 1993, 17,460 new housing units were authorized, with a value of over $1.8 billion. Monthly cost for owners with a mortgage in 1990 was $985 and $298 for those without a mortgage; median monthly rent was $580. In 1990, the median value of a home in Massachusetts was $162,800 (fourth highest of any state).

32 EDUCATION

Massachusetts has a long history of support for education. The Boston Latin School opened in 1635 as the first public school in the colonies. Harvard College—the first college in the US—was founded the following year. Today the state boasts some of the most highly regarded private secondary schools and colleges in the country.

As of the 1990 census, 78.6% of state residents age 25 or older were high school graduates and 29.1% had completed four or more years of college. As of 1993, there were about 874,000 students enrolled in public schools. Expenditures on education averaged $6,592 per pupil in 1993. Private preparatory schools include such prestigious institutions as Andover, Deerfield, and Groton. Enrollment in private schools in October 1992 totaled 123,305.

There are 116 colleges and universities in the state. The major public university system is the University of Massachusetts, with campuses at Amherst, Boston, Dartmouth, Lowell, and a medical school at Worcester. Harvard University is one of the country's premier institutions; its 1992 student population was 18,556. Also located in Cambridge are Radcliffe College (whose enrollment is included in Harvard's) and the Massachusetts Institute of Technology, or MIT (1861), with 9,790 students in 1992.

Mount Holyoke College, the first US college for women, was founded in 1837. Other prominent private schools include Amherst College, Boston College, Boston University, Brandeis University, the New England Conservatory of Music, Northeastern University, Smith College, Tufts University, and Wellesley College.

33 ARTS

Boston is the center of artistic activity in Massachusetts, and Cape Cod and the Berkshires are areas of significant seasonal artistic activity. Boston is the home of several small theaters, some of which offer previews of shows bound for Broadway. Of the regional theaters scattered throughout the state, the Williamstown Theater in the Berkshires and the Provincetown Theater on Cape Cod are especially noteworthy.

The Boston Symphony, one of the major orchestras in the US, was founded in 1881. During the summer, the symphony is the main attraction of the Berkshire Music Festival at Tanglewood in Lenox. An offshoot of the Boston Symphony, the Boston Pops Orchestra, gained fame under the conductorship of Arthur Fiedler. Boston is also the headquarters of the Opera Company of Boston. The Boston Ballet Company is the state's major dancing troupe. The state of Massachusetts generated $119,137,369 in federal and state funds for the arts from 1987 to 1991.

34 LIBRARIES AND MUSEUMS

The first public library in the US was established in Boston in 1653. Three regional library systems served 351 towns and cities with a total library circulation of 35 million in 1992. The major city libraries are in Boston, Worcester, and Springfield. Statewide in 1992 there were 28,459,354 volumes in all public libraries.

The Boston Athenaeum, with 650,000 volumes, is the most noteworthy private library in the state. Harvard University's library system is one of the largest in the world, with 12,394,894 volumes in 1992. Other major academic libraries are those of Boston University, the University of Massachusetts (Amherst), Smith College, and Boston College.

Boston houses a number of important museums, among them the Museum of Fine Arts with vast holdings of artwork. These include extensive Far East and French impressionist collections and American art and furniture, the Isabella Stewart Gardner Museum, and the Museum of Science. Plymouth Plantation in Plymouth is a re-creation of life in the 17th century, and Old Sturbridge Village, a working historical farm, displays 18th- and 19th-century artifacts. The state had over 328 museums in 1994.

35 COMMUNICATIONS

The first American post office was established in Boston in 1639. As of March 1993, 97.6% of the state's 2,316,000 occupied housing units had telephones, the highest percentage of any state. The state had 67 AM stations and 104 FM stations in 1993, when 15 commercial and 4 educational television stations were also in operation. Boston's WGBH is a major producer of programming for the Public Broadcasting Service. In 1993 there were 22 large cable television systems.

36 PRESS

Publishing milestones that occurred in the state include the first book printed in the English colonies (Cambridge, 1640) and the first regularly issued American newspaper, the *Boston News-Letter* (1704). As of 1994 there were 39 daily newspapers in the state (including 5 morning, 31 evening, and 3 all-day). The *Boston Globe,* the most widely read newspaper in the state, has won numerous awards for journalistic excellence on the local and national levels. The *Christian Science Monitor* is highly

Photo credit: Susan D. Rock.

A young spectator waits for the St. Patrick's Day parade to start. In 1990, over 25% of the population claimed Irish ancestry.

respected for its coverage of national and international news.

Major newspapers and their average daily circulations in 1994 were the *Boston Globe* (516,981); the *Boston Herald* (355,328); and the *Christian Science Monitor* (97,170). *The Atlantic,* which began publishing in 1857, *Harvard Law Review, Harvard Business Review,* and *New England Journal of Medicine* are other influential publications. Massachusetts is also a center of book publishing, with more than 100 publishing houses, including Little, Brown and Company,

Houghton Mifflin, Merriam-Webster, and Harvard University Press.

37 TOURISM, TRAVEL, AND RECREATION

Massachusetts beaches are a popular destination for summer travelers, but other areas have their own attractions. In 1993, tourists spent more than $7.4 billion in the state. The largest number of visitor-days are spent in Barnstable County (Cape Cod). Among its many attractions are beaches, fishing, good dining spots, artists' colonies, and summer theaters. Beaches, fishing, and quaint villages are also among the charms of Nantucket and Martha's Vineyard.

Boston is the second most popular area for tourists. A trip to the city might include visits to such old landmarks as Faneuil Hall, Old North Church, the USS *Constitution,* and Paul Revere's House, and such newer attractions as the John Hancock Observatory and the sky walk above the Prudential Tower. Boston Common is one of the oldest public parks in the country.

The Berkshires are the summer home of the Berkshire Music Festival at Tanglewood and the Jacob's Pillow Dance Festival in Lee, and during the winter also provide recreation for cross-country and downhill skiers. In Concord are the homes of Henry David Thoreau, Ralph Waldo Emerson, and Louisa May Alcott. Norfolk County, south of Boston, has the homes of three US presidents: John Adams and John Quincy Adams in Quincy, and John F. Kennedy in Brookline.

38 SPORTS

There are four major league professional sports teams in Massachusetts: the Boston Red Sox of Major League Baseball, the New England Patriots of the National Football League, the Boston Celtics of the National Basketball Association, and the Boston Bruins of the National Hockey League.

Probably the most famous amateur athletic event in the state is the Boston Marathon, a race of more than 26 miles (42 kilometers) held every Patriots' Day (third Monday in April). During the summer, a number of boat races are held, and rowing is also popular. Each October the traditional sport is celebrated in a regatta on the Charles River among college students from across the Northeast. Suffolk Downs in East Boston features thoroughbred horse-racing.

39 FAMOUS BAY STATERS

Massachusetts has produced an extraordinary collection of public figures and leaders of thought. Its four US presidents were John Adams (1735–1826), a signer of the Declaration of Independence; his son John Quincy Adams (1767–1848); John Fitzgerald Kennedy (1917–63), and George Herbert Walker Bush (b. 1924).

Massachusetts's great jurists include US Supreme Court Justices Joseph Story (1779–1845); Oliver Wendell Holmes, Jr. (1841–1935); Louis D. Brandeis (b.Kentucky, 1856–1941); and Felix Frankfurter (b.Austria, 1882–1965). David Souter (b.1939), a Supreme Court justice, appointed during the Bush administration, was born in Melrose.

Stephen Breyer (b. California, 1939), a Supreme Court justice, was first a Circuit Court of Appeals judge in Boston before his appointment.

Important federal officeholders at the cabinet level were Henry Knox (1750–1806), the first secretary of war; Daniel Webster (b.New Hampshire, 1782–1852), US senator from Massachusetts who served as secretary of state under William Henry Harrison, John Tyler, and Millard Fillmore; Henry Kissinger (b.Germany, 1923), secretary of state under Richard Nixon and Gerald Ford, and a Nobel Peace Prize winner in 1973; and Robert F. Kennedy (1925–68), attorney general under his brother John and later US senator from New York.

Other federal officeholders include John Hancock (1737–93), a Boston merchant and revolutionary, who was the Continental Congress's first president and later became the first elected governor of the state. In the 19th century, Massachusetts sent abolitionist Charles Sumner (1811–74) to the Senate. Massachusetts has provided two US House speakers: John W. McCormack (1891–1980) and Thomas P. "Tip" O'Neill, Jr. (1912–94). Other well-known legislators include Edward M. "Ted" Kennedy (b.1932), President Kennedy's youngest brother and a leading Senate liberal. Paul Tsongas (b.1941), a senator and presidential candidate during the 1992 election, was born in Lowell, Massachusetts. Michael S. Dukakis (b.1933), a former governor of the state and the 1988 Democratic nominee for president, was born in Brookline.

Literary genius has flourished in Massachusetts. In the 17th century, the colony was the home of poets Anne Bradstreet (1612–72) and Edward Taylor (1645–1729) and of the theologian Cotton Mather (1663–1728). During the 1800s, Massachusetts was the home of novelists Nathaniel Hawthorne (1804–64), Louisa May Alcott (b.Pennsylvania, 1832–88), and Henry James (b.New York, 1843–1916); essayists Ralph Waldo Emerson (1803–82) and Henry David Thoreau (1817–62); and poets Henry Wadsworth Longfellow (b.Maine, 1807–82) and Emily Dickinson (1830–86). Among 20th-century notables are novelist and short-story writer John Cheever (1912–82); and poets Robert Lowell (1917–77), Anne Sexton (1928–74), and Sylvia Plath (1932–63). Henry James's elder brother, William (b.New York, 1842–1910), pioneered psychology; and George Santayana (b.Spain, 1863–1952), philosopher and author, grew up in Boston. Mary Baker Eddy (b.New Hampshire, 1821–1910) founded the Church of Christ, Scientist, during the 1870s.

Reformers have abounded in Massachusetts, especially in the 19th century. William Lloyd Garrison (1805–79) was an outstanding abolitionist. Margaret Fuller (1810–50), and Susan Brownell Anthony (1820–1906) were leading advocates of women's rights. Horace Mann (1796–1859) led the fight for public education; and Mary Lyon (1797–1849) founded Mount Holyoke, the first women's college in the US.

Efforts to improve the care and treatment of the sick, wounded, and handicapped were led by Dorothea Lynde Dix (1802–87); and Clara Barton (1821–1912), founder of the American Red Cross. The 20th century reformer and National Association for the Advancement of Colored People (NAACP) leader William Edward Burghardt (W.E.B.) Du Bois (1868–1963) was born in Great Barrington.

Leonard Bernstein (1918–90) was a composer and conductor of worldwide fame. Arthur Fiedler (1894–79) was the celebrated conductor of the Boston Pops Orchestra. Composers include William Billings (1746–1800) and Alan Hovhaness (b.1911). Louis Henri Sullivan (1856–1924) was an important architect. Painters include John Singleton Copley (1738–1815), James Whistler (1834–1903), and Winslow Homer (1836–1910).

Among the notable scientists associated with Massachusetts are Samuel F. B. Morse (1791–1872), inventor of the telegraph; and Elias Howe (1819–67), who invented the sewing machine. Winners of the Nobel Prize include: Mertun Miller (b.1923), Nobel Prize winner in economics; Henry Kendall (b.1926), 1990 co-recipient of the Nobel Prize for physics; and Joseph E. Murray (b.1919), the 1990 winner of the Nobel Prize in medicine-physiology.

Massachusetts was the birthplace of television journalists Mike Wallace (b.1918) and Barbara Walters (b.1931). Massachusetts-born show business celebrities include director Cecil B. DeMille (1881–1959); actors Walter Brennan (1894–1974), Bette Davis (1908–84), and Jack Lemmon (b.1925); and singer James Taylor (b.1948).

40 BIBLIOGRAPHY

Brown, Richard D. *Massachusetts: A Bicentennial History*. New York: Norton, 1978.

Gross, Robert. *The Minutemen and Their World*. New York: Hill and Wang, 1976.

Whitehall, Walter M., and Norman Kotker. *Massachusetts: A Pictorial History*. New York: Scribner, 1981.

MICHIGAN

State of Michigan

ORIGIN OF STATE NAME: Possibly derived from the Fox Indian word *mesikami,* meaning "large lake."

NICKNAME: The Wolverine State.

CAPITAL: Lansing.

ENTERED UNION: 26 January 1837 (26th).

SONG: "Michigan, My Michigan" (unofficial).

MOTTO: *Si quaeris peninsulam amoenam circumspice* (If you seek a pleasant peninsula, look about you).

COAT OF ARMS: In the center, a shield depicts a peninsula on which a man stands, at sunrise, holding a rifle. At the top of the shield is the word "Tuebor" (I will defend), beneath it the state motto. Supporting the shield are an elk on the left and a moose on the right. Over the whole, on a crest, is an American eagle beneath the US motto, *E pluribus unum.*

FLAG: The coat of arms centered on a dark blue field, fringed on three sides.

OFFICIAL SEAL: The coat of arms surrounded by the words "The Great Seal of the State of Michigan" and the date "A.D. MDCCCXXXV." (1835, the year the state constitution was adopted).

BIRD: Robin.

FISH: Trout.

FLOWER: Apple blossom.

TREE: White pine.

GEM: Isle Royale Greenstone (Chlorastrolite).

STONE: Petoskey stone.

TIME: 7 AM EST = noon GMT; 6 AM CST = noon GMT.

1 LOCATION AND SIZE

Located in the eastern north-central US, Michigan is the third-largest state east of the Mississippi River and ranks 23d in size among the 50 states. The total area of Michigan (excluding Great Lakes waters) is 58,527 square miles (151,585 square kilometers). The state consists of the upper peninsula adjoining three of the Great Lakes—Superior, Huron, and Michigan—and the lower peninsula, projecting northward between Lakes Michigan, Erie, and Huron. Michigan has islands in Lakes Superior, Huron, and Michigan, and also in the St. Mary's and Detroit Rivers. The state's total boundary length is 1,673 miles (2,692 kilometers).

2 TOPOGRAPHY

Michigan's two peninsulas are generally level land masses, including flat lowlands in the eastern portion of both peninsulas, higher land in the western part of the lower peninsula, and hilly uplands in the upper peninsula, attaining elevations of 1,800 feet (550 meters). The state's highest point, at 1,979 feet (603 meters), is Mt. Arvon, in Baraga County.

Michigan's political boundaries extend into four of the five Great Lakes (all but Lake Ontario), giving the state jurisdiction over portions of these lakes. In addition, Michigan has about 35,000 inland lakes and ponds. The state's leading river is the Grand, flowing through the lower peninsula into Lake Michigan. Other major rivers of the lower peninsula include the Kalamazoo, Muskegon, Saginaw, and Huron. Most major rivers in the upper peninsula (including the longest, the Menominee) flow southward into Lake Michigan. Most of the many islands belonging to Michigan are located in northern Lake Michigan and in Lake Huron.

3 CLIMATE

Michigan has a temperate climate with well-defined seasons. The warmest temperatures and longest frost-free period are found most generally in the southern part of the lower peninsula. Detroit's temperatures range from 23°F (–5°C) in January to 72°F (22°C) in July. Colder temperatures and a shorter growing season prevail in the more northerly regions. Sault Ste. Marie ranges from 13°F (–11°C) in January to 64°F (18°C) in July. The coldest temperature ever recorded in the state (in 1934) is –51°F (–46°C). The all-time high of 112°F (44°C) was recorded in 1936.

Detroit has an average annual precipitation of 31 inches (79 centimeters). Rainfall tends to decrease as one moves

Michigan Population Profile

Estimated 1995 population:	9,575,000
Population change, 1980–90:	0.4%
Leading ancestry group:	German
Second leading group:	Irish
Foreign born population:	3.8%
Hispanic origin†:	2.2%
Population by race:	
White:	83.4%
Black:	13.9%
Native American:	0.6%
Asian/Pacific Islander:	1.1%
Other:	1.0%

Population by Age Group

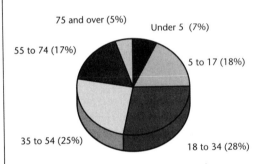

75 and over (5%)
Under 5 (7%)
55 to 74 (17%)
5 to 17 (18%)
35 to 54 (25%)
18 to 34 (28%)

Top Cities with Populations Over 25,000

City	Population	National rank	% change 1980–90
Detroit	1,012,110	9	–14.6
Grand Rapids	191,230	85	4.0
Warren	142,404	123	–10.1
Flint	139,311	132	–11.8
Lansing	126,722	146	–2.4
Sterling Heights	118,314	156	8.1
Ann Arbor	109,766	175	1.5
Livonia	101,375	196	–3.8
Dearborn	88,296	238	–1.5
Westland	85,524	254	0.1

Notes: †A person of Hispanic origin may be of any race. NA indicates that data are not available.
Sources: Economic and Statistics Administration, Bureau of the Census. *Statistical Abstract of the United States, 1994–95.* Washington, DC: Government Printing Office, 1995; Courtenay M. Slater and George E. Hall. *1995 County and City Extra: Annual Metro, City and County Data Book.* Lanham, MD: Bernan Press, 1995.

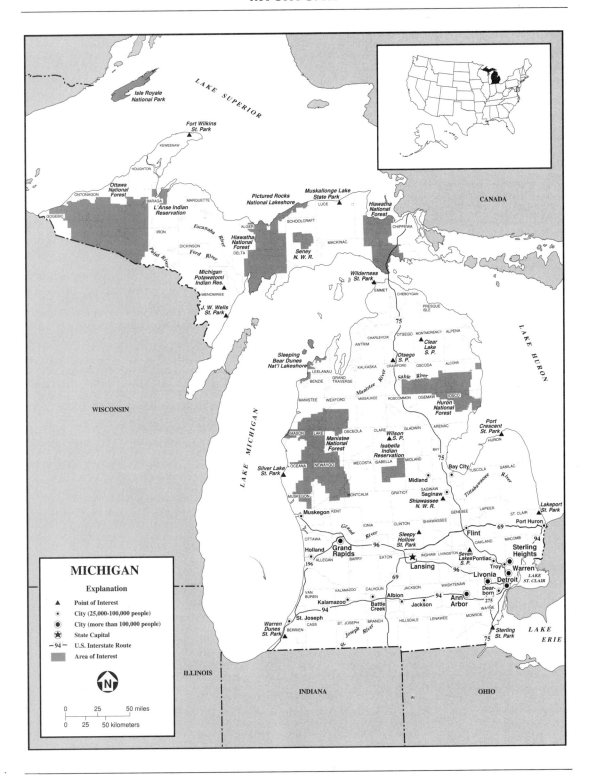

northward. The greatest snowfall is found in the extreme northern areas.

4 PLANTS AND ANIMALS

Maple, birch, hemlock, aspen, spruce, and fir predominate in the upper peninsula. Maple, birch, aspen, pine, and beech are common in the lower. Elms have largely disappeared because of the ravages of disease, while the white pine (the state tree) and red pine have been replaced in cutover lands by aspen and birch.

Strawberries, raspberries, blueberries, and cranberries are among the fruit-bearing plants and shrubs that grow wild in many areas of the state, as do mushrooms and wild asparagus. The state flower is the apple blossom. Wild flowers also abound, with as many as 400 varieties found in a single county. Protected plants include all members of the orchid, trillium, and gentian families.

Despite intensive hunting, the deer population remains high. Other game animals include the common cottontail, snowshoe hare, and raccoon. In addition to the raccoon, important native furbearers are the river otter and the beaver. More than 300 types of birds have been observed. The robin is the state bird. Ruffed grouse, bob-white quail, and various ducks and geese are hunted extensively. Reptiles include the massasauga, the state's only poisonous snake.

Whitefish, perch, and lake trout (the state fish) are native to the Great Lakes, while perch, bass, and pike are found in inland waters. Rainbow and brown trout have been introduced, and in the late 1960s, the state enjoyed its most spectacular success with the introduction of several species of salmon.

The Michigan list of threatened or endangered animals includes the gray wolf, Kirtland's water snake, blue pike, and five species of cisco.

5 ENVIRONMENTAL PROTECTION

The environmental protection program area encompasses five divisions: air quality; environmental response; surface water quality; underground storage tanks; and waste management. The Michigan Department of Natural Resources (DNR) is the state's fourth largest department, employing approximately 3,700 persons.

The Environmental Response Act provides for the identification of sites of environmental contamination throughout the state and an appropriation procedure to support their cleanup. The Solid Waste Management Act and the Hazardous Waste Management Act provide the legal basis for the separate management of hazardous wastes under a detailed regulatory program. There were 77 hazardous waste sites in Michigan as of 1994. The DNR also seeks to provide quality recreational opportunities to the people of Michigan through the effective management of state recreational lands and parks, boating facilities, and fish and wildlife.

6 POPULATION

Michigan ranked eighth among the 50 states in the 1990 census, with a population of 9,295,297. The estimated population for 1995 was 9,575,000. Population density for the entire state in 1990 was 163.6 persons per square mile (62.9 persons per square kilometer). Half the population was concentrated in the Detroit metropolitan area. With 70.5% of its population classified as urban in 1990, Michigan's percentage was below the national average.

Since 1950, Detroit has lost population, dropping to 1,012,110 in 1992, when it held seventh place among U.S. cities. As Detroit lost population, however, many of its suburban areas grew at an even greater rate and the Detroit metropolitan area population totaled 4,665,000 in 1990, up from 3,950,000 in 1960.

Other Michigan cities with 1992 populations in excess of 100,000 include: Grand Rapids, 191,230; Warren, 142,404; Flint, 139,311; Lansing (the capital), 126,722; Sterling Heights, 118,314; and Ann Arbor, 109,766.

7 ETHNIC GROUPS

The black population of Michigan in 1990 was 1,291,706, 13.9% of the state's total population and second highest among the midwestern states. Nearly two-thirds lived in Detroit, where they made up 75.7% of the population, the highest percentage in any US city of one million or more.

There were 201,596 persons of Hispanic origin living in the state in 1990, of whom 118,424 were of Mexican descent. The state's Asian population has been increasing: as of 1990 there were 18,100 Asian Indians, 16,086 Filipinos, 17,100 Chinese, 17,738 Koreans, 13,309 Japanese, and 5,229 Vietnamese. The 1990 census counted about 56,000 Native Americans. The Ottawa, Ojibwa, and Potawatomi were the principal groups with active tribal organizations.

8 LANGUAGES

Except for the huge industrial area in southeastern Michigan, English in the state is remarkably uniform in its retention of the major Northern dialect features of upper New York and western New England. Southern blacks have introduced into the southeastern automotive manufacturing areas a regional variety of English that has become a controversial educational concern.

In 1990, only 6.6% of the state's population five years old or older spoke a language other than English at home. Other languages spoken at home, with the number of speakers, included Spanish, 137,490; Polish, 64,527; German, 57,328; and Italian, 38,023.

9 RELIGIONS

Michigan had 2,338,608 Roman Catholics in 1990, and an estimated 107,116 Jews. Among Protestant denominations, a census taken in 1990 showed various Lutheran groups with a combined total of 421,029 members and Methodist groups with 252,129 members. Among other major denominations, the Presbyterian Church had 126,326 members; the Episcopal Church, 71,727, and the Reformed Church in America, 100,680. The Seventh Day Adventists, who had their world headquarters in Battle Creek from 1855 to 1903, numbered 37,949 in 1980; the Salvation Army, 7,896; and the Church of

Jesus Christ of Latter-day Saints (Mormon), 23,475.

10 TRANSPORTATION

Because of Michigan's location, its inhabitants have always depended heavily on the Great Lakes for transportation. Although extensive networks of railroads and highways now reach into all parts of the state, the Great Lakes remain major avenues of commerce.

There were 1,940 miles (3,128 kilometers) of Class I rail trackage by December 1992. Most railroad passenger service is provided by Amtrak, which operates five trains through the state and carried 659,027 Michigan passengers in 1991/92.

As of 1 January 1994, the state had 89,485 miles (143,981 kilometers) of rural roads and 28,174 miles (45,332 kilometers) of urban roads. There were 1,240 miles (1,995 kilometers) of interstate highway open to traffic. In 1993 there were 5,730,607 registered passenger cars, 1,644,321 trucks, 23,630 buses, and 137,406 motorcycles.

The opening of the St. Lawrence Seaway in 1959 made it possible for a large number of oceangoing vessels to dock at Michigan ports. In 1991, the port of Detroit handled 14,320,909 tons of cargo. The major airport is Detroit Metropolitan, which in 1991 boarded 9,618,283 passengers and handled 132,025 aircraft departures.

11 HISTORY

In the early 17th century, when European exploration began, Michigan's lower peninsula was practically uninhabited. The Algonkian-speaking Ojibwa and Menomini inhabited portions of the upper peninsula. Other groups, including the Winnebago, Sioux, and Huron, later settled in the area. For two centuries after the first Europeans came to Michigan, the Native Americans remained a vital force in the area's development, providing furs for trade and serving as potential allies in wars between rival colonial powers. However, after the War of 1812, when the fur trade declined and the possibility of war receded, the value of the Indians to the white settlers diminished. Between 1795 and 1842, tribal lands in Michigan were ceded to the federal government, and the Huron, Miami, and many Potawatomi were removed from the area.

The first European explorer known to have reached Michigan was a Frenchman, Etienne Brulé, who explored the Sault Ste. Marie area around 1620. Missionary and fur trading posts—and, later, military forts—were established at Sault Ste. Marie by Father Jacques Marquette in 1668. In 1701, Antoine Laumet de la Mothe Cadillac founded a permanent settlement at the site of present-day Detroit.

Following France's defeat in the French and Indian War, and an unsuccessful Native American rebellion, the British were in firm control of the area by 1764 and continued to occupy it until 13 years after the American Revolution, in which the need to protect the fur trade from encroachment by American farmers had placed the people of Michigan solidly on the British side.

Courtesy Michigan Travel Bureau.

A cargo ship passes through the Soo Locks at Sault Ste. Marie. The locks enable cargo ships to travel between Lake Superior and Lake Huron.

Statehood

After occupation by the British in the War of 1812, the Michigan territory was finally returned to American authority under the terms of the Treaty of Ghent at the end of 1814. With the opening in 1825 of the Erie Canal, settlers for the first time pushed into the interior of southern Michigan. By 1833, Michigan had attained a population of 60,000 qualifying it for statehood. After the settlement of boundary disputes with Indiana and Ohio—including the so-called Toledo War, in which no one was killed—Michigan became part of the Union on 26 January 1837.

In July 1854, antislavery Democrats joined with members of the Whig and Free-Soil parties to organize Michigan's Republican Party, which swept into office that year and, with rare exceptions, controlled the state until the 1930s. Approximately 90,000 Michigan men served in the Union army, taking part in all major actions of the Civil War.

Michigan grew rapidly in economic importance. Agriculture sparked the initial growth of the new state and was responsible for its rapid increase in population. By 1850, the southern half of the lower peninsula was filling up. Less than two decades later, exploitation of vast pine forests in northern Michigan had made the state the top lumber producer in the US. Settlers were also attracted to the area by the discovery of rich mineral deposits.

Industrialization

Toward the end of the 19th century, new opportunities in manufacturing opened up. The sudden popularity of Ransom E. Olds's Oldsmobile inspired a host of Michiganians to produce similar practical, relatively inexpensive automobiles. By 1904, Detroit's Cadillac (initially a cheap car), the first Fords, and the Oldsmobile made Michigan the leading automobile producer in the country—and, later, in the world.

Industrialization brought with it urbanization; the census of 1920 for the first time showed a majority of Michiganians living in towns and cities. Nearly all industrial development was concentrated in the southern third of the state, particularly the southeastern Detroit area. The northern two-thirds of the state, where nothing took up the slack left by the decline in lumber and mining output, steadily lost population and became increasingly troubled economically.

The onset of the depression of the 1930s had devastating effects in Michigan. The market for automobiles collapsed; by 1932, half of Michigan's industrial workers were unemployed. The ineffectiveness of the Republican state and federal governments during the crisis led to a landslide victory for the Democrats. Factory workers, driven by the desire for greater job security, joined the recruiting campaign launched by the new Congress of

Industrial Organizations (CIO). By 1941, the United Automobile Workers (UAW) had organized the entire auto industry, and Michigan had been converted to a strongly pro-union state.

By the mid-1950s, the Democrats controlled practically all statewide elective offices. However, Republicans maintained their control of the legislature and frustrated the efforts of Democratic administrations to institute social reforms. In the 1960s, as a result of US Supreme Court rulings, the legislature was reapportioned. This shifted a majority of legislative seats into urban areas and enabled the Democrats generally to control the legislature since that time.

1980s–1990s

The nationwide recession of the early 1980s hit Michigan harder than most other states because of its effect on the auto industry. Auto makers had already suffered heavy losses as a result of their inability to foresee the decline of the big luxury cars and because of the increasing share of the American auto market captured by foreign, mostly Japanese, manufacturers. During the late 1970s and the first two years of the 1980s, US automakers were forced to lay off hundreds of thousands of workers, tens of thousands of whom left the state. Many smaller businesses, dependent on the auto industry, closed their doors, adding to the unemployment problem.

When Governor James J. Blanchard took office in 1983, he was faced with the immediate tasks of saving Michigan from bankruptcy and reducing the unemployment rate, which had averaged more than 15% in 1982 (60% above the US average). The new governor was forced to institute budget cuts totaling $225 million and to lay off thousands of government workers. Also, at his urging, the state legislature increased Michigan's income tax by 38%.

By May 1984, Michigan's unemployment rate dropped to 11.3%, but the state faced the difficult task of restructuring its economy to lessen its dependence on the auto industry. By the late 1980s, there were signs of success. Less than 25% of wage earners worked in factories in 1988, a drop from 30% in 1978. Despite continued layoffs and plant closings by auto manufacturers between 1982 and 1988, Michigan added half a million more jobs than it lost. The state established a $100 million job-retraining program to upgrade the skills of displaced factory workers, and contributed $5 million to a joint job-training program created by General Motors and the United Automobile Workers.

12 STATE GOVERNMENT

The legislature consists of a senate of 38 members, elected for terms of four years, and a house of representatives of 110 members, elected for two-year terms. Legislation may be adopted by a majority of each house, but to override a governor's veto, a two-thirds vote of the members of each house is required. Elected executive officials include the governor and lieutenant governor (who run jointly), secretary of state, and attorney general, all serving four-year terms.

Legislative action is completed when a bill has been passed by both houses of the legislature and signed by the governor. A bill also becomes law if not signed by the governor after a 14-day period when the legislature is in session. The governor may stop passage of a bill by vetoing it or, if the legislature adjourns before the 14-day period expires, by refusing to sign it.

13 POLITICAL PARTIES

From its birth in 1854 through 1932, the Republican Party dominated state politics. The problems caused by the economic depression of the 1930s revitalized the Democratic Party and made Michigan a strong two-party state. Most labor organizations, led by the powerful United Automobile Workers union, have generally supported the Democratic Party since the 1930s. But in recent years, moderate Republicans have had considerable success in attracting support among previously Democratic voters.

Ronald Reagan won 49% of the state's popular vote in 1980 and 59% in 1984. Michigan elected Republican George Bush in 1988, but gave Democrat Bill Clinton 44% of the vote in 1992. In that election, Bush trailed with 36% of the vote. Independent Ross Perot picked up 19%. In the 1994 mid-term elections, Republican governor John Engler was reelected, and three-term Democratic Senator Carl Levin was joined by newly elected Republican Spencer Abraham, replacing retiring Democrat Donald Riegel. In 1995, the state's 16-member US House delegation consisted of 9 Democrats and 7 Republicans. There were 22 Republicans and 16 Democrats in the Michigan state senate, and 54 Democrats and 56 Republicans in the state house.

14 LOCAL GOVERNMENT

In 1992 there were 2,727 separate units of local government in Michigan, including 83 counties, 534 municipal governments, and 1,242 townships. Each county is administered by a county board of commissioners. Executive authority is vested in five officers elected for four-year terms: the sheriff, prosecuting attorney, treasurer, clerk, and registrar of deeds. An increasing number of counties are placing overall administrative responsibility in the hands of a county manager or administrator.

Most cities establish their own form of government under an adopted charter. Some charters provide for the election of a mayor; other cities have chosen the council-manager system. Township government, its powers strictly limited by state law, consists of a supervisor, clerk, treasurer, and up to four trustees.

15 JUDICIAL SYSTEM

Michigan's highest court is the state supreme court, consisting of seven justices elected for eight-year terms. The chief justice is elected by the members of the court. The high court hears cases on appeal from lower state courts and also administers the state's entire court system. Unless the supreme court agrees to review a court of appeals ruling, the latter's decision is final.

Michigan Presidential Vote by Political Parties, 1948–92

YEAR	MICHIGAN WINNER	DEMOCRAT	REPUBLICAN	PROGRESSIVE	SOCIALIST	PROHIBITION
1948	Dewey (R)	1,003,448	1,038,595	46,515	6,063	13,052
					SOC. WORKERS	
1952	*Eisenhower (R)	1,230,657	1,551,529	3,922	655	10,331
1956	*Eisenhower (R)	1,359,898	1,713,647	—	—	6,923
				SOC. LABOR		
1960	*Kennedy (D)	1,687,269	1,620,428	1,718	4,347	2,029
1964	*Johnson (D)	2,136,615	1,060,152	1,704	3,817	
						AMERICAN IND.
1968	Humphrey (D)	1,593,082	1,370,665	1,762	4,099	331,968
						AMERICAN
1972	*Nixon (R)	1,459,435	1,961,721	2,437	1,603	63,321
				PEOPLE'S		LIBERTARIAN
1976	Ford (R)	1,696,714	1,893,742	3,504	1,804	5,406
				CITIZENS	COMMUNIST	
1980	*Reagan (R)	1,661,532	1,915,225	11,930	3,262	41,597
1984	*Reagan (R)	1,529,638	2,251,571	1,191	—	10,055
				NEW ALLIANCE	WORKERS LEAGUE	
1988	*Bush (R)	1,675,783	1,965,486	2,513	1,958	18,336
				IND. (Perot)	TISCH IND. CITIZENS	
1992	*Clinton (D)	1,871,182	1,554,940	824,813	8,263	10,175

*Won US presidential election

The major trial courts in the state as of 1994 were the 55 circuit courts. The circuit courts have original jurisdiction in all felony criminal cases, civil cases involving sums of more than $10,000, and divorces. They also hear appeals from lower courts and state administrative agencies. Probate courts have original jurisdiction in cases involving juveniles and dependents, and also handle wills and estates, adoptions, and commitments of the mentally ill.

Michigan had an overall 1994 crime rate of 5,445.2 per 100,000 population. There were 39,318 prisoners in state or federal correctional facilities in 1993.

16 MIGRATION

After World War II, many Europeans immigrated to Michigan. Smaller groups of Mexicans, Spanish-speaking peoples from Latin America, and Arabic-speaking peoples, who by the late 1970s were more numerous in Detroit than in any other US city, also arrived. Between 1940 and 1970, a net total of 518,000 migrants were drawn to Michigan. The economic problems of the auto industry in the 1970s and 1980s caused a significant reversal of this trend, with the state suffering a net loss of over 460,000 in the 1980s.

Most parts of northern Michigan have suffered a loss of population since the early years of this century as a result of rural-to-urban migration. However, since 1950, the central cities have experienced a steady loss of population to the suburbs, in part caused by the migration of whites from areas that were becoming increasingly black.

17 ECONOMY

Michigan's dependence on automobile production has caused grave and persistent economic problems since the 1950s. Michigan's unemployment rates in times of recession have far exceeded the national average, since auto sales are among the hardest hit in such periods. Although the state was relatively prosperous during the record automotive production years of the 1960s and 1970s, the high cost of gasoline and the encroachment of imports on domestic car sales had disastrous effects by 1980. At that time it became apparent that the state's future economic health required greater diversification of industry.

Employment in car manufacturing dropped 16.5% between 1981 and 1991, and manufacturing employment as a whole dropped 6% in those years. Jobs in the nonmanufacturing sector, on the other hand, increased 59.9%. Service jobs increased 5% and wholesale and retail trade grew 3%. By 1991, both the trade and service sectors employed more people than the manufacturing industry.

18 INCOME

In 1994, Michigan had a per capita (per person) income of $22,173 (18th among the states). Total personal income was $210.6 billion. Some 15.4% of the population lived below the federal poverty level in 1993.

19 INDUSTRY

The rise of the auto industry in the early 20th century completed the transformation of Michigan into one of the most important manufacturing areas in the world. In 1992, the total value of shipments totaled $143.1 billion.

Motor vehicles and equipment dominate the state's economy. The value of shipments by automotive manufacturers was $56.5 billion, or 39% of the total. As of 1993, Michigan had 19 auto production facilities which accounted for about 25% of US car and truck production. Production of nonelectrical machinery and metal products was directly related to automobile production. The Detroit metropolitan area is the major industrial region: this area includes not only a heavy concentration of auto-related plants, but also major steel, chemical, and pharmaceutical industries, among others.

20 LABOR

Michigan's civilian labor force in 1994 included 4,753,000 workers. Of these, an average of 280,000, or 5.9%, were unemployed.

Michigan had 18 national labor unions operating in its borders in 1993. Its most powerful and influential industrial union since the 1930s has been the United Automobile Workers (UAW), with nearly 1,197,000 members in 1992. Its national headquarters is in Detroit. Some 23.8% of all workers in the state were union members in 1994.

21 AGRICULTURE

In 1994 Michigan had 52,000 farms occupying 10,100,000 acres (4,087,000 hectares). In 1994, Michigan's agricultural income was estimated at over $3.4 billion, placing Michigan 20th among the 50 states. About 59% came from crops and the rest from livestock and livestock products. Dairy products, cattle, corn, and soybeans were the principal commodities. The state in 1994 ranked first in output of tart cherries, blueberries, and dry edible beans; and third in commercial apples.

The southern half of the lower peninsula is the principal agricultural region, and the area along Lake Michigan is a leader in fruit-growing. Leading field crops in 1994 included 260,910,000 bushels of corn for grain, 58,250,000 bushels of soybeans, and 30,740,000 bushels of wheat. Output of commercial apples totaled 930,000,000 pounds.

22 DOMESTICATED ANIMALS

The same areas of southern Michigan that lead in crop production also lead in livestock and livestock products. At the end of 1994 there were 1,200,000 cattle in the state, 1,220,000 hogs, 94,000 sheep, and 333,000 milk cows. During 1994, production of cattle accounted for 8.9% of Michigan's agricultural receipts. In 1994, milk production was 5,545,000,000 pounds, valued at $746,000,000. Mink pelts are also marketed.

23 FISHING

Commercial fishing, once an important factor in the state's economy, is relatively minor today. The commercial catch in 1992 was 15,057,000 pounds valued at $10,337,000. Principal species landed in 1991 were silver salmon and alewives. Sport fishing continues to flourish and is one of the state's major tourist attractions. A state salmon-planting program, begun in the mid-1960s, has made salmon the most popular game fish for Great Lakes sport-fishers.

24 FORESTRY

In 1993, Michigan's forestland totaled 19.3 million acres (7.8 million hectares), or more than half the state's total land area. The major wooded regions are in the northern two-thirds of the state, where great pine forests enabled Michigan to become the leading lumber-producing state in the last four decades of the 19th century. State and national forests cover 6.2 million acres (2.5 million hectares).

25 MINING

Nonfuel mineral production was valued at $1.6 billion in 1994 in Michigan. Michigan continued to lead the nation in the quantity and value of crude iron oxide pigments, magnesium chloride, and peat produced, and ranked second in the nation in the production of bromine, iron ore, and industrial sand. In 1992, the production of 5.3 million short tons of cement was worth $250.6 million. Over 40 million short tons of sand and gravel were valued at $136.9 million. Crushed stone, production, at 39 million short tons, was worth $126.9 million.

26 ENERGY AND POWER

In 1992, energy consumption per capita (per person) totaled 295.1 million Btu. Coal is the principal source of fuel used in generating electric power, while natural gas is the major fuel used for other energy needs. In 1993, electric energy production totaled 92.3 billion kilowatt hours.

Hydroelectric plants, which had produced more than 10% of the state's electric energy in 1947, yielded less than 1% in 1991. Coal-fired steam units produced 69%; nuclear-powered units, 29%; and other units, about 2%.

Michigan is dependent on outside sources for most of its fuel needs. Petroleum production in 1993 totaled 13.4 million barrels, and natural gas output was 205 billion cubic feet, less than one-fourth the natural gas consumed in the state. Proven petroleum reserves were 119 million barrels at the end of 1991; natural gas reserves, 1.3 trillion cubic feet. The state had five nuclear power plants as of 1993.

27 COMMERCE

Michigan had 1992 wholesale sales of $125.7 billion; 1993 retail sales of $79.2 billion; and 1992 service establishment receipts of $39 billion. Leading categories were motor vehicles and automobile parts and supplies (accounting for nearly one-fifth of all sales by value), groceries, metals and minerals, and machinery. With its ports open to oceangoing vessels through the St. Lawrence Seaway, Michigan is a major exporting and importing state for foreign as well as domestic markets. Exports of Michigan's manufactured goods totaled $20.4 billion in 1992, fifth in the US.

28 PUBLIC FINANCE

The state constitution requires the governor to submit a budget proposal to the legislature each year. The estimated revenues for 1994/95 were $26,749.7 million; expenditures were $27,232.1 million.

The harbor at Mackinac Island.

The total state debt in 1993 was $8.8 billion, or $935 per capita (per person). was $44.9 billion, the eighth largest among the US states.

29 TAXATION

Sales and income taxes are now the main sources of state revenues. Property taxes are reserved entirely to local governments. In 1994, Michigan's school system eliminated its use of property taxes for funds, which could mean a property tax decrease of up to 65%.

Other state taxes and fees are levied on inheritances, corporate and financial-institution income, cigarettes, alcoholic beverages, parimutuel wagering, and gasoline and other fuels. Michigan's share of the federal tax burden in 1992

30 HEALTH

Major causes of death in 1992 included heart disease, cancer, cerebrovascular diseases, accidents, (of which motor vehicle accidents accounted for 50%), and suicide. In 1993, Michigan had 167 community hospitals, with 30,900 beds. The average expense of hospitals for care was $902 per inpatient day, or $6,147 for an average cost per stay. Michigan had 18,500 nonfederal physicians and 65,500 nurses as of 1993. Some 11.2% of state residents did not have health insurance in 1993.

31 HOUSING

In 1993 there were an estimated 3,965,000 housing units in Michigan. During the 1980s, the housing stock increased by only 7%. In 1993, the number of new privately owned housing units authorized was valued at over $3.3 billion. A limited amount of state aid for low-income housing is available through the State Housing Development Authority.

32 EDUCATION

Historically, Michigan has strongly supported public education, which helps account for the fact that the percentage of students attending public schools is one of the highest in the US. But the cost of maintaining this extensive public educational system has become a major problem in recent years because of the declining school-age population. In 1993, total expenditures for public schools amounted to $6,402 per pupil on average (13th in the nation).

In 1990, 76.8% of persons 25 years and over had completed four years of high school. In 1993/94 there were 3,301 public schools, including 2,065 elementary schools, 1,205 secondary schools, and 31 combined elementary and secondary schools. Public school enrollment totaled 1,618,000 in 1993. In 1993/94 there were 169,113 pupils in private schools. The largest number of these were enrolled in Catholic schools, which had 95,047 students in 1993/94.

In the fall of 1993, Michigan had 15 public universities and 29 community colleges with a combined enrollment of 483,029. The oldest state school is the University of Michigan, founded at its Ann Arbor campus in 1837. Other public universities are Michigan State and Wayne State. Michigan also has 54 independent, nonprofit colleges and universities with a total enrollment of 85,412. Among the state's private colleges and universities, are the University of Detroit, Kalamazoo College, and Albion College (1835).

33 ARTS

Michigan's major center of arts and cultural activities is the Detroit area. Orchestra Hall is the home of the Detroit Symphony Orchestra; the Music Hall and the Masonic Auditorium present a variety of musical productions; and the Fisher Theater is the major home for Broadway productions. Nearby Meadow Brook, in Rochester, has a prestigious summer music program.

The University of Michigan, Michigan State, Wayne State, and Eastern Michigan University have notable art schools. The Cranbrook Academy of Arts, which was created by the architect Eliel Saarinen, is a significant art center, and the Ann Arbor Art Fair, begun in 1959, is one of the largest and most prestigious summer outdoor art shows in the country.

The Meadow Brook Theater at Rochester is perhaps the largest professional theater company. Detroit also has a number of little theater groups. Successful summer theaters include the Cherry County Playhouse at Traverse City and the Star Theater in Flint.

The Detroit Symphony Orchestra is nationally known. Grand Rapids and Kalamazoo have regional orchestras. The National Music Camp at Interlochen is a major center for young musicians throughout the country. There are local ballet and opera groups in Detroit and in a few other communities.

Michigan's best-known contribution to popular music was that of Berry Gordy, Jr., whose Motown recording company in the 1960s popularized the "Detroit sound" and featured such artists as Diana Ross and the Supremes, Smokey Robinson and the Miracles, the Four Tops, the Temptations, and Stevie Wonder.

The state of Michigan generated $66,828,928 in federal and state funds for its arts programs from 1987–1991.

34 LIBRARIES AND MUSEUMS

Michigan in 1991/92 had 377 public libraries, 74 academic libraries, and numerous special libraries. In 1991/92, public libraries in the state had a total of nearly 26 million volumes and a circulation exceeding 46.1 million. The largest public library is the Detroit Public Library. Among academic libraries, the University of Michigan at Ann Arbor had 658,574 book titles and 52,460 periodical subscriptions in 1991/92. In 1980, the Gerald R. Ford Presidential Library was opened on the university campus.

The Detroit Institute of Arts is the largest art museum in the state and has an outstanding collection of African art. The Kalamazoo Institute of Art, the Flint Institute of Art, the Grand Rapids Art Museum, and the Hackley Art Gallery in Muskegon are important art museums.

The Detroit Historical Museum heads the more than 224 museums in the state. In Dearborn, the privately run Henry Ford Museum and Greenfield Village are leading tourist attractions. The major historical sites open to the public include the late-18th-century fort on Mackinac Island and the reconstructed early-18th-century fort at Mackinaw City.

35 COMMUNICATIONS

By March 1993, 96.3% of the 3,557,000 occupied housing units in the state had telephones. Michigan had 138 AM radio stations and 225 FM stations in 1993. As of 1993 there were 38 commercial television stations and 12 educational stations in the state. There were also 29 large cable television systems serving the state in 1993.

36 PRESS

In 1994 there were 55 daily newspapers in Michigan. In addition, 15 Sunday editions were published in the state and there were also 316 weekly or other non-daily newspapers. The number of daily papers has declined in recent decades. Since 1959, Detroit has been the only Michigan city with more than one daily. Leading daily newspapers in Michigan with average daily circulation in 1994 are the *Detroit Free Press* (622,349); the *Detroit News* (418,766); and the *Grand Rapids Press* (146,749). Workers at the two daily Detroit newspapers went on strike in July 1995.

37 TOURISM, TRAVEL, AND RECREATION

Tourism has been an important source of economic activity in Michigan since the 19th century and now rivals agriculture as the second most important segment of the state's economy. In 1990, out-of-state visitors were estimated to have spent over $16.5 billion in Michigan.

The opportunities offered by Michigan's water resources are the number one attraction. No part of the state is more than 85 miles (137 kilometers) from one of the Great Lakes, and most of the population lives only a few miles away from one of the thousands of inland lakes and streams.

Historic attractions have been heavily promoted in recent years, following the success of Dearborn's Henry Ford Museum and Greenfield Village, which attract about 1.5 million paying visitors each year. Tours of Detroit automobile factories and other industrial sites, such as Battle Creek's breakfast-food plants, are also important attractions.

Camping and recreational facilities are provided by the federal government at three national forests, comprising 2.8 million acres (1.1 million hectares). Three facilities are operated by the National Park Service (Isle Royale National Park, the Pictured Rocks National Lakeshore, and Sleeping Bear Dunes National Lakeshore). There are also several federally-operated wildlife sanctuaries. State-operated facilities include 89 parks and recreational areas with 264,000 acres (107,000 hectares), and state forests and wildlife areas totaling 4,250,000 acres (1,720,000 hectares).

38 SPORTS

Michigan has four major league professional sports teams, all of them centered in Detroit: the Tigers of Major League Baseball, the Lions of the National Football League, the Pistons of the National Basketball Association, and the Red Wings of the National Hockey League.

Horse-racing, Michigan's oldest organized spectator sport, is controlled by the state racing commissioner, who regulates thoroughbred and harness-racing seasons at tracks in the Detroit area and at Jackson. Auto-racing is also popular in Michigan. The state hosts two major races, the Detroit Grand Prix and the Michigan 500 stock-car race.

Interest in college sports centers on the football and basketball teams of the University of Michigan and Michigan State University, which usually are among the top-ranked teams in the country. The University of Michigan's football stadium, seating 104,001, is the largest college-owned stadium in the country.

39 FAMOUS MICHIGANIANS

Only one Michiganian has held the offices of US president and vice-president: Gerald R. Ford (Leslie King, Jr., b.Nebraska, 1913), the 38th US president, who was appointed to the vice-presidency by Richard M. Nixon in 1973 upon the resignation of Vice-President Spiro T. Agnew. When Nixon resigned on 9 August 1974, Ford became president, the first to hold

Mackinac Bridge, Mackinaw City.

that post without having been elected to high national office.

Two Michiganians have served as associate justices of the Supreme Court: Henry B. Brown (b.Massachusetts, 1836–1913), author of the 1896 segregationist decision in *Plessy v. Ferguson;* and Frank Murphy (1890–1949), who also served as US attorney general and was a notable defender of minority rights during his years on the court. Another justice, Potter Stewart (1915–85), was born in Jackson but appointed to the court from Ohio.

Other Michiganians who have held high federal office include Robert S. McNamara (b.California, 1916), secretary of defense;

and W. Michael Blumenthal (b.Germany, 1926), secretary of the treasury. Recent well-known US representatives include John Conyers, Jr. (b.1929), and Martha W. Griffiths (b.Missouri, 1912), a representative for 20 years who served as the state's lieutenant governor in the 1980s. Detroit's first black mayor, Coleman A. Young (b.Alabama, 1918), promoted programs to revive the city's tarnished image while in office during 1974–93.

The most famous figure in the early development of Michigan is Jacques Marquette (b.France, 1637–75). Laura Haviland (b.Canada, 1808–98) was a noted leader in the fight against slavery and for black rights, while Lucinda Hinsdale

Stone (b.Vermont, 1814–1900) and Anna Howard Shaw (b.England, 1847–1919) were important in the women's rights movement.

Nobel laureates from Michigan include diplomat Ralph J. Bunche (1904–71), winner of the Nobel Peace Prize in 1950; and Glenn T. Seaborg (b.1912), Nobel Prize winner in chemistry in 1951. Among leading educators, James B. Angell (b.Rhode Island, 1829–1916), president of the University of Michigan, led that school to the forefront among American universities.

In the business world, William C. Durant (b.Massachusetts, 1861–1947), Henry Ford (1863–1947), and Ransom E. Olds (b.Ohio 1864–1950) are the three most important figures in making Michigan the center of the American auto industry. Ford's grandson, Henry Ford II (1917-87), was the dominant personality in the auto industry from 1945 through 1979. Two brothers, John Harvey Kellogg (1852–1943) and Will K. Kellogg (1860–1951), helped make Battle Creek the center of the breakfast-food industry. Pioneer aviator Charles A. Lindbergh (1902–74) was born in Detroit.

Among prominent labor leaders in Michigan were Walter Reuther (b.West Virginia, 1907–70), president of the United Automobile Workers, and his controversial contemporary, James Hoffa (b.Indiana, 1913–75?), president of the Teamsters Union, whose disappearance and presumed murder remain a mystery.

The best-known literary figures who were either native or adopted Michiganians include Ring Lardner (1885–1933), master of the short story; Edna Ferber (1885–1968), best-selling novelist; Howard Mumford Jones (1892–1980), critic and scholar; and Bruce Catton (1899–1978), Civil War historian.

Other prominent Michiganians past and present include Frederick Stuart Church (1842–1924), painter; Albert Kahn (b.Germany, 1869–1942), innovator in factory design; and (Gottlieb) Eliel Saarinen (b.Finland, 1873–1950), architect and creator of the Cranbrook School of Art. Malcolm X (Malcolm Little, b.Nebraska, 1925–65) developed his black separatist beliefs while living in Lansing.

Popular entertainers born in Michigan include Danny Thomas (Amos Jacobs, 1914–91); Ed McMahon (b.1923); Julie Harris (b.1925); Ellen Burstyn (Edna Rae Gilhooley, b.1932); Della Reese (Dellareese Patricia Early, b.1932); William "Smokey" Robinson (b.1940); Diana Ross (b.1944); Bob Seger (b.1945); Stevie Wonder (Stevland Morris, b.1950); and Madonna (Madonna Louise Ciccone, b.1959); along with film director Francis Ford Coppola (b.1939).

Among sports figures who had notable careers in the state were Joe Louis (Joseph Louis Barrow, b.Alabama, 1914–81); heavyweight boxing champion from 1937 to 1949; "Sugar Ray" Robinson (1921–89), who held at various times the welterweight and middleweight boxing titles; and baseball Hall of Famer Al Kaline (b.Maryland, 1934), a Detroit Tigers star. Basketball star Earvin "Magic" Johnson (b. 1959), who broke Oscar Robertson's record for most assists, was born in Lansing.

40 BIBLIOGRAPHY

Dunbar, Willis F., and George S. May. *Michigan: A History of the Wolverine State*. Rev. ed. Grand Rapids: Eerdmans, 1980.

League of Women Voters of Michigan. *The State We're In: A Citizen's Guide to Michigan State Government*. Lansing, 1979.

May, George S. *Pictorial History of Michigan*. 2 vols. Grand Rapids: Eerdmans, 1967/1969.

MINNESOTA

State of Minnesota

ORIGIN OF STATE NAME: Derived from the Sioux Indian word *minisota*, meaning "sky-tinted waters."

NICKNAME: The North Star State.

CAPITAL: St. Paul.

ENTERED UNION: 11 May 1858 (32d).

SONG: "Hail! Minnesota."

MOTTO: *L'Etoile du Nord* (The North Star).

FLAG: On a blue field bordered on three sides by a gold fringe, a version of the state seal is surrounded by a wreath with the statehood year (1858), the year of the establishment of Ft. Snelling (1819), and the year the flag was adopted (1893). Five clusters of gold stars and the word "Minnesota" fill the outer circle.

OFFICIAL SEAL: A farmer, with a powder horn and musket nearby, plows a field in the foreground, while in the background, before a rising sun, an Indian on horseback crosses the plains; pine trees and a waterfall represent the state's natural resources. The state motto is above, and the whole is surrounded by the words "The Great Seal of the State of Minnesota 1858." Another version of the seal in common use shows a cowboy riding across the plains.

BIRD: Common loon.

FISH: Walleye.

FLOWER: Pink and white lady's-slipper.

TREE: Red (Norway) pine.

GEM: Lake Superior agate.

GRAIN: Wild rice.

MUSHROOM: Morel or sponge mushroom.

DRINK: Milk.

TIME: 6 AM CST = noon GMT.

1 LOCATION AND SIZE

Situated in the western north-central US, Minnesota is the largest midwestern state and ranks 12th in size among the 50 states, with a total area of 84,402 square miles (218,601 square kilometers). The state extends 406 miles (653 kilometers) north-south and 358 miles (576 kilometers) east-west. Its boundary length totals 1,783 miles (2,870 kilometers).

2 TOPOGRAPHY

Minnesota consists mainly of flat prairie. There are rolling hills and deep river valleys in the southeast. The northeast, known as Arrowhead Country, is more rugged and includes the Vermilion Range and the Mesabi Range. Eagle Mountain, in the extreme northeast, rises to a height of 2,301 feet (701 meters), the highest point in the state.

With more than 15,000 lakes and extensive wetlands, rivers, and streams, Minnesota has more inland water than any other state except Alaska. A total of 2,212 square miles (5,729 square kilometers) of Lake Superior lies within Minnesota's jurisdiction. The Mississippi River drains about three-fifths of the state. Other rivers include the Minnesota and the Red River.

3 CLIMATE

Minnesota has a continental climate, with cold, often frigid winters and warm summers. Normal daily mean temperatures range from 11°F (–12°C) in January to 73°F (23°C) in July in the Twin Cities of Minneapolis–St. Paul. The lowest temperature recorded in the state of Minnesota was –59°F (–51°C) in 1903; the highest, 114°F (46°C) in 1936.

Mean annual precipitation ranges from 19 inches (48 centimeters) in the northwest to 32 inches (81 centimeters) in the southeast. Heavy snowfalls occur from November to April, averaging between 30 inches (76 centimeters) and 70 inches (178 centimeters) annually. Blizzards hit Minnesota twice each winter on the average.

4 PLANTS AND ANIMALS

Minnesota is divided into three main life zones: the wooded lake regions of the north and east, the prairie lands of the west and southwest, and a transition zone in between. Oak, maple, elm, birch, pine, ash, and poplar still thrive, although much of the state's woodland has been cut down since the 1850s. Common shrubs include thimbleberry, sweetfern, and several

Minnesota Population Profile

Estimated 1995 population:	4,501,000
Population change, 1980–90:	7.3%
Leading ancestry group:	German
Second leading group:	Norwegian
Foreign born population:	2.6%
Hispanic origin†:	1.2%
Population by race:	
White:	94.4%
Black:	2.2%
Native American:	1.1%
Asian/Pacific Islander:	1.8%
Other:	0.5%

Population by Age Group

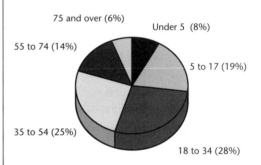

75 and over (6%)
55 to 74 (14%)
Under 5 (8%)
5 to 17 (19%)
35 to 54 (25%)
18 to 34 (28%)

Top Cities with Populations Over 25,000

City	Population	National rank	% change 1980–90
Minneapolis	362,696	47	–0.7
St. Paul	268,266	60	0.7
Duluth	85,431	255	–7.9
Bloomington	85,181	256	5.5
Rochester	73,913	310	22.2
Coon Rapids	59,945	402	47.9
Brooklyn Park	57,399	424	30.1
Plymouth	54,834	459	61.0
Burnsville	53,742	478	43.8
Eagan	52,886	491	129.0

Notes: †A person of Hispanic origin may be of any race. NA indicates that data are not available.
Sources: Economic and Statistics Administration, Bureau of the Census. *Statistical Abstract of the United States, 1994–95.* Washington, DC: Government Printing Office, 1995; Courtenay M. Slater and George E. Hall. *1995 County and City Extra: Annual Metro, City and County Data Book.* Lanham, MD: Bernan Press, 1995.

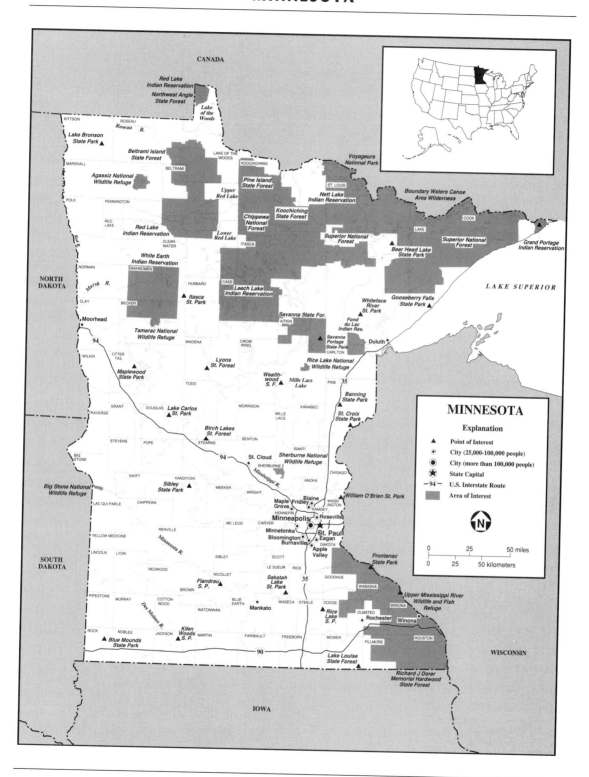

CANADA

Red Lake
Indian Reservation
Northwest Angle
State Forest

Lake
of the
Woods

KITTSON

ROSEAU
Roseau R.

Lake Bronson
State Park ▲

MARSHALL

Beltrami Island
State Forest

LAKE OF THE
WOODS

BELTRAMI

KOOCHICHING

Agassiz National
Wildlife Refuge

POLK

PENNINGTON

RED
LAKE

Red Lake
Indian Reservation

Upper
Red Lake

Pine Island
State Forest

Koochiching
State Forest

ST. LOUIS

Nett Lake
Indian Reservation

Voyageurs
National Park

Boundary Waters Canoe
Area Wilderness

Chippewa
National
Forest

Lower
Red Lake

Superior National
Forest

COOK

CLEAR-
WATER

White Earth
Indian Reservation

NORMAN

MAHNOMEN

ITASCA

LAKE

Bear Head Lake
State Park ▲

Superior National
Forest

Grand Portage
Indian Reservation ▲

NORTH
DAKOTA

Marsh R.

HUBBARD

CASS

▲ Itasca
St. Park

Leech Lake
Indian Reservation

LAKE SUPERIOR

CLAY

BECKER

Whiteface
River
St. Park

Gooseberry Falls
State Park ▲

■ Moorhead

Tamarac National
Wildlife Refuge

Savanna State For.

AITKIN

Fond
du Lac
Indian Res.

94

WADENA

CROW
WING

Savanna
Portage
State Park ▲

Duluth ●

WILKIN

OTTER
TAIL

Lyons
St. Forest

CARLTON

▲ Maplewood
State Park

TODD

Wealth-
wood
S. F.

Mille Lacs
Lake

Rice Lake National
Wildlife Refuge

PINE

35

Banning
State Park ▲

GRANT

DOUGLAS

Lake Carlos
▲ St. Park

MORRISON

MILLE
LACS

KANABEC

St. Croix
State Park ▲

TRAVERSE

Birch Lakes
St. Forest

BENTON

STEVENS

POPE

STEARNS

ISANTI

Sherburne National
Wildlife Refuge

BIG
STONE

94

St. Cloud ●

SHERBURNE

CHISAGO

William O'Brien St. Park ▲

SWIFT

KANDIYOHI

Sibley
State Park ▲

MEEKER

Mississippi R.

ANOKA

Big Stone National
Wildlife Refuge

LAC QUI PARLE

CHIPPEWA

WRIGHT

Maple ● Blaine
Grove ● Fridley

HENNEPIN

RAMSEY

WASH-
INGTON

MC LEOD

CARVER

Minneapolis ●

Roseville ●

YELLOW MEDICINE

RENVILLE

Minnetonka ●
Bloomington ●
Burnsville ●

St. Paul ★

Eagan ●

SOUTH
DAKOTA

LINCOLN

LYON

Minnesota R.

SIBLEY

Apple
Valley

DAKOTA

Frontenac
State Park ▲

REDWOOD

NICOLLET

SCOTT

LE SUEUR

RICE

GOODHUE

WABASHA

Flandrau
S. P. ▲

Sakatah
Lake
St. Park ▲

35

Upper Mississippi River
Wildlife and Fish
Refuge ▲

PIPESTONE

MURRAY

COTTON-
WOOD

BROWN

BLUE
EARTH

WATONWAN

Mankato ●

WASECA

STEELE

DODGE

Rice
Lake
S. P. ▲

OLMSTED

WINONA

Rochester ●

Winona ●

ROCK

NOBLES

JACKSON

Kilen
Woods
▲ S. P.

MARTIN

FARIBAULT

FREEBORN

MOWER

FILLMORE

HOUSTON

WISCONSIN

▲ Blue Mounds
State Park

Des Moines R.

90

Lake Louise
State Forest ▲

Richard J Dorer
Memorial Hardwood
State Forest

IOWA

MINNESOTA

Explanation

▲ Point of Interest

● City (25,000-100,000 people)

◉ City (more than 100,000 people)

★ State Capital

–94– U.S. Interstate Route

Area of Interest

Ⓝ

0   25   50 miles

0   25   50 kilometers

varieties of honeysuckle. Familiar among some 1,500 native flowering plants are prairie phlox and blazing star. Pink and white lady's-slipper is the state flower.

Among Minnesota's common mammals are the opossum, raccoon, and white-tailed deer. The western meadowlark, Brewer's blackbird, and Carolina wren are among some 240 resident bird species. Minnesota's many lakes are filled with such game fishes as walleyed pike, northern pike, and rainbow trout. Endangered species include the gray (timber) wolf, trumpeter swan, and American peregrine falcon.

5 ENVIRONMENTAL PROTECTION

The state's northern forests have been greatly depleted by fires, lumbering, and farming, but efforts to replenish them began as early as 1876, with the formation of the state's first forestry association. The present Department of Natural Resources is responsible for the management of forests, fish and game, public lands, minerals, and state parks and waters. A separate Pollution Control Agency enforces air and water quality standards and oversees solid waste disposal and pollution-related land-use planning. In fiscal year 1991/92, the state spent 2.46% of its budget on the environment and natural resources, or $23.31 per capita (per person).

Minnesotans dump 4,400 tons of waste a year (0.99 tons per capita) into 53 municipal landfills. There were 41 hazardous waste sites in the state in 1994. To control the state's solid waste, Minnesotans have established 488 curbside

Photo credit: ©Minnesota Office of Tourism.

The headwaters of the Mississippi River at Itasca State Park.

recycling programs. During the early 1980s, the state's Pollution Control Agency approved plans by FMC, a munitions maker, to clean up a hazardous waste site at Fridley (near Minneapolis), which the Environmental Protection Agency claimed was the country's most dangerous hazardous waste area.

6 POPULATION

The 1990 census gave Minnesota a population of 4,375,099, ranking it 20th among the 50 states. The 1995 estimated population was 4,501,000, yielding an average density for the state of 55 persons per square mile (21 persons per square kilometer).

In 1990, two out of three Minnesotans lived in metropolitan areas. The Minneapolis-St. Paul metropolitan area was the country's 16th largest in 1990, with a population of 2,464,000. Minneapolis itself had 362,696 residents in 1992, while St. Paul had a population of 268,266. The estimates for other leading cities were as follows: Duluth, 85,431; and Bloomington, 85,181.

7 ETHNIC GROUPS

Minnesota has more ethnic Norwegians than any other state, and is second in number of ethnic Swedes, behind California. The other ethnic groups are concentrated in Minneapolis–St. Paul or in the iron country of the Mesabi Range.

As of 1990, there were 50,000 Native Americans in Minnesota. Besides those living in seven small reservations and four villages, a cluster of urban dwellers (chiefly Ojibwa) lived in St. Paul. In 1990, blacks numbered 95,000, or 2.2% of the total population. In 1990 there were 78,000 Asian and Pacific peoples, mostly Hmong, Korean, and Vietnamese. There also were 54,000 Hispanic Americans.

8 LANGUAGES

English in the state is basically Northern, with minor infiltrations of Midland terms. Among older residents, traces of Scandinavian and Eastern European pronunciation persist. Minnesotans call the grass strip between street and sidewalk the *boulevard*

and a rubber band a *rubber binder,* and many *cook coffee* when they brew it. In 1990, 3,811,700 Minnesotans five years old or older spoke only English at home. Other leading languages spoken at home were German, 45,409; Spanish, 42,362; French, 13,693; and various Scandinavian languages, 25,758.

9 RELIGIONS

As of 1990, there were 1,693,568 known Protestants, including 1,069,703 Lutherans, 142,771 United Methodists, 66,715 Presbyterians, 55,497 members of the United Church of Christ, and 31,980 Episcopalians. Roman Catholics numbered 1,110,071 in 1990, when the estimated Jewish population was 33,779.

10 TRANSPORTATION

By the start of 1993, Minnesota had a total of 4,684 rail miles (7,357 kilometers) of track, including 3,490 miles (5,615 kilometers) of Class I track. Amtrak serves Minneapolis–St. Paul en route from Chicago to Seattle. The total number of Minnesota riders in 1991/92 came to 142,242. Minnesota had 129,959 miles (209,104 kilometers) of state and local roads and streets in 1993 (fifth highest in the US). In 1993 there were 2,905,647 registered automobiles, 795,728 trucks, and 14,728 buses.

The port of Duluth-Superior, at the western terminus of the Great Lakes–St. Lawrence Seaway, is the 17th busiest US port, handling 37.7 million tons of domestic and international cargo in 1991. The ports of Minneapolis and St. Paul handle more than 15 million tons of cargo each year. As of 1991, the state had 377 airports and 66 seaplane bases. Minneapolis–St. Paul International Airport handled 115,634 departing flights, boarding 8,862,052 passengers.

11 HISTORY

At the time of European penetration in the 17th and early 18th centuries, the two principal Native American nations were the Dakota and, after 1700, the Ojibwa. The first Europeans whose travels through the region have been documented were Pierre Esprit Radisson and his brother-in-law, Médart Chouart, Sieur de Groseilliers, who probably reached the interior of northern Minnesota in the 1650s. In 1679, Daniel Greysolon, Sieur Duluth, formally claimed the region for King Louis XIV of France.

In the two centuries before statehood, French, English, and American explorers, fur traders, and missionaries came to Minnesota. Competition for control of the upper Mississippi Valley ended with the British victory in the French and Indian War, which placed the portion of Minnesota east of the Mississippi under British control. The land west of the Mississippi was ceded by France to Spain in 1762. Although the Spanish paid little attention to their northern territory, the British immediately sent in fur traders and explorers.

US Claims

There was little activity in the region during the Revolutionary War, and for a few decades afterward, the British continued to pursue their interests there. After the War of 1812, the US Congress passed an act curbing British participation in the fur trade. Under the Northwest Ordinance of 1787, Minnesota east of the Mississippi became part of the Northwest Territory. Most of western Minnesota was acquired by the US as part of the Louisiana Purchase of 1803. The Red River Valley became a secure part of the US after an agreement with England on the northern boundary was reached in 1818.

In 1819, a military post was established on land acquired from the Dakota by Lieutenant Zebulon Pike, on a bluff overlooking the junction of the Mississippi and Minnesota rivers. For three decades, Ft. Snelling served as the principal center of civilization in Minnesota and the key frontier outpost in the northwest.

Beginning in 1837, a series of treaties with the Dakota and Ojibwa transferred large areas of tribal land to the US government, cutting off the profitable relationship between fur traders and Native Americans and opening the land for lumbering, farming, and settlement. In 1849, the Minnesota Territory was established, and in 1851 the legislature named St. Paul as the capital. As lumbering grew and additional treaties opened up more land, the population boomed, reaching a total of more than 150,000 by 1857.

Statehood

On 11 May 1858, Minnesota officially became the 32d state. In the first presidential election in which Minnesota participated, Abraham Lincoln, the Republican candidate, easily carried the state. When the Civil War broke out, Minnesota was the first state to answer Lincoln's call for troops. In all, Minnesota supplied more than 20,000 men to fight for the Union.

More challenging to the defense of Minnesota was the Dakota uprising of 1862, led by chief Little Crow, in which more than 300 whites and an unknown number of Native Americans were killed. In the aftermath, 38 Dakota captives were hanged and the Dakota remaining in Minnesota were removed to reservations in Nebraska. Also during 1862, Minnesota's first railroad joined St. Anthony (Minneapolis) and St. Paul with 10 miles (16 kilometers) of track.

The railroads soon ushered in an era of large-scale commercial farming. Wheat provided the biggest cash crop, as exports rose from 2 million bushels in 1860 to 95 million in 1890. Meanwhile, the falls of St. Anthony (Minneapolis) became the major US flour-milling center. By 1880, 27 Minneapolis mills were producing more than 2 million barrels of flour annually. Despite these signs of prosperity, discontent grew among Minnesota farmers, who were plagued by high railroad rates and damaging droughts. The first national farmers' movement, the National Grange of the Patrons of Husbandry, was founded in 1867 by a Minnesotan, Oliver H. Kelley, and spread more rapidly in Minnesota than in any other state.

Industrialization

Most immigrants during the 1860s and 1870s settled on the rich farmland of the north and west, but after 1880 the cities and industries grew more rapidly. When iron ore was discovered in the 1880s in the sparsely settled northeast, even that part of the state attracted settlers, many of them immigrants from eastern and southern Europe. Before the turn of the century, Duluth had become a major lake port, and by the eve of World War I, Minnesota had become a national iron-mining center.

The economic picture changed after the war. Facing the depletion of their forests and an agricultural depression, Minnesotans adapted to the new realities in various ways. Farmers planted corn, soybeans, and sugar beets along with wheat, and new food-processing industries developed. In 1948, for the first time, the dollar value of all manufactured products exceeded total cash farm receipts. Later were added business machines, electronics, computers, and other high-technology industries.

Economic disruption and the growth of cities and industries encouraged challenges to the Republican leadership from Democrats and third parties. John Johnson, a progressive Democratic governor first elected in 1904, was especially active in securing legislation to regulate the insurance industry. His successor, Republican Adolph Eberhart, promoted numerous progressive measures, including one establishing direct primary elections. The Farmer-Labor Party had many electoral successes in the 1920s and reached its peak with the election of Floyd B. Olson to the governorship in 1930. Olson introduced a graduated income tax and other progressive measures, but his death in office in 1936 was a crippling blow to the party.

In 1938, the Republicans recaptured the governorship with the election of Harold E. Stassen. However, a successful merger of the Farmer-Labor and Democratic parties was engineered in 1943–44. After World War II, Hubert Humphrey (later a US vice-president) and his colleagues Orville Freeman, Eugene McCarthy, and Eugenie Anderson emerged as leaders of this new coalition. Their political heir, Walter Mondale, was vice-president in 1977–81 but, as the Democratic presidential candidate in 1984, lost the election in a Republican landslide, carrying only his native state and the District of Columbia.

12 STATE GOVERNMENT

The Minnesota legislature consists of a 67-member senate and a 134-member house of representatives. Senators serve four years and representatives two years. The governor and lieutenant governor are jointly elected for four-year terms. Other constitutional officers are the secretary of state, auditor, treasurer, and attorney general, all serving for four years.

Once a bill is passed by a majority of both houses, the governor may sign it, veto it in whole or in part, or pocket-veto it by failing to act within 14 days of adjournment. A two-thirds vote of both houses is sufficient to override a veto. Constitutional amendments require the approval of a majority of both houses of the legislature and are subject to ratification by the electorate.

Minnesota Presidential Vote by Political Parties, 1948–92

YEAR	MINNESOTA WINNER	DEMOCRAT(1)	REPUBLICAN(2)	PROGRESSIVE	SOCIALIST	SOCIALIST LABOR(3)
1948	*Truman (D)	692,966	483,617	27,866	4,646	2,525
1952	*Eisenhower (R)	608,458	763,211	2,666	—	2,383
					Soc. Workers	
1956	*Eisenhower (R)	617,525	719,302	—	1,098	2,080
1960	*Kennedy (D)	779,933	757,915	—	3,077	962
1964	*Johnson (D)	991,117	559,624	—	1,177	2,544
						American Ind.
1968	Humphrey (D)	857,738	658,643	—	—	68,931
				People's		American
1972	*Nixon (R)	802,346	898,269	2,805	4,261	31,407
				Libertarian		
1976	*Carter (D)	1,070,440	819,395	3,529	4,149	13,592
					Citizens	
1980	Carter (D)	954,173	873,268	31,593	8,406	6,136
1984	Mondale (D)	1,036,364	1,032,603	2,996	1,219	—
					Minn. Prog.	Socialist Workers
1988	Dukakis (D)	1,109,471	962,337	5,109	5,403	2,155
					Ind. (Perot)	Constitution
1992	*Clinton (D)	1,020,997	747,841	3,373	562,506	3,363

*Won US presidential election.
1 Called Democratic-Farmer-Labor Party in Minnesota.
2 Since 1976, called Independent-Republican in Minnesota.
3 Appeared as Industrial Government Party on the ballot.

13 POLITICAL PARTIES

The two major political parties are the Democratic-Farmer-Labor Party (DFL) and the Independent-Republican Party (IR), as Minnesota's Republican Party is now officially called. The Republican Party dominated Minnesota politics from the 1860s through the 1920s, except for a period around the turn of the century. The DFL, formed in 1944 by merger between the Democratic Party and the Farmer-Labor Party, rose to prominence in the 1950s under US Senator Hubert Humphrey.

Minnesota is famous as a breeding ground for presidential candidates, who include Republican Governor Harold Stassen (1948, 1952, and later years); and Democrats Vice-President Hubert Humphrey (1968), US Senator Eugene McCarthy (1968, 1976), and Walter Mondale (1976, 1980, 1984). Mondale was chosen in 1976 by Jimmy Carter as his vice-presidential running mate; he again ran with Carter in 1980, when the two lost their bid for reelection. In the 1984 election, Minnesota was the only state to favor the Walter Mondale-Geraldine Ferraro ticket.

In 1990, after serving four terms, Democrat Rudy Perpich lost the governorship to Independent-Republican Arne Carlson, who was reelected in 1994. In 1992, the two US Senate seats were held by Democrat Paul Wellstone and Republican David Durenberger, while the Democrats controlled the state's congressional delegation. In 1994, Durenberger retired and Rod Grams, a 46-year-old Republican, was elected to the seat. The Democrats continued to control the congressional delegation. In 1995, there were 44 members of the DFL party serving in the Minnesota state senate, and 23 Independent-Republicans. Party representation in the state house consisted of 71 Democratic-Farmer- Labor members and 63 Independent- Republicans.

14 LOCAL GOVERNMENT

Minnesota is divided into 87 counties and 13 regional administrations. As of 1992, the state had 1,804 townships (more than any other state) and 854 municipal governments. Each of Minnesota's counties is governed by a board of commissioners. Other elected officials include the auditor, treasurer, recorder, and sheriff. Regional development commissions, or RDCs, prepare and adopt regional development plans and review applications for loans and grants. The mayor-council system is the most common form of city government. Townships are governed by a board of three supervisors and other officials.

15 JUDICIAL SYSTEM

Minnesota's highest court is the supreme court, consisting of a chief justice and eight associate justices. The district court, divided into ten judicial districts, is the principal court of original jurisdiction. County courts, operating in all counties of the state except two, exercise civil jurisdiction in cases where the amount in contention is $5,000 or less, and criminal jurisdiction in preliminary hearings and misdemeanors. They also hear cases involving family disputes, and have joint

Photo credit: ©Minnesota Office of Tourism.

The Split Rock Lighthouse shines a welcome to ships on Lake Superior.

jurisdiction with the district court in divorces, adoptions, and certain other proceedings.

The probate division of the county court system presides over guardianship and incompetency proceedings and all cases relating to the disposing of estates. Crime rates are generally below the national average. In 1994, Minnesota's total crime rate per 100,000 was 4,341. Federal and state correctional institutions had a total population of 4,200 in 1993.

16 MIGRATION

Especially since 1920, new arrivals from other states and countries have been relatively few. The state experienced a net loss from migration of 80,000 between 1970 and 1980, but nearly halted the trend in the 1980s when immigration nearly equaled emigration. As of 1990, 73.6% of all Minnesota residents were native-born. Within the state, there has been a long-term movement to metropolitan areas and especially to the suburbs of major cities. From 1970 to 1990, the population of the Minneapolis-St. Paul metropolitan area grew by 24%.

17 ECONOMY

Furs, wheat, pine lumber, and high-grade iron ore were once the basis of Minnesota's economy. As these resources diminished, however, the state turned to wood pulp, dairy products, corn and soybeans, taconite, and manufacturing, often in such food-related industries as meat-packing, canning, and the processing of dairy products.

The leading sources of income in Minnesota have shifted again in recent years. Manufacturing remains central to the state's economy, but finance, real estate, and insurance have also come to play a dominant role. Government and trade activities rose significantly between the late 1960s and early 1980s, while the role played by manufacturing and construction declined.

18 INCOME

In 1994, Minnesota ranked 16th among the 50 states in income per capita (per person), amounting to $22,257. Total personal income increased to $101.7 billion in 1994. In 1993, 11.6% of all state residents lived below the poverty level.

19 INDUSTRY

In the early 20th century, canning and meat-packing were among the state's largest industries. While food and food products remain important, the state's economy has diversified significantly from its early beginnings. Today, Minnesota looks to high-technology industries such as computer-manufacturing, scientific instruments, and medical products as well as resource-based industries such as food products and wood products.

The total value of shipments by manufacturers in 1991 exceeded $53.3 billion. Industry is concentrated in the state's southeast region, especially in the Twin Cities (Minneapolis-St. Paul) area. Among the well-known national firms with headquarters in Minnesota are 3M, General Mills, Honeywell, and Hormel Foods.

20 LABOR

About one-third of the state's labor force is employed in agriculture or agriculture-related industries, most notably food processing. In 1994, the civilian labor force totaled 2,565,000 persons, of whom 4% were unemployed. As of 1993, Minnesota had ten national labor unions operating in its borders. Some 19.7% of all workers were union members in 1994.

21 AGRICULTURE

Cash receipts from farm marketings totaled $6.5 billion in 1994, placing Minnesota seventh among the 50 states. For 1994, Minnesota ranked first in the production of sugar beets, second in sunflower seeds; and third in flaxseed and soybeans. As of 1994, the state had 85,000 farms, covering 25,700,000 acres (10,400,000 hectares), or 50.4% of the state's total land area. Minnesota's farmers faced acute financial troubles during the early 1980s as a result of heavy debts, high interest rates, and generally low crop prices.

The main farming areas are in the south and southwest, where corn, soybeans, and oats are important, and in the Red River Valley along the western border, where oats, wheat, sugar beets, and potatoes are among the chief crops. The following table shows selected major crops in 1994:

CROP	PRODUCTION
Soybeans	229,600,000 bushels
Corn for grain	915,900,000 bushels
Hay	7,530,000 tons
Wheat	71,948,000 bushels
Oats	24,750,000 bushels
Barley	30,000,000 bushels
Sunflowers	600,000,000 pounds
Sugar beets	8,467,000 tons

22 DOMESTICATED ANIMALS

Excluding the northeast, livestock-raising is dispersed throughout the state. In 1994, Minnesota had 2,800,000 cattle, 4,850,000 hogs (fourth in the US), and 190,000 sheep.

During 1994, dairy products accounted for 18.3% of the state's agricultural receipts. Production of chickens was 249 million pounds, and the turkey output was 847 million pounds.

23 FISHING

Commercial fishers in 1992 landed 269,000 pounds of fish, valued at $101,000. The catch included herring and smelts from Lake Superior, whitefish and yellow pike from large inland lakes, and carp and catfish from the Mississippi and Minnesota rivers. Sport-fishing attracts some 1.5 million anglers annually to the state's 2.6. million acres (1.1 million hectares) of fishing lakes and 7,000 miles (11,000 kilometers) of fishing streams. These are stocked with trout, bass, pike, muskie, and other fish.

24 FORESTRY

Forests, which originally occupied two-thirds of Minnesota's land area, have been depleted by lumbering, farming, and forest fires. As of 1990, forestland covered 16,718,000 acres (6,854,380 hectares), or one-third of the state's total area. Over half the timber that is harvested is used in paper products; 10% is used in furniture; and 30% is used in wood products. Mills that process raw logs account for half of forest and forest-product employment in Minnesota.

The state's two national forests are Superior (2,054,022 acres—831,236 hectares—in 1984) and Chippewa (661,218 acres—267,586 hectares). More than 3 million acres (1.2 million hectares) are planted each year—more than enough to replace those harvested or destroyed by fire, insects, or disease.

25 MINING

The value of nonfuel mineral production in Minnesota in 1994 was estimated to be about $1.4 billion. Iron ore, Minnesota's leading mineral commodity, accounted for nearly 90% ($1.2 billion) of the state's total mineral value. The combined value of construction sand and gravel, and crushed stone—the two other leading mineral commodities produced—accounted for less than 8% of Minnesota's mineral value in 1992. Minnesota ranked third nationally in the production of metals.

26 ENERGY AND POWER

Minnesota produced 41.3 billion kilowatt hours of electricity in 1993. Steam-generating plants accounted for 67% of total installed capacity; most plants were coal-fired. There are three nuclear reactors. Minnesota's 7 million acres (2.8 million hectares) of peat lands, the state's only known fossil fuel resource, constitute nearly half of the US total (excluding Alaska). Energy expenditures were $1,712 per capita (per person) in 1992.

27 COMMERCE

Access to the Great Lakes, the St. Lawrence Seaway, and the Atlantic Ocean, as well as to the Mississippi River and the Gulf of Mexico, helps make Minnesota a major marketing and distribution center for the upper Midwest. The state's wholesale sales totaled $72.5 billion in 1992; retail sales were $39.6 billion in 1993; and service establishment receipts were $21.1 billion in 1992. Exports to foreign countries amounted to $6.1 billion in 1992 (17th among the 50 states).

28 PUBLIC FINANCE

In 1990/91, Minnesota ranked seventh among the 50 states in total state and local general expenditures per capita (per person) at $4,250.

Estimated general fund revenues for the 1994/95 two-year period were $16,609.1 million; expenditures were

$16,855.1 million. As of 1993, the state's outstanding debt totaled $4.1 billion, or $916 per capita (per person).

29 TAXATION

Minnesota ranked 14th among the 50 states in 1991 in total receipts from state taxes ($7.0 billion), and 6th in taxes collected per person ($1,558). Corporate profits and individual income are taxed at graduated rates. There is also a 6.5% state sales tax, a gasoline tax, and a cigarette tax. Gift and inheritance taxes were repealed in 1980.

Minnesota has an estate tax, generally only on amounts above $200,000, with an additional $250,000 exemption for a surviving spouse. Commercial, industrial, and residential property is subject to property tax, the principal source of revenue for local governing units. Minnesota paid out more than $27.7 billion in federal taxes in 1992.

30 HEALTH

The death rates in 1992 per 100,000 population for the two leading causes, heart disease and cancer, were 229.4 and 191.3, respectively. Rates for these causes of death were below the national norms, while the death rate from cerebrovascular diseases (64.4) exceeded the national average. In 1993, Minnesota had 145 community hospitals, with 18,400 beds. The average hospital expense in 1993 was $652 per inpatient day, or $5,867 for an average cost per stay. Minnesota had 10,500 nonfederal physicians and 40,000 nurses as of 1993. Some 10.1% of state residents did not have health insurance in that year.

The Mayo Clinic, developed by Drs. Charles H. and William J. Mayo in the 1890s and early 1900s, was the first private clinic in the US and became a world-renowned center for surgery.

31 HOUSING

According to a 1993 estimate based on the 1990 census, Minnesota had 1,919,000 year-round housing units. The median valuation of an owner-occupied house in 1990 was $74,000. In 1993, 27,265 new units valued at $2.6 billion were authorized. The median monthly cost for an owner with a mortgage was $724 in 1990, and $186 for an owner without a mortgage. Renters paid a median amount of $422 per month in 1990.

32 EDUCATION

In 1990, according to state data, 84.9% of Minnesotans aged 25 or older were high school graduates. In 1992/93, Minnesota had an estimated 788,836 public school students, and 45,311 teachers. Expenditures on education averaged $5,626 per pupil (20th in the nation) in 1993. The state has four major systems of public post-secondary education. The state university system had an enrollment of 52,047 in 1992/93. The community college system, consisting of 18 two-year colleges and three other centers, had 35,150 students.

In 1992/93, a statewide network of 33 area vocational-technical institutes enrolled 35,388 students, the University of Minnesota had 52,930 students, and there were

Dancers at the Red Lake Native American Pow Wow. The two historic nations in Minnesota were the Dakota and the Ojibwa, or Chippewa.

26 private colleges, including Carleton College, a notable independent institution. In 1992/93, state expenditures for education totaled $6.6 billion.

33 ARTS

The recently built Ordway Music Theater in St. Paul is the home of the Minnesota Opera Company and of the St. Paul Chamber Orchestra. The Minnesota Orchestra enlisted Eiji Ouie as musical director in 1995; Hugh Wolf became music director of the St. Paul Chamber Orchestra in 1992. Bobby McFerrin became creative chair of the St. Paul Chamber Orchestra in 1994. The Minnesota Opera, conducted by Phillip Brunelle, and the St. Olaf College Choir, at Northfield, also have national reputations. The Tyrone Guthrie Theater, founded in Minneapolis in 1963, is one of the nation's most prestigious repertory companies.

The Walker Art Center in Minneapolis is an innovative museum with an outstanding contemporary collection, while the Minneapolis Institute of Arts exhibits more traditional works. The art gallery of the University of Minnesota is in Minneapolis, and the Minnesota Museum of Art is in St. Paul. The State of Minnesota received $148,555,214 in federal and state assistance for its arts programs from 1987 to 1991.

34 LIBRARIES AND MUSEUMS

Minnesota has 133 public libraries. The total number of books and audiovisual items was 15,805,838 in 1991, when the state's public library circulation reached 40,923,366. The largest single public library system is the Minneapolis Public Library and Information Center; the leading academic library, with 4,651,111 volumes, is maintained by the University of Minnesota at Minneapolis. There are 150 museums and historic sites. In addition to several noted museums of the visual arts, Minnesota is home to the Mayo Medical Museum at the Mayo Clinic in Rochester. Historic sites include the boyhood home of Charles Lindbergh in Little Falls and the Sauk Centre home of Sinclair Lewis.

35 COMMUNICATIONS

As of March 1993, 97.6% of Minnesota's 1,792,000 occupied housing units had telephones. Commercial broadcasting began with the opening of the first radio station in 1922. As of 1993 there were 261 radio stations—100 AM and 161 FM—and 29 television stations, including 7 educational stations. As of 1993, eight major cable television systems served the state.

36 PRESS

In April 1982, Minneapolis's only daily newspapers were merged into the *Minneapolis Star and Tribune*. As of 1994, the state had 11 morning dailies, 14 evening dailies, and 13 Sunday papers. The leading dailies, with their daily circulations in 1994 are the *St. Paul Pioneer Press* (201,861); the *Duluth News-Tribune* (60,431); and the *Minneapolis Star and Tribune* (42,871). As of 1994, 337 weekly newspapers and 176 periodicals were being published in Minnesota.

37 TOURISM, TRAVEL, AND RECREATION

With its lakes and parks, ski trails and campsites, and historical and cultural attractions, Minnesota provides ample recreational opportunities for residents and visitors alike.

Besides the museums, sports stadiums, and concert halls in the big cities, Minnesota's attractions include the 220,000-acre (80,000-hectare) Voyageurs National Park, near the Canadian border; Grand Portage National Monument, in Arrowhead Country, a former fur-trading center with a restored trading post; and Lumbertown USA, a restored 1870s lumber community.

The state maintains and operates 66 parks, 9,240 miles (14,870 kilometers) of trails, 10 scenic and natural areas, 5 recreation areas, and 18 canoe and boating routes. Minnesota also has 288 primary wildlife refuges. An estimated 723,000 people enjoy boating each year on Minnesota's scenic waterways. Winter sports have gained in popularity, and many parks are now used heavily all year round.

38 SPORTS

All the major league professional sports have teams in Minnesota: The Minnesota Twins of Major League Baseball, the Minnesota Vikings of the National Football

League, and the Minnesota Timberwolves of the National Basketball Association. In collegiate sports, the University of Minnesota Golden Gophers are a Big Ten football team. The university is probably best known for its ice hockey team, which supplied the coach, Herb Brooks, and many of the players for the gold medal–winning US team in the 1980 Winter Olympics.

39 FAMOUS MINNESOTANS

No Minnesotan has been elected to the US presidency, but several have sought the office, including two who served as vice-president. Hubert Horatio Humphrey (b.South Dakota, 1911–78) was vice-president under Lyndon Johnson and a serious contender for the presidency in 1960, 1968, and 1972.

Humphrey's protégé, Walter Frederick "Fritz" Mondale (b.1928)—after serving as vice-president under Jimmy Carter (and as Carter's running mate in his unsuccessful bid for reelection in 1980)—won the Democratic presidential nomination in 1984. Mondale chose US Representative Geraldine A. Ferraro of New York as his running mate, making her the first woman to be nominated by a major party for national office. Warren Earl Burger (1907–95) of St. Paul was named chief justice of the US Supreme Court in 1969. Three other Minnesotans have served on the court: Pierce Butler (1866–1939); William O. Douglas (1898–1980); and Harry A. Blackmun (b.Illinois, 1908).

The first woman ambassador in US history was Eugenie M. Anderson (b.Iowa, 1909).

The Mayo Clinic was founded in Minnesota by Dr. William W. Mayo (b.England, 1819–1911) and developed through the efforts of his sons, Drs. William H. (1861–1939) and Charles H. (1865–1939) Mayo. Oil magnate J. Paul Getty (1892–1976) was a Minnesota native, as was Richard W. Sears (1863–1914), founder of Sears, Roebuck.

The first US citizen ever to be awarded the Nobel Prize for literature was Sinclair Lewis (1885–1951), whose novel *Main Street* (1920) was modeled on life in his hometown of Sauk Centre. Prominent literary figures besides Sinclair Lewis include F. Scott Fitzgerald (1896–1940), well known for his classic novel *The Great Gatsby*.

Minnesota-born entertainers include Judy Garland (Frances Gumm, 1922–69), Bob Dylan (Robert Zimmerman, b.1941), and Jessica Lange (b.1949). Football star Bronislaw "Bronco" Nagurski (b.Canada, 1908–1990) played for the University of Minnesota. Minnesotan Roger Maris (1934–85) set the record for the most home runs hit in a baseball season in 1961.

40 BIBLIOGRAPHY

Hazard, Evan B. *The Mammals of Minnesota*. Minneapolis: University of Minnesota Press, 1982.
Lass, William E. *Minnesota: A Bicentennial History*. New York: Norton, 1977.
Spadaccini, Victor M., ed. *Minnesota Pocket Data Book, 1985-86*. St. Paul: Blue Sky, 1983.

MISSISSIPPI

State of Mississippi

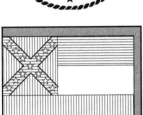

ORIGIN OF STATE NAME: Derived from the Ojibwa Indian words *misi sipi*, meaning great river.

NICKNAME: The Magnolia State.

CAPITAL: Jackson.

ENTERED UNION: 10 December 1817 (20th).

SONG: "Go, Mississippi."

MOTTO: *Virtute et armis* (By valor and arms).

COAT OF ARMS: An American eagle clutches an olive branch and a quiver of arrows in its talons.

FLAG: Crossed blue bars, on a red field, bordered with white and emblazoned with 13 white stars—the motif of the Confederate battle flag—cover the upper left corner. The field consists of three stripes of equal width, blue, white, and red.

OFFICIAL SEAL: The seal consists of the coat of arms surrounded by the words "The Great Seal of the State of Mississippi."

MAMMAL: White-tailed deer.

WATER MAMMAL: Porpoise.

BIRD: Mockingbird.

WATERFOWL: Wood duck.

FISH: Largemouth or black bass.

INSECT: Honeybee.

FOSSIL: Prehistoric whale.

FLOWER: Magnolia.

TREE: Magnolia.

STONE: Petrified wood.

BEVERAGE: Milk.

TIME: 6 AM CST = noon GMT.

1 LOCATION AND SIZE

Located in the eastern south-central US, Mississippi ranks 32d in size among the 50 states. The total area of Mississippi is 47,233 square miles (122,333 square kilometers). Mississippi's maximum east-west extension is 188 miles (303 kilometers); its greatest north-south distance is 352 miles (566 kilometers). The total boundary length of Mississippi is 1,015 miles (1,634 kilometers). Several small islands lie off the coast.

2 TOPOGRAPHY

Mississippi lies entirely within two low-land plains: the Mississippi Alluvial Plain (popularly known as the Delta), extending eastward from the Mississippi, and the Gulf Coastal Plain, covering the rest of the state. Mississippi's maximum elevation is

806 feet (246 meters) at Woodall Mountain in the north.

The state's largest lakes—Grenada, Sardis, Enid, and Arkabutla—are all artificial. Mississippi's longest inland river, the Pearl, flows about 490 miles (790 kilometers) from the eastern center of the state to the Gulf of Mexico.

3 CLIMATE

Mississippi has short winters and long, humid summers. Summer temperatures vary little from one part of the state to another, averaging around 80°F (27°C). During the winter, however, because of the temperate influence of the Gulf of Mexico, the southern coast is much warmer than the north. In January, Biloxi averages 52°F (11°C) to Oxford's 41°F (5°C). The lowest temperature ever recorded in Mississippi was –19°F (–28°C) in 1966; the highest, 115°F (46°C), was set in 1930. The north-central region averages 53 inches (135 centimeters) of precipitation a year; the coastal region, 62 inches (157 centimeters). Mississippi lies in the path of hurricanes moving northward from the Gulf of Mexico during the late summer and fall.

4 PLANTS AND ANIMALS

Post and white oaks, hickory, and magnolia grow in the forests of the uplands. Various willows and gums (including the tupelo) are in the Delta; and longleaf pine is in the Piney Woods. Wildflowers include the black-eyed Susan and Cherokee rose. Common among the state's mammals are the opossum, armadillo, and coyote. Birds include varieties of wren,

Mississippi Population Profile

Estimated 1995 population:	2,717,000
Population change, 1980–90:	2.1%
Leading ancestry group:	African American
Second leading group:	Irish
Foreign born population:	0.8%
Hispanic origin†:	0.6%
Population by race:	
White:	63.5%
Black:	35.6%
Native American:	0.3%
Asian/Pacific Islander:	0.5%
Other:	0.1%

Population by Age Group

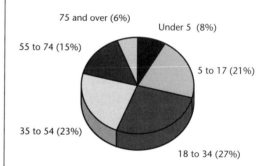

75 and over (6%)
Under 5 (8%)
55 to 74 (15%)
5 to 17 (21%)
35 to 54 (23%)
18 to 34 (27%)

Top Cities with Populations Over 25,000

City	Population	National rank	% change 1980–90
Jackson	196,231	80	–3.1
Biloxi	47,232	560	–6.1
Greenville	44,029	604	11.4
Hattiesburg	42,768	623	2.6
Gulfport	41,494	651	2.8
Meridian	40,895	663	–11.9
Tupelo	31,934	883	28.4
Pascagoula	28,288	981	–11.7

Notes: †A person of Hispanic origin may be of any race. NA indicates that data are not available.
Sources: Economic and Statistics Administration, Bureau of the Census. *Statistical Abstract of the United States, 1994–95.* Washington, DC: Government Printing Office, 1995; Courtenay M. Slater and George E. Hall. *1995 County and City Extra: Annual Metro, City and County Data Book.* Lanham, MD: Bernan Press, 1995.

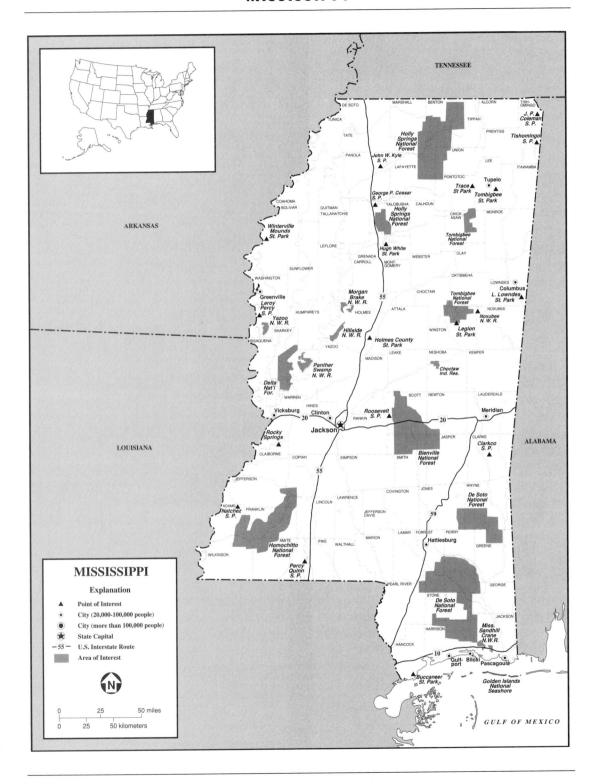

TENNESSEE

DE SOTO | MARSHALL | BENTON | ALCORN | TISH-OMINGO

TUNICA | TIPPAH

J. P. Coleman S. P. ▲

Holly Springs National Forest

TATE | PRENTISS

Tishomingo S. P. ▲

PANOLA | John W. Kyle S. P. ▲ | LAFAYETTE | UNION | LEE | ITAWAMBA

PONTOTOC

ARKANSAS

George P. Cossar S. P. ▲

YALOBUSHA | CALHOUN

Tupelo ⊙

Trace ▲ St Park

Tombigbee St. Park ▲

COAHOMA | BOLIVAR | QUITMAN | TALLAHATCHIE

Holly Springs National Forest

CHICK-ASAW | MONROE

Winterville Mounds St. Park

LEFLORE

Hugh White St. Park ▲

GRENADA | CARROLL | MONT-GOMERY | WEBSTER | CLAY

Tombigbee National Forest

SUNFLOWER

OKTIBBEHA

LOWNDES ⊙

Columbus L. Lowndes ⊙ St. Park ▲

WASHINGTON

Greenville ⊙ Leroy Percy S. P. ▲

Yazoo N. W. R.

HUMPHREYS

Morgan Brake N. W. R.

HOLMES

CHOCTAW | ATTALA

Tombigbee National Forest

NOXUBEE

Noxubee N. W. R.

Legion St. Park ▲

WINSTON

SHARKEY

Hillside N. W. R.

YAZOO

Holmes County St. Park ▲

LEAKE | NESHOBA | KEMPER

ISSAQUENA

Panther Swamp N. W. R.

MADISON

Choctaw Ind. Res.

Delta Nat'l For.

WARREN | HINDS

SCOTT | NEWTON | LAUDERDALE

Vicksburg ⊙

Clinton ⊙

Roosevelt S. P. ▲

Meridian ⊙

20 | RANKIN | 20

LOUISIANA

Jackson ★

Rocky Springs ▲

JASPER | CLARKE | Clarkco S. P. ▲ | ALABAMA

CLAIBORNE | COPIAH | SIMPSON | SMITH

Bienville National Forest

55

JEFFERSON

LINCOLN

LAWRENCE

JONES | WAYNE

De Soto National Forest

Natchez ▲ S. P.

ADAMS | FRANKLIN

JEFFERSON DAVIS

59

AMITE

Homochitto National Forest

PIKE | WALTHALL | MARION | LAMAR | FORREST | PERRY | GREENE

COVINGTON

Hattiesburg ⊙

WILKINSON

Percy Quinn S. P. ▲

PEARL RIVER

GEORGE

STONE

De Soto National Forest

JACKSON

HARRISON

Miss. Sandhill Crane N.W.R.

HANCOCK

10

Gulf-port | Biloxi | Pascagoula ⊙

Buccaneer St. Park ▲

Golden Islands National Seashore

GULF OF MEXICO

MISSISSIPPI

Explanation

▲   Point of Interest
⊙   City (20,000-100,000 people)
◉   City (more than 100,000 people)
★   State Capital
— 55 —   U.S. Interstate Route
▮   Area of Interest

N

| 0 | 25 | 50 miles |
| 0 | 25 | 50 kilometers |

163

thrush, and hawk, along with numerous waterfowl and seabirds. Black bass, perch, and mullet are common freshwater fish. The Florida panther and gray bat are among the state's endangered species.

5 ENVIRONMENTAL PROTECTION

The Mississippi Department of Environmental Quality (MDEQ) is responsible for most environmental regulatory programs in the state. The agency implements one of the premier pollution prevention programs in the nation. As of 1994, Mississippi had five hazardous waste sites.

6 POPULATION

With a 1990 census population of 2,573,216, Mississippi ranked 31st among the 50 states. In 1995, the population was estimated to be 2,717,000. In 1990, the population density was 55 persons per square mile (21 persons per square kilometer). Mississippi is one of the most rural states in the US. Mississippi's largest city, Jackson, had a 1992 population of 196,231. Biloxi had a population of 47,232, and Greenville, 44,029.

7 ETHNIC GROUPS

Since 1860, blacks have constituted a larger proportion of the population of Mississippi than of any other state. Because of out-migration, the proportion of black Mississippians declined to 35.6% in 1990, when the state had 1,633,000 whites, 915,000 blacks, 13,000 Asians and Pacific Islanders, and 9,000 Native Americans. Of the total population, 16,000 (0.6%) were of Hispanic origin.

8 LANGUAGES

English in the state is largely Southern, with some South Midland speech in northern and eastern Mississippi because of population drift from Tennessee. In 1990, 97.2% of Mississippi residents five years old and older spoke only English in the home. Other languages spoken at home, and the number of people who spoke them, included Spanish, 25,061, and French, 13,215.

9 RELIGIONS

Protestants have dominated Mississippi since the late 18th century. During 1990, membership in the two principal Protestant denominations was: Southern Baptist Convention, 869,942 known members; and United Methodist Church, 240,325. There were 94,948 Roman Catholics and an estimated 2,466 Jews in 1990.

10 TRANSPORTATION

In 1995, there were 2,841 rail miles (4,571 kilometers) of track in the state. Amtrak operated two long-distance trains through Mississippi, with stops at 13 stations in the state. The total number of Mississippi riders was 100,196 in 1991/92.

Mississippi had 72,834 miles (117,190 kilometers) of roads at the end of 1993. In addition, there were 685 miles (1,102 kilometers) of interstate highways. In 1993 there were 1,999,639 registered motor vehicles, including 1,526,480 automobiles and 464,109 trucks. Mississippi has two deepwater seaports, Gulfport and Pascagoula. The Tennessee-Tombigbee Waterway links the Ohio River and the Gulf Coast. The Yazoo is also open to river traffic. The most important airfield, Allen C. Thompson Field (near Jackson) boarded 347,435 passengers in 1991.

11 HISTORY

Upon the appearance of the first Spanish explorers in the early 16th century, Mississippi's Native Americans numbered some 30,000 and were divided into 15 tribes. Soon after the French settled in 1699, however, only three large tribes remained: the Choctaw, the Chickasaw, and the Natchez. The French destroyed the Natchez in 1729–30 in retaliation for the massacre of a French settlement.

Spaniards, of whom Hernando de Soto in 1540–41 was the most notable, explored the area that is now Mississippi in the first half of the 16th century. The French explorer Robert Cavelier, Sieur de la Salle, entered the lower Mississippi Valley in 1682 and named the entire area Louisiana in honor of the French King, Louis XIV. Soon the French opened settlements at Biloxi Bay (1699), Mobile (1702), Natchez (1716), and finally New Orleans (1718). After losing the French and Indian War, France ceded Louisiana to Spain, which ceded the portion of the colony east of the Mississippi to England, which governed the new lands as West Florida.

During the Revolutionary War, Spain once again seized West Florida, which it continued to rule almost to the end of the century, although the US claimed the region after 1783. The US Congress organized the Mississippi Territory in 1798. The territory's large size convinced Congress to organize the eastern half as the Alabama Territory in 1817. Congress then offered admission to the western half, which became the nation's 20th state—Mississippi—on 10 December.

State Development

After the opening of fertile Choctaw and Chickasaw lands for sale and settlement in the 1820s, cotton agriculture increased. Slavery was used to make farming profitable. As the profitability and number of slaves increased, so did attempts by ruling white Mississippians to justify slavery morally, socially, and economically. After Lincoln's election to the US presidency, Mississippi became, on 9 January 1861, the second southern state to secede. Union forces maneuvered before Vicksburg for more than a year before Grant besieged the city and forced its surrender on 4 July 1863. Along with Vicksburg went the western half of Mississippi. Of the 78,000 Mississippians who fought in the Civil War, nearly 30,000 died.

Reconstruction was a tumultuous period during which the Republican Party encouraged blacks to vote and hold political office, while the native white Democrats resisted full freedom for their former slaves. The era from the end of Reconstruction (1875) to World War II was a period of economic, political, and social stagnation for Mississippi. White Mississippians discriminated against blacks through segregation laws and customs and a new state constitution that removed the last vestiges of their political rights. Mississippi's agricultural economy, dominated by cotton and tenant farming, provided little economic opportunity for landless black farmworkers. According to the

Vicksburg National Military Park. Vicksburg was the site of a major battle during the Civil War.

Tuskegee Institute, 538 blacks were lynched in Mississippi between 1883 and 1959, more than in any other state.

The Great Depression of the 1930s drove the state's agricultural economy to the brink of disaster. In 1932, cotton sank to five cents a pound, and one-fourth of the state's farmland was forfeited for non-payment of taxes. World War II brought the first prosperity in a century to Mississippi. The war stimulated industrial growth and agricultural mechanization. By the early 1980s, Mississippi had become an industrial state.

Post-War Politics

Politics in Mississippi have also changed considerably since World War II. Within little more than a generation, legal segregation was destroyed, and black people exercised full political rights for the first time since Reconstruction. However, the "Mississippi Summer" campaign that helped win these rights also resulted in the abduction and murder of three civil rights activists in June 1964, in Philadelphia, Mississippi.

In 1987, Mississippi elected a young reformist governor, Ray Mabus, who enacted the nation's largest teacher pay increase in 1988. As of 1990, the Mississippi Legislature was nearly 23% black in a state in which blacks constitute 33% of the population.

12 STATE GOVERNMENT

Mississippi's two-chamber legislature includes a 52-member senate and a 122-member house of representatives. All state legislators are elected to four-year terms. The governor, lieutenant governor, secretary of state, attorney general, and state treasurer are independently elected for four-year terms.

13 POLITICAL PARTIES

Mississippi has traditionally been a Democratic state during most of the period since the end of Reconstruction. However, its Democratic Party has periodically been splintered along racial lines. During the 1950s and early 1960s, the segregationist White Citizens' Councils were so widespread and influential in the state as to rival the major parties in political importance.

In 1980, Ronald Reagan edged Jimmy Carter by a plurality of fewer than 12,000 votes. In 1984, however, Reagan won the state by a landslide, polling 62% of the vote. In the 1992 election, Republican George Bush won 50% of the vote; Democrat Bill Clinton received 41%; and Independent Ross Perot, 9%.

In 1995, Mississippi's governor, Kirk Fordice, was a Republican as were its two senators, Thad Cochran and Trent Lott. All of its five U.S. Representatives were Democrats until the 1994 mid-term elections when Republican Roger Wicker won a House seat that had been in Democratic hands since Reconstruction. Mike Parker, the Democratic Representative from the

Mississippi Presidential Vote by Political Parties, 1948–92

YEAR	MISSISSIPPI WINNER	DEMOCRAT	REPUBLICAN	STATES' RIGHTS DEMOCRAT	SOCIALIST WORKERS	LIBERTARIAN
1948	Thurmond (SRD)	19,384	4,995	167,538	—	—
1952	Stevenson (D)	172,553	112,966	—	—	—
				INDEPENDENT		
1956	Stevenson (D)	144,453	60,683	42,961	—	—
				UNPLEDGED		
1960	Byrd**	108,362	73,561	116,248	—	—
1964	Goldwater (R)	52,616	356,512	—	—	—
				AMERICAN IND.		
1968	Wallace (AI)	150,644	88,516	415,349	—	—
				AMERICAN		
1972	*Nixon (R)	126,782	505,125	11,598	2,458	—
1976	*Carter (D)	381,309	366,846	6,678	2,805	2,788
				WORKERS' WORLD		
1980	*Reagan (R)	429,281	441,089	2,402	2,240	4,702
1984	*Reagan (R)	352,192	582,377	—	—	2,336
1988	*Bush (R)	363,921	557,890			3,329
				IND. (Perot)	NEW ALLIANCE	
1992	Bush (R)	400,258	487,793	85,626	2,625	2,154

* Won US presidential election.
** Unpledged electors won plurality of votes and cast Mississippi's electoral votes for Senator Harry F. Byrd of Virginia.

southwest and central parts of the state, switched to the Republican Party in 1995. Prior to the 1994 elections, the state senate contained 38 Democrats and 14 Republicans. The state house had 93 Democrats, 27 Republicans, and 2 Independents.

14 LOCAL GOVERNMENT

Each of Mississippi's 80 counties is divided into five districts, each of which elects a member to the county board of supervisors. As of 1992, Mississippi had 294 municipal governments. Most cities, including most of the larger ones, have a mayor and city council.

15 JUDICIAL SYSTEM

The Mississippi supreme court consists of a chief justice, two presiding justices, and six associate justices. The principal trial courts are 20 chancery courts, which try civil cases, and 20 circuit courts, which try both civil and criminal cases. Small-claims courts are presided over by justices of the peace, who need not be lawyers. In 1994, Mississippi had a total FBI Crime Index rate of 4,837.1 per 100,000 population. There were 10,078 prisoners in state and federal prisons in Mississippi as of 1993.

16 MIGRATION

Out-migration from Mississippi was heavy during the 1940s and 1950s, when at least 720,000 people, nearly three-quarters of them black, left the state. Black out-migration slowed considerably during the 1970s, and more whites settled in the state than left. Also during the 1970s, there was considerable intrastate migration to Hinds County (Jackson) and the Gulf Coast. Between 1980 and 1990, Mississippi had a net loss from migration of 144,128 (38% whites).

17 ECONOMY

Once the turmoil of the 1950s and early 1960s had subsided, the impressive industrial growth of the immediate postwar years resumed. By the mid-1960s, manufacturing—attracted to the state, in part, because of low wage rates and a weak labor movement—surpassed farming as a source of jobs. During the following decade, the balance of industrial growth changed somewhat. The relatively low-paying garment, textile, and wood-products industries, based on cotton and timber, grew less rapidly than a number of heavy industries, including transportation equipment and electric and electronic goods. Still, Mississippi remains a poor state.

18 INCOME

As it has for much of this century, Mississippi ranked last among the 50 states in per capita (per person) income in 1994, at $15,793. Total personal income was $42.2 billion in 1994. As of 1993, 24.7% of all state residents lived below the federal poverty level.

19 INDUSTRY

In 1991, the value of shipments totaled $31 billion. Food and kindred products contributed the largest amount of the 1991 total, 15%. The state's biggest manufacturing concern is Litton Industries' Ingalls shipyard at Pascagoula. In addition

Photo credit: Courtesy of Mississippi Division of Tourism.

Cotton fields in the Mississippi Delta. In 1994, Mississippi ranked third in the nation in cotton production.

to merchant vessels, this yard builds US Navy ships, including nuclear-powered submarines.

20 LABOR

Data for 1994 showed a civilian labor force of approximately 1,254,000 in Mississippi. The unemployment rate was 6.6%. As of 1994, 6.4% of all workers in the state were union members.

21 AGRICULTURE

In 1994, Mississippi ranked 25th among the states in income from agriculture, with marketings of over $2.9 billion. Crops accounted for $1.2 billion and livestock and livestock products $1.7 billion in 1994. From the 1830s through World War II, cotton was Mississippi's principal cash crop. During the postwar period, however, as mechanized farming replaced the sharecropper system, agriculture became more diversified. In 1994 Mississippi ranked 3d in cotton production, 5th in rice production, and 11th in soybeans. About 2,132,000 bales of cotton worth $744 million were harvested in 1994. Soybean output in 1994 totaled 59,500,000 bushels, worth $308.8 million. Rice production was estimated at 16,200,000 hundredweight in 1995, with a value of $140.5 million.

22 DOMESTICATED ANIMALS

Cattle are raised throughout the state, though principally in the west. There were

1,340,000 head of cattle and 214,000 hogs on Mississippi farms at the end of 1994. In that year the state produced an estimated 3,900,000 pounds of cattle marketings. Mississippi is a leading producer of broilers, ranking fifth in 1994, when 2.7 billion pounds of chickens and broilers, worth over $900 million, were produced.

23 FISHING

In 1992, Mississippi ranked ninth among the 50 states in the size of its commercial fish landings. These totaled 187,634,000 pounds, with a value of $31,348,000. Shrimp and blue crab made up the bulk of the commercial landings. The saltwater catch also includes mullet and red snapper; the freshwater catch is dominated by buffalo fish, carp, and catfish. As of 1 July 1993, Mississippi ranked first among the states in catfish farming, mostly from ponds in the Yazoo River basin.

24 FORESTRY

Mississippi had approximately 17,000,000 acres (6,900,000 hectares) of protected forested land in 1992, 57% of the total land area of the state. Six national forests extend over 2,300,000 acres (930,000 hectares). Timber production was valued at $905 million in 1993.

25 MINING

Mississippi's nonfuel mineral production in 1994 was valued at $112 million. In 1993, 1.1 million short tons of clays were produced for a value of $38 million. Almost ten million short tons of sand and gravel produced were worth $44.1 million. A quantity of 2.5 million short tons of crushed stone was worth $10.4 million.

26 ENERGY AND POWER

Mississippi generated a total of 23.2 billion kilowatt hours of electricity in 1993. Mississippi is a major petroleum producer, and its 1993 crude production totaled 23,000,000 barrels. Mississippi produced 81 billion cubic feet of natural gas during 1993. State energy expenditures were $1,883 per capita (per person) in 1992.

27 COMMERCE

Mississippi had 1992 wholesale sales of $15.8 billion; 1993 retail sales of $15.3 billion; and 1992 service establishment receipts of $6.3 billion. Mississippi was the 34th-leading exporter of products in 1992, accounting for $2 billion.

28 PUBLIC FINANCE

As of 1993, the state's outstanding debt was $1.7 billion, or $628 per capita (per person).

Total general revenues for 1992 were $6,177,000,000; total expenditures were $5,762,000,000.

29 TAXATION

In 1995, Mississippi collected slightly more than $3.3 billion in state taxes. The state taxes individual and corporate income and also imposes taxes on oil, natural gas, and timber. A 7% retail sales tax is levied, along with taxes on inheritance, gasoline, tobacco, beer, wine, and other items. In 1992, Mississippians paid $5.1 billion in federal taxes.

30 HEALTH

In 1992, Mississippi's death rates from heart disease, cancer, and cerebrovascular diseases exceeded national rates. Traffic fatalities per 100 million vehicle miles (160 million vehicle kilometers) of travel were 2.47, higher than in any other state. Mississippi had 97 community hospitals, with 12,500 beds, in 1993. The average hospital cost per inpatient day was $555 in 1993, while the average cost per stay was $4,053. The 1992 ratio of 149 physicians per 100,000 civilian population was lower than that in every other state but Alaska. Mississippi had 3,400 nonfederal physicians and 13,400 nurses in 1993. Some 17.8% of state residents did not have health insurance in that year.

31 HOUSING

The 1993 estimate based on the 1990 census amounted to 1,025,000 year-round housing units. Over 8,100 new housing units worth $495 million were authorized during 1993. In 1990, Mississippi had the lowest median home value of any state except South Dakota, at $45,600. The median monthly costs for owners (with a mortgage) and renters in 1990 were $511 and $309, respectively. Both costs were lower than in any other state but West Virginia.

32 EDUCATION

Only 68% of adult Mississippians 25 and older had completed high school in 1993. As of the fall of 1993, there were 500,000 students enrolled in public schools in Mississippi. Of these, 363,000 were elementary (including kindergarten), and 137,000 were secondary. Expenditures on education averaged $3,390 per pupil (50th in the nation) in 1993. During 1993 there were 42 institutions of higher education with a total enrollment of 109,038. Eight were public universities, 16 were public junior colleges, and 18 (including 4 Bible colleges and theological seminaries) were private institutions. Important institutions of higher learning include The University of Mississippi, Mississippi State University, and Southern Mississippi University. Predominantly black institutions include Tougaloo College and Jackson State University.

33 ARTS

Jackson has two ballet companies, a symphony orchestra, and two opera companies. Opera South, an integrated but predominantly black company, mounts two major productions yearly. There are local symphony orchestras in Meridian, Starkville, Tupelo, and Greenville. The established professional theaters in the state are the Sheffield Ensemble in Biloxi and the New Stage in Jackson. The Greater Gulf Coast Arts Center has been very active in bringing arts programs into the coastal area.

A distinctive contribution to US culture is the music of black sharecroppers from the Delta, known as "the blues." The Delta Blues Museum in Clarksdale has an extensive collection documenting blues history.

The State of Mississippi generated a total of $5,998,512 from federal and state sources to support its arts programs from 1987 to 1991.

34 LIBRARIES AND MUSEUMS

There were 45 county or multicounty (regional) public libraries in 1995. There were 5.2 million volumes in Mississippi libraries, and total public library circulation was over 8 million. In the Vicksburg-Warren County Public Library are collections on the Civil War, state history, and oral history. Tougaloo College has special collections of African materials, civil rights papers, and oral history.

There are 61 museums, including the distinguished Mississippi State Historical Museum at Jackson, the Mississippi Blues Museum at Clarksdale, and the Lauren-Rogers Museum of Art in Laurel. Beauvoir, Jefferson Davis's home at Biloxi, is a state shrine and includes a museum. The Mississippi governor's mansion, said to be the second-oldest executive residence in the US, is a National Historical Landmark.

35 COMMUNICATIONS

In March 1993, only 86.7% of the state's 971,000 occupied housing units had telephones, the lowest rate in the US. In 1993, the state had 221 operating radio stations (98 AM, 123 FM) and 26 commercial television stations. Four large cable television systems also served Mississippi.

36 PRESS

In 1994, Mississippi had 21 daily newspapers which included 5 morning dailies and 16 evening dailies. In addition there were 11 Sunday papers in the state. The state's leading newspaper is in Jackson: the *Clarion–Ledger* has a daily circulation of 107,787 (127,440 Sunday). A monthly,

Mississippi Magazine, is published in Jackson; and a bimonthly, *Mississippi: A View of the Magnolia State,* in Jackson.

37 TOURISM, TRAVEL, AND RECREATION

During 1989, out-of-state visitors spent $1.5 billion in Mississippi. Among Mississippi's major tourist attractions are its mansions and plantations, many of them in the Natchez area. At Greenwood is the Florewood River Plantation, a museum re-creating 19th-century plantation life. The Natchez Trace Parkway, Gulf Islands National Seashore, and Vicksburg National Military Park attract the most visitors annually. There are also 6 national forests and 27 state parks.

38 SPORTS

There are no major league professional teams in Mississippi. Jackson has a minor league baseball team in the Texas League. The University of Mississippi has long been prominent in college football. The Dixie National Livestock Show and Rodeo is held in Jackson in January.

39 FAMOUS MISSISSIPPIANS

Mississippi's most famous political figure, Jefferson Davis (b.Kentucky, 1808–89), was president of the Confederacy from 1861 until the defeat of the South in 1865. Imprisoned for two years after the Civil War (though never tried), Davis lived the last years of his life at Beauvoir, an estate on the Mississippi Gulf Coast. Lucius Quintus Cincinnatus Lamar (b.Georgia, 1825–93), who served as Confederate minister to Russia, was appointed secretary of

Photo credit: Courtesy of Mississippi Division of Tourism.

Jackson, the state capital of Mississippi.

the interior in 1885 and later named to the US Supreme Court.

Some of the foremost authors of 20th-century America had their origins in Mississippi. Supreme among them is William Faulkner (Falkner, 1897–1962), whose novels include such classics as *The Sound and the Fury* (1929) and *Light in August* (1932). Faulkner received two Pulitzer Prizes and in 1949 was awarded the Nobel Prize for literature. Richard Wright (1908–60), a powerful writer and leading spokesperson for the black Americans of his generation, is best remembered for his novel *Native Son* (1940) and for *Black Boy* (1945), an autobiographical account of his Mississippi childhood.

Other native Mississippians of literary renown (and Pulitzer Prize winners) are Eudora Welty (b.1909); Tennessee Williams (Thomas Lanier Williams, 1911–83); and playwright Beth Henley (b.1952). Other Mississippi authors are Shelby Foote (b.1916); Walker Percy (b.Alabama, 1916-1990); and Willie Morris (b.1934).

Among the state's numerous musicians are Leontyne Price (Mary Leontine Price, b.1927), a distinguished opera soprano; and famous blues singers Muddy Waters (McKinley Morganfield, 1915–83); John Lee Hooker (b.1917); and Riley "B. B." King (b.1925). Mississippi's contributions to music also include Jimmie Rodgers (1897–1933), Bo Diddley (Ellas McDaniels, b.1928), Conway Twitty (1933–94), and Jimmy Buffet (b.1946). Elvis Presley (1935–77), born in Tupelo, was one of the most popular singers in US history. Other entertainers from Mississippi include Jim Henson (1936–90) and Oprah Winfrey (b.1954).

40 BIBLIOGRAPHY

Loewen, James W., and Charles Saillis. *Mississippi: Conflict and Change.* Rev. ed. New York: Pantheon, 1982.

Skates, John Ray. *Mississippi: A Bicentennial History.* New York: Norton, 1979.

Welty, Eudora. *One Time, One Place: Mississippi in the Depression.* New York: Random House, 1971.

MISSOURI

State of Missouri

ORIGIN OF STATE NAME: Probably derived from the Iliniwek Indian word *missouri,* meaning "owners of big canoes."

NICKNAME: The Show Me State.

CAPITAL: Jefferson City.

ENTERED UNION: 10 August 1821 (24th).

SONG: "Missouri Waltz."

MOTTO: *Salus populi suprema lex esto* (The welfare of the people shall be the supreme law).

COAT OF ARMS: Two grizzly bears stand on a scroll inscribed with the state motto and support a shield portraying an American eagle and a constellation of stars, a grizzly bear on all fours, and a crescent moon, all encircled by the words "United We Stand, Divided We Fall." Above are a six-barred helmet and 24 stars; below is the roman numeral MDCCCXX (1820), when Missouri's first constitution was adopted.

FLAG: Three horizontal stripes of red, white, and blue, with the coat of arms encircled by 24 white stars on a blue band in the center.

OFFICIAL SEAL: The coat of arms is surrounded by the words "The Great Seal of the State of Missouri."

BIRD: Bluebird.

FLOWER: Hawthorn blossom.

TREE: Flowering dogwood.

INSECT: Honeybee.

ROCK: Mozarkite (chert, or flint rock).

FOSSIL: Crinoid.

MINERAL: Galena.

TIME: 6 AM CST = noon GMT.

1 LOCATION AND SIZE

Located in the western north-central US, Missouri ranks 19th in size among the 50 states. The total area of Missouri is 69,697 square miles (180,516 square kilometers). Missouri extends 284 miles (457 kilometers) east-west; its greatest north-south extension is 308 miles (496 kilometers). The total boundary length of Missouri is 1,438 miles (2,314 kilometers).

2 TOPOGRAPHY

Missouri is divided into four major land regions: the Dissected Till Plains, which comprise rolling hills, open fertile flatlands, and well-watered prairie; the Osage Plains, covering the western part of the state; the Mississippi Alluvial Plain, made up of fertile black lowlands; and the Ozark Plateau, which comprises most of southern Missouri and contains Taum

Sauk Mountain, the highest elevation in the state at 1,772 feet (540 meters).

Missouri has more than 1,000 miles (1,600 kilometers) of navigable waterways. The Mississippi and Missouri rivers, the two largest in the US, form the state's eastern border and part of its western border. The largest lake is the artificial Lake of the Ozarks, covering a total of 93 square miles (241 square kilometers).

3 CLIMATE

Missouri has a continental climate, but with considerable local and regional variation. The average annual temperature is 50°F (10°C) in the northwest, but is about 60°F (16°C) in the southeast. The coldest temperature ever recorded in Missouri was –40°F (–40°C) in 1905; the hottest, 118°F (48°C) in 1954. The average annual precipitation for the state is about 40 inches (100 centimeters). Springtime is the peak tornado season.

4 PLANTS AND ANIMALS

Representative trees of Missouri include the shortleaf pine, scarlet oak, peachleaf willow, and dogwood (the state tree). Various types of wild grasses proliferate in the northern plains region. Missouri's state flower is the hawthorn blossom. Other wildflowers include Queen Anne's lace, meadow rose, and white snakeroot. The American elm, common throughout the state, is considered endangered because of Dutch elm disease.

Native mammals include the common cottontail, muskrat, and white-tailed deer. The state bird is the bluebird. Other

Missouri Population Profile

Estimated 1995 population:	5,286,000
Population change, 1980–90:	4.1%
Leading ancestry group:	German
Second leading group:	Irish
Foreign born population:	1.6%
Hispanic origin†:	1.2%
Population by race:	
White:	87.7%
Black:	10.7%
Native American:	0.4%
Asian/Pacific Islander:	0.8%
Other:	0.4%

Population by Age Group

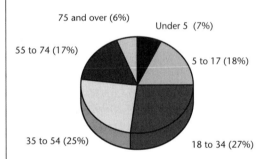

75 and over (6%)
Under 5 (7%)
55 to 74 (17%)
5 to 17 (18%)
35 to 54 (25%)
18 to 34 (27%)

Top Cities with Populations Over 25,000

City	Population	National rank	% change 1980–90
Kansas City	431,553	32	–2.9
St. Louis	383,733	38	–12.4
Springfield	145,438	119	5.5
Independence	112,713	169	0.4
Columbia	73,078	312	11.3
St. Joseph	71,929	323	–6.3
St. Charles	57,274	426	46.0
FLorissant	51,456	504	–7.5
Lee's Summit	51,327	506	61.5
St. Peters	49,932	528	191.6

Notes: †A person of Hispanic origin may be of any race. NA indicates that data are not available.
Sources: Economic and Statistics Administration, Bureau of the Census. *Statistical Abstract of the United States, 1994–95.* Washington, DC: Government Printing Office, 1995; Courtenay M. Slater and George E. Hall. *1995 County and City Extra: Annual Metro, City and County Data Book.* Lanham, MD: Bernan Press, 1995.

MISSOURI

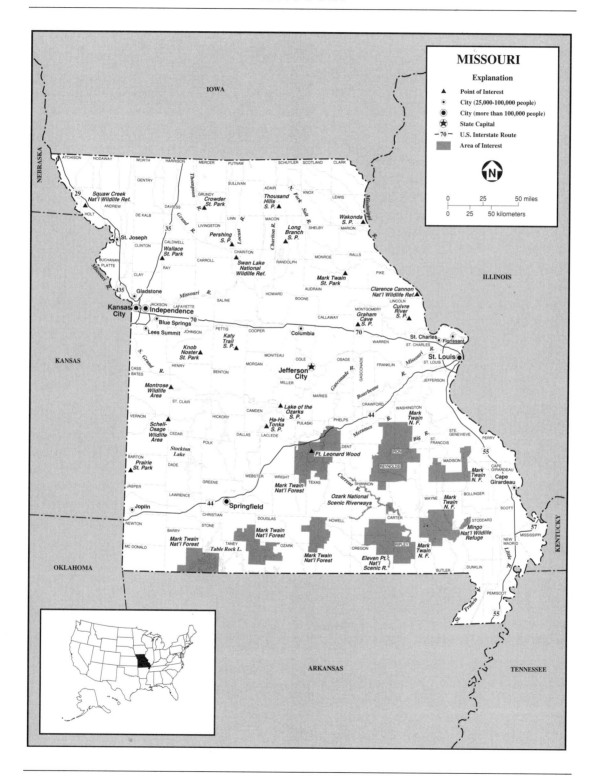

MISSOURI
Explanation

▲ Point of Interest
◦ City (25,000-100,000 people)
◉ City (more than 100,000 people)
★ State Capital
—70— U.S. Interstate Route
▨ Area of Interest

N

| 0 | 25 | 50 miles |
| 0 | 25 | 50 kilometers |

IOWA

NEBRASKA

ILLINOIS

KANSAS

OKLAHOMA

ARKANSAS

TENNESSEE

KENTUCKY

ATCHISON NODAWAY WORTH HARRISON MERCER PUTNAM SCHUYLER SCOTLAND CLARK

GENTRY

SULLIVAN

ADAIR KNOX LEWIS

29 Squaw Creek Nat'l Wildlife Ref. ANDREW DE KALB DAVIESS GRUNDY Crowder St. Park Thousand Hills S. P. ▲

Thompson R.

Grand R.

HOLT

35 Pershing S. P. ▲ Wakonda S. P. ▲

St. Joseph BUCHANAN CLINTON CALDWELL Wallace St. Park ▲

LIVINGSTON LINN MACON SHELBY MARION

Locust R. Chariton R. Salt R. E. Fork

Long Branch S. P. ▲

PLATTE CLAY RAY CARROLL CHARITON RANDOLPH MONROE RALLS

Swan Lake National Wildlife Ref. ▲

435 Gladstone Missouri R. SALINE HOWARD AUDRAIN PIKE

Mark Twain St. Park ▲

Kansas City ◉ JACKSON LAFAYETTE BOONE

Independence ◉

Clarence Cannon Nat'l Wildlife Ref. ▲ LINCOLN

Blue Springs ◦ 70 PETTIS COOPER CALLAWAY MONTGOMERY Graham Cave ▲ Cuivre River S. P. ▲

Lees Summit ◦ JOHNSON Columbia ◉ 70 WARREN ST. CHARLES St. Charles ◉ Florissant ◉

Katy Trail S. P. ▲ MONITEAU COLE OSAGE FRANKLIN Missouri R. ST. LOUIS St. Louis ◉

Knob Noster St. Park ▲ MORGAN Jefferson City ★ Gasconade R. GASCONADE

S. Grand R. HENRY BENTON MILLER MARIES Bourbeuse R. JEFFERSON

Montrose Wildlife Area ▲ ST. CLAIR HICKORY CAMDEN Lake of the Ozarks S. P. ▲ PULASKI PHELPS CRAWFORD WASHINGTON Mark Twain N. F.

Ha-Ha Tonka S. P. ▲ 44 R. Meramec R. Big R. STE. GENEVIEVE

Schell-Osage Wildlife Area ▲ CEDAR DALLAS LACLEDE DENT ST. FRANCOIS PERRY

Stockton Lake POLK Ft. Leonard Wood ▲ IRON MADISON 55 CAPE GIRARDEAU

VERNON BARTON Prairie St. Park ▲ DADE REYNOLDS Mark Twain N. F. Cape Girardeau ◦

GREENE WEBSTER WRIGHT TEXAS Current R. SHANNON WAYNE BOLLINGER SCOTT

JASPER LAWRENCE Mark Twain Nat'l Forest Ozark National Scenic Riverways Mark Twain N. F. 57

Joplin ◦ 44 Springfield ◉ CHRISTIAN DOUGLAS HOWELL CARTER STODDARD Mingo Nat'l Wildlife Refuge NEW MADRID

NEWTON BARRY STONE Mark Twain Nat'l Forest OZARK REPLEY Mark Twain N. F. MISSISSIPPI

MC DONALD Table Rock L. TANEY Mark Twain Nat'l Forest Eleven Pt. Nat'l Scenic R. OREGON BUTLER DUNKLIN Little R. 55

St. Francis R. PEMISCOT 57

177

common birds are the cardinal and solitary vireo. A characteristic amphibian is the plains leopard frog. Native snakes include garter, ribbon, and copperhead. Bass, carp, perch, jack salmon (walleye), and crayfish abound in Missouri's waters. The chigger, a minute insect, is a notorious pest. Listed as endangered in Missouri are the Ozark big-eared, gray, and Indiana bats; bald eagle; and whooping crane.

5 ENVIRONMENTAL PROTECTION

Today, Missouri's principal environmental protection agencies are the Department of Conservation, which manages the state forests and fish hatcheries and maintains wildlife refuges, and the Department of Natural Resources, responsible for state parks, energy conservation, and environmental quality programs.

An important environmental problem is soil erosion. Rain washes away an average of 12.2 tons of soil from each cropland acre in Missouri every year—the third-highest erosion rate in the nation. St. Louis ranks high among US cities for the quantities of lead and suspended particles found in the atmosphere, but conditions improved between the mid-1970s and early 1980s. The state had 23 hazardous waste sites as of 1994.

6 POPULATION

Missouri ranked 15th among the 50 states at the 1990 census. It had a population of 5,117,073, with a density of 74.3 persons per square mile (28.5 persons per square kilometer). The estimated population in 1995 was 5,286,000, and the population projection for the year 2000 is 5,473,000.

In 1990, 68.7% of all Missourians lived in urban areas and 31.3% in rural areas. The largest cities and their 1992 populations were Kansas City, 431,553; and St. Louis, 383,733. The St. Louis metropolitan area, embracing parts of both Missouri and Illinois, comprised 2,444,000 people in 1990 (17th in the US), while metropolitan Kansas City, in Missouri and Kansas, had a population of 1,566,000 (25th).

7 ETHNIC GROUPS

Of those claiming descent from at least one specific ancestry group in 1990, over 1,840,000 named German, 743,232 English, and 1,037,658 Irish. Black Americans have represented a rising proportion of Missouri's population in recent decades, accounting for 10.7% in 1990. Of 548,000 blacks, 34% lived in St. Louis (which was more than 47% black). In 1990 Missouri also had 62,000 people of Hispanic origin, including 35,860 of Mexican ancestry. The Asian community in 1990 included 8,006 Chinese, 7,181 Filipinos, 6,452 Koreans, 6,233 Japanese, and 4,030 Asian Indians. The 1990 census showed a Native American population of 20,000.

8 LANGUAGES

Four westward-flowing language streams met and partly merged in Missouri. Northern and North Midland speakers settled north of the Missouri River and in the western border counties, bringing their Northern *pail* and *sick to the stomach* and their North Midland *fishworm* (earthworm), *gunnysack* (burlap bag), and *sick at the stomach*. South

The St. Louis Arch and city skyline.

of the Missouri River, and notably in the Ozark Highlands, South Midland dominates, though with a few Southern forms, especially in the cotton-growing floodplain of the extreme southeast.

About 96% of state residents five years old or older spoke only English at home in 1990. Of those who claimed to speak another language at home, the leading languages and number of speakers were Spanish, 59,585; German, 32,286; and French, 20,135.

9 RELIGIONS

In 1990, Missouri had 802,083 Roman Catholics. The principal Protestant denominations in 1990 were the Southern Baptist Convention, with 789,183 members; United Methodist Church, 255,111; Lutheran Church—Missouri Synod, 145,741; and the Christian Church (Disciples of Christ), 101,756. In 1990, Missouri's estimated Jewish population was 53,092.

10 TRANSPORTATION

Centrally located, Missouri is a leading US transportation center. Both St. Louis and Kansas City are hubs of rail, truck, and airline transportation. In 1992, there were 4,233 rail miles (6,811 kilometers) of track in the state. In 1991/92, the total number of Missouri Amtrak riders was 489,341. In 1993 there were 121,787 miles (195,955 kilometers) of roadway, sixth among the states. Motor vehicle registration for the state in 1993 was 4,065,686, including 2,857,878 passenger cars, 1,195,728 trucks, and 12,080 buses.

The Mississippi and Missouri rivers have long been important transportation routes. The Mississippi still serves considerable barge traffic, making metropolitan St. Louis an active inland port area, with 29,262,653 tons of cargo handled in 1991. Charles A. Lindbergh, having spent a few years in the St. Louis area, had the backing of business owners from that city when he flew his *Spirit of St. Louis* across the Atlantic in 1927. Today, Kansas City International Airport and Lambert-St. Louis Municipal Airport are among the busiest airports in the country. These two boarded 3,288,900 and 9,351,652 passengers, respectively, in 1991, when the state had 355 airports and 101 heliports.

11 HISTORY

When the first Europeans arrived in the late 17th century, most of the few thousand Native Americans living in Missouri belonged to two main linguistic groups: Algonkian-speakers, mainly the Sauk, Fox, and Iliniwek (Illinois) in the northeast; and a Siouan group, including the Osage, Missouri, Iowa, Kansas, and other tribes, to the south and west. The flood of white settlers into Missouri after 1803 forced the Native Americans to move into Kansas and into what became known as Indian Territory (present-day Oklahoma). During the 1820s, the US government negotiated treaties with the Osage, Sauk, Fox, and Iowa tribes whereby they surrendered all their lands

in Missouri. By 1836, few Native Americans remained.

The first Europeans to pass through land that was eventually included within Missouri's boundaries were Jacques Marquette and Louis Jolliet, who in 1673 passed the mouth of the Missouri River on their journey down the Mississippi. Robert Cavelier, Sieur de la Salle, claimed the entire Mississippi Valley for France in 1682. Missouri passed into Spanish hands with the rest of the Louisiana Territory in 1762. In 1764, the French fur trader Pierre Laclède established a trading post on the present site of St. Louis.

Although the Spanish did not attempt to settle Missouri, they did allow Americans to migrate freely into the territory. Spanish authorities granted free land to the new settlers, relaxed their restrictions against Protestants, and welcomed slaveholding families from southern states. Spanish rule ended abruptly in 1800 when Napoleon forced Spain to return Louisiana to France. Included in the Louisiana Purchase, Missouri then became part of the US in 1803.

Statehood

Missouri was part of the Louisiana Territory until 1 October 1812, when the Missouri Territory (including present-day Arkansas) was established. A flood of settlers between 1810 and 1820 more than tripled Missouri's population from 19,783 to 66,586, leading Missourians to petition the US Congress for statehood as early as 1818. But Congress, divided over the slavery issue, withheld permission for three years, finally approving statehood for Maine and Missouri under the terms of the Missouri Compromise (1820), which sanctioned slavery in the new state but banned it in the rest of the former Louisiana Territory north of Arkansas. Missouri became the 24th state on 10 August 1821.

Aided by the advent of steamboat travel on the Mississippi and Missouri rivers, settlers continued to arrive in the new state, whose population surpassed one million by 1860. There was a great deal of proslavery sentiment in the state, and thousands of Missourians crossed into neighboring Kansas in the mid-1850s to help elect a proslavery government in that territory. During the Civil War, Missouri remained loyal to the Union, though not without difficulty, supplying some 110,000 soldiers to the Union and 40,000 to the Confederacy. At a constitutional convention held in January 1865, Missouri became the first slave state to free all blacks.

Photo credit: Convention & Visitors Bureau of Greater Kansas City.

Dedicated in 1921, the Liberty Memorial in Kansas City honors the soldiers of the First World War.

1870s–1990s

In addition to conflicts caused by the Republican Reconstruction government, the 1870s saw a period of lawlessness, typified by the exploits of Jesse and Frank James, that earned Missouri the epithet of the "robber state." Of more lasting importance were the closing of the frontier in Missouri, the decline of the fur trade and steamboat traffic, and the rise of the railroads. The state's economy increasingly shifted from agriculture to industry, and Missouri's rural population declined from about three-fourths of the total in 1880 to less than one-third by 1970. Although the overall importance of mining declined, Missouri remained the world's top lead producer, and the state has emerged as second only to Michigan in US automobile manufacturing.

Postwar prosperity was threatened beginning in the 1960s by the deterioration of several cities, notably St. Louis, which lost 47% of its population between 1950 and 1980. Both St. Louis and Kansas City undertook urban renewal programs to cope with the serious problems of air pollution, traffic congestion, crime, and substandard housing. During the early 1980s, millions of dollars in federal, state, and private funds were used to rehabilitate abandoned and dilapidated apartment buildings and houses.

In the spring and summer of 1993, Missouri was hit by devastating floods. Over half of the state was declared a disaster area and 19,000 people were evacuated from their homes. Damage to the state was estimated at $3 billion.

12 STATE GOVERNMENT

The legislative branch, or general assembly, consists of a 34-member senate and a 163-seat house of representatives. Senators are elected to staggered four-year terms; representatives for two. The state's elected executives are the governor and lieutenant governor (who run separately), secretary of state, auditor, treasurer, and attorney general. All serve four-year terms.

A bill becomes law when signed by the governor within 15 days of legislative passage. A two-thirds vote by both houses is required to override a gubernatorial veto. Constitutional amendments require a majority vote of both houses of the legislature and ratification by the voters.

13 POLITICAL PARTIES

Except for the Civil War and Reconstruction periods, the Democratic Party held the governorship from the late 1820s to the early 1900s. The outstanding figures of 20th century Missouri politics were both Democrats: Thomas Pendergast, the Kansas City political boss; and Harry S Truman, who began his political career as a Jackson County judge in the Kansas City area and in 1945 became the 33d president of the US.

Between 1980 and 1988, the state voted consistently for Republican presidential

Missouri Presidential Vote by Political Parties, 1948–92

YEAR	MISSOURI WINNER	DEMOCRAT	REPUBLICAN	PROGRESSIVE	SOCIALIST
1948	*Truman (D)	917,315	655,039	3,998	2,222
1952	*Eisenhower (R)	929,830	959,429	—	—
1956	Stevenson (D)	918,273	914,289	—	—
1960	*Kennedy (D)	972,201	962,218	—	—
1964	*Johnson (D)	1,164,344	653,535	—	—
				AMERICAN IND.	
1968	*Nixon (R)	791,444	811,932	206,126	—
1972	*Nixon (R)	698,531	1,154,058	—	—
1976	*Carter (D)	998,387	927,443	—	—
				LIBERTARIAN	SOC. WORKERS
1980	*Reagan (R)	931,182	1,074,181	14,422	1,515
1984	*Reagan (R)	848,583	1,274,188	—	—
					NEW ALLIANCE
1988	*Bush (R)	1,001,619	1,084,953	434	6,656
					IND. (Perot)
1992	*Clinton (D)	1,053,873	811,159	7,497	518,741

*Won US presidential election.

candidates. In 1992, however, Bill Clinton won 44% of the vote; George Bush received 34%; and Ross Perot collected 22%. Democrat Mel Carnahan won the governorship in 1992. As of the mid-term elections in 1994, Missouri's US Senators were both Republicans—Christopher Bond, reelected in 1992, and former Governor John Ashcroft, newly elected to fill the seat formerly held by senior senator John Danforth. Six of the US Representatives are Democrats; three are Republicans. In the state senate in 1995, there were 19 Democrats and 15 Republicans. In the state house, there were 87 Democrats and 76 Republicans.

14 LOCAL GOVERNMENT

As of 1994, Missouri had 110 counties, 933 municipalities, 324 townships, 553 school districts, and 1,443 special districts. Elected county officials generally include a public administrator, prosecuting attorney, sheriff, assessor, and treasurer. The city of St. Louis, which is administratively independent of any county, has an elected mayor, a comptroller, and a 29-member board of aldermen (including the president). Most other cities are governed by an elected mayor and council.

15 JUDICIAL SYSTEM

As of 1994, the supreme court, the state's highest court, consisted of seven judges and three commissioners. The court of appeals consisted in 1994 of 32 judges in three districts. The circuit court is the only trial court and has original jurisdiction over all cases and matters, civil and municipal. Many circuit courts have established municipal divisions, presided over by judges paid locally. The 1994 crime rate for the state was 5,307.7 per 100,000. As of 1993, there were 16,178 inmates in Missouri federal and state prisons.

16 MIGRATION

In recent decades, Missouri has been losing population through migration— 322,000 people were lost to net migration between 1940 and 1970, followed by a net gain of 22,000 during the 1970s and a net loss of nearly 100,000 during the 1980s. The dominant intrastate migration pattern has been the concentration of blacks in the major cities, especially St. Louis and Kansas City, and the exodus of whites from those cities to the suburbs and, more recently, to small towns and rural areas. As of 1990, just under 70% of all state residents had been born in Missouri.

17 ECONOMY

Missouri's central location and access to the Mississippi River contributed to its growth as a commercial center. The state's current economy is diversified, with manufacturing, farming, trade, tourism, services, government, and mining as prime sources of income. Today, automobile and aerospace manufacturing are the state's leading industries, while soybeans and meat and dairy products are the most important agricultural commodities. The state's historic past, varied physical terrain, and modern urban attractions— notably the Gateway Arch in St. Louis— have made tourism a growth industry in recent decades.

18 INCOME

With an income per capita (per person) of $20,562 in 1994, Missouri ranked 25th among the 50 states. Total personal income for Missouri was $108.5 billion in 1994. About 16.1% of state residents lived below the federal poverty level in 1993.

19 INDUSTRY

The leading industry groups, by employment, are transportation equipment (mainly automobiles, aircraft, and rockets and missiles); food and food products; electric and electronic equipment; printing and publishing; and fabricated metal products. Shipments by Missouri manufacturers during 1991 amounted to $66.4 billion. McDonnell Douglas, with headquarters in St. Louis, is a leading manufacturer of aerospace products, including all the Mercury and Gemini space capsules.

20 LABOR

In 1994, Missouri's civilian labor force averaged 2,695,000. The unemployment rate was 4.9%. Missouri is a strong union state. Some 14.8% of all workers in the state belonged to labor unions in 1994. In 1993, there were seven national labor unions operating in its borders.

21 AGRICULTURE

Missouri had 105,000 farms (second in the US) covering 28.5 million acres (11.5 million hectares) in 1994. Missouri's agricultural income reached $4.5 billion in 1994, 15th among the 50 states. Of this total, about 20% came from soybeans.

In 1994, Missouri was fourth among the states in grain sorghum production and sixth in soybean and rice production. In that year, cash receipts from all crops totaled $2 billion. Farmers harvested 173.2 million bushels of soybeans, 273.7 million bushels of corn, 49.5 million bushels of wheat, 49.5 million bushels of grain sorghum, 595,000 bales of cotton, and 6.8 million tons of hay. Tobacco, oats, rye, apples, peaches, grapes, watermelons, and various seed crops are also grown in commercial quantities.

22 DOMESTICATED ANIMALS

Missouri is a leading livestock-raising state. Cash receipts from sales of livestock and livestock products totaled $2.4 billion in 1994. Hog-raising is concentrated north of the Missouri River, cattle-raising in the western counties, and dairy farming in the southwest. At the end of 1994, Missouri farms and ranches had 4.5 million cattle, 3.4 million hogs, and 8.3 million chickens.

In the same year, the state's 195,000 milk cows produced about $191 million in dairy products. In 1994, broiler production was 658 million pounds, and turkey production was 478 million pounds.

23 FISHING

Commercial fishing takes place mainly on the Mississippi, Missouri, and St. Francis rivers. Sport fishing is enjoyed throughout the state, but especially in the Ozarks, whose waters harbor walleye, rainbow trout, bluegill, and largemouth bass.

24 FORESTRY

Missouri has about 13,998,200 acres (5,665,100 hectares) of forestland (31% of the state). Of the commercial forests, approximately three-fourths are of the oak/hickory type. Shortleaf pine and oak/pine forests comprise about 5%, while the remainder consists of cedar and bottomland hardwoods. Missouri leads the US in the production of charcoal, cedar products, and nutmeats. Railroad ties, veneers, wine and bourbon casks, and other forest-related items are also produced. Timber production in 1991 totaled 189 million cubic feet.

More than 300,000 acres (120,000 hectares) of conservation areas, managed by the Forestry Division, are used for timber production, wildlife and watershed protection, hunting, fishing, and other recreational purposes. A state-run nursery sells seedling trees and shrubs to Missouri landowners.

25 MINING

Nonfuel mineral production in Missouri was estimated at over $1 billion in 1994. Missouri ranked first of 11 states producing lead in 1992. In 1991, Missouri's lead production comprised 75% of the US market and 10% of the world market. The state also ranked first in lime and fire clay production. Items of high value in 1992 include lead, $238.8 million; crushed stone, $186.7 million; and zinc, $56.4 million.

26 ENERGY AND POWER

In 1993, electrical output totaled 53.2 billion kilowatt hours. Coal-fired plants accounted for 80% of all power production in 1991. The state had one operating nuclear plant as of 1993. Fossil fuel resources are limited. Reserves of bituminous coal totaled six billion tons as of 1 January 1992, but only a small portion was considered recoverable. Small quantities of crude petroleum are also produced commercially. In 1992, such production totaled 142,000 barrels. The state's energy expenditures were $1,779 per capita (per person) in 1992.

27 COMMERCE

Missouri has been one of the nation's leading trade centers ever since merchants in Independence began provisioning wagon trains for the Santa Fe Trail. The state's wholesale sales totaled $68.4 billion in 1992; retail sales were $44.8 billion in 1993; and service establishment receipts were $22.4 billion in 1992. Foreign exports of Missouri products exceeded $3.7 billion in 1992 (24th among the states).

28 PUBLIC FINANCE

The debt of Missouri state government in 1993 was $6.5 billion, or $1,245 per capita (per person). The actual revenues for 1992 were $11,619 million; expenditures were $10,446 million.

29 TAXATION

Missouri's total state tax revenues, traditionally low, ranked 20th in the nation in 1991. On a per capita (per person) basis, state general revenue of $968.70 ranked 43rd in the US in 1991. Missouri taxes personal and corporate income. The basic state sales tax in 1991 was 4.125%; cities and towns may add an additional tax. Other taxes levied by the state include charges on motor fuel, cigarettes, and alcoholic beverages along with motor vehicle and operator's license fees and taxes on inheritances. Property and sales taxes are the leading sources of local revenue. During 1992, Missouri contributed $27.3 billion in federal taxes.

30 HEALTH

The overall death rate of 982.3 per 100,000 population in 1992 was the sixth-highest in the US, reflecting the relatively high proportion of elderly Missourians in the population as a whole. Deaths from heart disease, cancer, stroke, and accidents—the major causes of death—were all above the national average. In 1993, Missouri had 130 community hospitals, with 23,600 beds. The average expense of hospitals for care in 1993 was $863 per inpatient day, or $6,161 for an average cost per stay. The state had 10,800 non-federal physicians and 40,000 nurses in 1993. Some 12.2% of state residents did not have health insurance in 1993.

31 HOUSING

In 1993, Missouri had an estimated 2,258,000 housing units. The median price of a single-family home in Missouri was $59,800 in 1990 (33d among the states). The median costs for owners (including a mortgage) and renters in 1990 were $600 and $368, respectively, per month.

32 EDUCATION

In 1990, 78.7% of all Missourians 25 years of age or older were high school graduates. About 860,000 students were enrolled in Missouri's 538 public elementary and secondary school districts in 1993. There were about 54,100 public school teachers in the state in 1994. Expenditures on education averaged $4,489 per pupil (40th in the nation) in 1993.

Missouri had 13 public and 54 private four-year institutions of higher education in 1992. Total full-time enrollment in the fall of 1992 was 297,154 students. The University of Missouri, the first state-supported university west of the Mississippi River, has four campuses with a combined full-time enrollment of 40,000 in 1991/92. There are five regional state universities and three state colleges. Two leading independent universities, Washington University and St. Louis University, are located in St. Louis.

33 ARTS

Theatrical performances are offered throughout the state, mostly during the summer. In Kansas City, productions of Broadway musicals and light opera are staged at the Starlight Theater. In St. Louis, the 12,000-seat Municipal Opera puts on outdoor theater, while the *Goldenrod*, built in 1909 and said to be the largest showboat ever constructed, is used today for vaudeville, melodrama, and ragtime shows.

Leading orchestras are the St. Louis Symphony and Kansas City Symphony.

The Opera Theatre of St. Louis and the Lyric Opera of Kansas City are distinguished musical organizations. Springfield has a regional opera company.

Between World Wars I and II, Kansas City was the home of a thriving jazz community that included Charlie Parker and, later, Count Basie. Country music predominates in rural Missouri: the Ozark Opry at Osage Beach and the Baldknobbers Hillbilly Jamboree and Mountain Music Theater in Branson have seasons from May to October. The state of Missouri generated $37,074,960 to support its arts programs from 1987 to 1991.

34 LIBRARIES AND MUSEUMS

Missouri had 37 county and 11 regional library systems in 1991/92, when the combined book stock of all public libraries in the state was 17,255,266, and their combined circulation 34,927,322. The Missouri State Library, in Jefferson City, is the center of the state's interlibrary loan network. The University of Missouri-Columbia has the leading academic library, with 2,579,253 volumes in 1991/92.The federally-administered Harry S Truman Library and Museum is at Independence.

Missouri has over 150 museums and historic sites. The William Rockhill Nelson Gallery/Atkins Museum of Fine Arts in Kansas City and the St. Louis Art Museum both house distinguished general collections. The Mark Twain Home and Museum in Hannibal has a collection of manuscripts and other memorabilia.

35 COMMUNICATIONS

As of March 1993, Missouri had approximately 1,898,000 residences with telephones. About 92.9% of all state residences had telephone service. As of 1993 there were 113 commercial AM stations and 165 FM stations in service. Missouri had 27 commercial and 5 noncommercial television stations. In 1993, the state had nine major cable systems in service.

36 PRESS

Many Missouri journalists have achieved national recognition. The best known is Samuel Clemens (later Mark Twain). Hungarian-born Joseph Pulitzer created the *St. Louis Post–Dispatch* in 1878 and established the Pulitzer Prizes, which annually honor journalistic and artistic achievement. As of 1994, Missouri had 9 morning newspapers, 33 evening dailies, and 21 Sunday papers. The leading dailies with their 1994 daily circulations are the *St. Louis Post-Dispatch* (585,681) and the *Kansas City Star* (423,305). Periodicals include the St. Louis-based *Sporting News*, the bimonthly "bible" of baseball fans.

37 TOURISM, TRAVEL, AND RECREATION

During 1991, travelers spent more than $7.8 billion in Missouri on transportation, accommodations, meals, entertainment, recreation, and other items. The principal attraction in St. Louis is the Gateway Arch; at 630 feet (192 meters) it is the tallest man-made national monument in the US. Designed by Eero Saarinen in 1948 but not

Photo credit: Convention & Visitors Bureau of Greater Kansas City.

The Negro Leagues Baseball museum in Kansas City documents the history of black baseball. It is located a few blocks from where the Negro National League was founded by Andrew "Rube" Foster in 1920. The color line in organized baseball was broken in 1947 when Kansas City Monarchs shortstop Jackie Robinson signed with the Brooklyn Dodgers.

constructed until 1964, three years after his death, the arch and the Museum of Westward Expansion form part of the Jefferson National Expansion Memorial on the western shore of the Mississippi River. In the Kansas City area are the modern Crown Center hotels and shopping plaza, the Truman Sports Complex, Jesse James's birthplace near Excelsior Springs, and Harry Truman's hometown of Independence.

Memorabilia of Mark Twain are housed in and around Hannibal. The birthplace and childhood home of George Washington Carver is in Diamond. The Lake of the Ozarks, with 1,375 miles (2,213 kilome-

ters) of shoreline, is one of the most popular vacation spots in mid-America. Other attractions are the Pony Express Stables and Museum at St. Joseph and the "Big Springs Country" of the Ozarks, in the southeast.

As of 1991, Missouri had 47 state parks. Lake of the Ozarks State Park is the largest, covering 16,872 acres (6,828 hectares). There were also 27 historic sites in 1994, when state parks and historic sites covered 105,000 acres (43,050 hectares). They attract nearly 15 million visitors annually. Hunting and fishing are popular recreational activities.

38 SPORTS

There are four major league professional sports teams in Missouri: the Kansas City Royals and the St. Louis Cardinals of Major League Baseball; the Kansas City Chiefs of the National Football League; and the St. Louis Blues of the National Hockey League. In collegiate sports, the University of Missouri competes in the Big Eight Conference. Other annual sporting events include the National Intercollegiate Basketball Tournament, held in Kansas City in March. Thoroughbred-racing can be seen during a summer and fall season at Cahokia Downs, outside St. Louis.

39 FAMOUS MISSOURIANS

Harry S Truman (1884–1972) has been the only native-born Missourian to serve as US president or vice-president. Truman was Franklin D. Roosevelt's vice-presidential running mate in 1944 and succeeded to the presidency upon Roosevelt's death on 12 April 1945. The "man from Independence" was elected to the presidency in his own right in 1948, defeating Republican Thomas E. Dewey in one of the most surprising upsets in US political history. Charles Evans Whittaker (b.Kansas, 1901–73) was a federal district and appeals court judge in Missouri before his appointment as Supreme Court associate justice in 1957. Among the state's outstanding US military leaders are Generals John J. Pershing (1860–1948) and Omar Bradley (1893–1981).

Missouri's best-known senator was Thomas Hart Benton (b.North Carolina, 1782–1858), who championed the interests of Missouri and the West for 30 years.

W. Stuart Symington (b.Massachusetts, 1901–88) was a US senator from 1953 to 1977 and earlier was the nation's first secretary of the Air Force. Thomas F. Eagleton (b.1929) has been a US senator since 1969 and, briefly, was the Democratic vice-presidential nominee in 1972, until publicity about his having received electroshock treatment for depression forced him off the ticket.

Meriwether Lewis (b.Virginia, 1774–1809) and William Clark (b.Virginia, 1770–1838) explored Missouri and the West during 1804–6. Lewis later served as governor of Louisiana Territory, with headquarters at St. Louis, and Clark was governor of Missouri Territory from 1813 to 1821. Dred Scott (b.Virginia, 1795–1858), a slave owned by a Missourian, figured in a Supreme Court decision that set the stage for the Civil War. Missourians with unsavory reputations include such desperadoes as Jesse James (1847–82) and his brother Frank (1843–1915). Another well-known native was Kansas City's political boss, Thomas Joseph Pendergast (1872–1945), a power among Missouri Democrats until convicted of income tax evasion in 1939 and sent to Leavenworth prison.

Distinguished scientists include agricultural chemist George Washington Carver (1864–1943); astronomer Edwin P. Hubble (1889–1953); Nobel Prize-winning nuclear physicist Arthur Holly Compton (b.Ohio, 1892–1962); and mathematician-cyberneticist Norbert Wiener (1894–1964). Charles A. Lindbergh (b.Michigan 1902–74) was a pilot and aviation instructor in the St. Louis area during the 1920s before winning worldwide acclaim for his solo New York-Paris flight.

Prominent Missouri businessmen include Joseph Pulitzer (b.Hungary, 1847–1911), who established the *St. Louis Post-Dispatch* (1878) and later endowed the journalism and literary prizes that bear his name; and James Cash Penney (1875–1971), founder of the J. C. Penney Company. Noteworthy journalists from Missouri include television newscaster Walter Cronkite (b.1916). Other distinguished Missourians include theologian Reinhold Niebuhr (1892–1971) and civil rights leader Roy Wilkins (1901–81).

Missouri's most popular author is Mark Twain (Samuel Langhorne Clemens, 1835–1910), whose *Adventures of Tom Sawyer* (1876) and *Adventures of Huckleberry Finn* (1884) evoke his boyhood in Hannibal. Robert Heinlein (1907–88) was a noted writer of science fiction. Poet-critic T(homas) S(tearns) Eliot (1888–1965), awarded the Nobel Prize for literature in 1948, was born in St. Louis but became a British subject in 1927. Other Missouri-born poets include Marianne Moore (1887–1972) and Langston Hughes (1902–67).

Distinguished painters who lived in Missouri include James Carroll Beckwith (1852–1917). Among the state's important musicians are ragtime pianist-composer Scott Joplin (b.Texas, 1868–1917); W(illiam) C(hristopher) Handy (b.Alabama, 1873–1958); composer-critic Virgil Thompson (b.1896); jazzman Coleman Hawkins (1907–69); and popular songwriter Burt Bacharach (b.1929). Photographer Walker Evans (1903–75) was a St. Louis native.

Missouri-born entertainers include actors Dick Van Dyke (b.1925) and Edward Asner (b.1929); dancer Josephine Baker (1906–75); actress-dancer Ginger Rogers (1911–95); film director John Huston (1906–84); and opera star Grace Bumbry (b.1937). In popular music, the state's most widely known singer-songwriter is Charles "Chuck" Berry (b.California, 1926).

St. Louis Cardinals stars who became Hall of Famers include Jerome Herman "Dizzy" Dean (b.Arkansas, 1911–74); Stanley Frank "Stan the Man" Musial (b.Pennsylvania, 1920); Robert "Bob" Gibson (b.Nebraska, 1935), and Louis "Lou" Brock (b.Arkansas, 1939). Among the native Missourians who achieved stardom in the sports world are baseball manager Charles Dillon "Casey" Stengel (1890–1975); catcher Lawrence Peter "Yogi" Berra (b.1925); sportscaster Joe Garagiola (b.1926); and golfer Tom Watson (b.1949).

40 BIBLIOGRAPHY

Greene, Lorenzo J., et al. *Missouri's Black Heritage.* St. Louis: Forum, 1980.

Nagel, Paul C. *Missouri: A Bicentennial History.* New York: Norton, 1977.

State Historical Society of Missouri. *Historic Missouri: A Pictorial Narrative.* Columbia, 1977.

M O N T A N A

State of Montana

ORIGIN OF STATE NAME: Derived from the Latin word meaning "mountainous."

NICKNAME: The Treasure State. (Also: Big Sky Country.)

CAPITAL: Helena.

ENTERED UNION: 8 November 1889 (41st).

SONG: "Montana."

MOTTO: *Oro y Plata* (Gold and silver).

FLAG: A blue field, fringed in gold on the top and bottom borders, surround the state coat of arms, with "Montana" in gold letters above the coat of arms.

OFFICIAL SEAL: In the lower center are a plow and a miner's pick and shovel; mountains appear above them on the left, the Great Falls of the Missouri River on the right, and the state motto on a banner below. The words "The Great Seal of the State of Montana" surround the whole.

ANIMAL: Grizzly bear.

BIRD: Western meadowlark.

FISH: Black-spotted (cutthroat) trout.

FLOWER: Bitterroot.

TREE: Ponderosa pine.

GEMS: Yogo sapphire; Montana agate.

GRASS: Bluebunch wheatgrass.

TIME: 5 AM MST = noon GMT.

1 LOCATION AND SIZE

Located in the northwestern US, Montana is the largest of the eight Rocky Mountain states and ranks fourth in size among the 50 states. The total area of Montana is 147,046 square miles (380,849 square kilometers). The state's maximum east-west extension is 570 miles (917 kilometers); its extreme north-south distance is 315 miles (507 kilometers). Its total boundary length is 1,947 miles (3,133 kilometers).

2 TOPOGRAPHY

Montana has an approximate mean elevation of 3,400 feet (1,000 meters). The Rocky Mountains cover the western two-fifths of the state, with the Bitterroot Range along the Idaho border. The high, gently rolling Great Plains occupy most of central and eastern Montana. The highest point in the state is Granite Peak, at an elevation of 12,799 feet (3,901 meters). The Continental Divide passes through the western part of the state. Ft. Peck Reservoir is Montana's largest body of inland water; Flathead Lake is the largest natural lake. The state's most important rivers are the Missouri and the Yellowstone.

3 CLIMATE

The Continental Divide separates the state into two distinct climatic regions: the west generally has a milder climate than the east, where winters can be especially harsh. Montana's maximum daytime temperature averages 27°F (–2°C) in January and 85°F (29°C) in July. The all-time low temperature in the state, –70°F (–57°C) in 1954, is the lowest ever recorded in the continental US. The all-time high, 117°F (47°C), was set in 1937. Great Falls receives an average annual precipitation of 15 inches (38 centimeters), but much of north-central Montana is arid.

4 PLANTS AND ANIMALS

The subalpine region, in the northern Rocky Mountains, is rich in wildflowers during a short midsummer growing season. The plants of the montane zone consists largely of coniferous forests, principally alpine fir, and a variety of shrubs. The plains are characterized by an abundance of grasses, cacti, and sagebrush species. Game animals of the state include elk, moose, and mountain goat. Rattlesnakes and other reptiles occur in most of the state. The black-footed ferret, Eskimo curlew, and greenback cutthroat trout are on the endangered list.

5 ENVIRONMENTAL PROTECTION

Montana's major environmental concerns are management of mineral and water

Montana Population Profile

Estimated 1995 population:	862,000
Population change, 1980–90:	1.6%
Leading ancestry group:	German
Second leading group:	Irish
Foreign born population:	1.7%
Hispanic origin†:	1.5%
Population by race:	
White:	92.7%
Black:	0.3%
Native American:	6.0%
Asian/Pacific Islander:	0.5%
Other:	0.5%

Population by Age Group

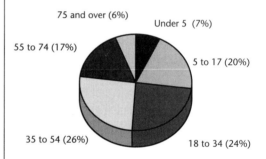

75 and over (6%)
Under 5 (7%)
55 to 74 (17%)
5 to 17 (20%)
18 to 34 (24%)
35 to 54 (26%)

Top Cities with Populations Over 25,000

City	Population	National rank	% change 1980–90
Billings	84,011	265	21.5
Great Falls	56,628	441	–2.9
Missoula	44,522	597	28.5
Butte–Silver Bow	34,128	809	na

Notes: †A person of Hispanic origin may be of any race. NA indicates that data are not available.
Sources: Economic and Statistics Administration, Bureau of the Census. *Statistical Abstract of the United States, 1994–95.* Washington, DC: Government Printing Office, 1995; Courtenay M. Slater and George E. Hall. *1995 County and City Extra: Annual Metro, City and County Data Book.* Lanham, MD: Bernan Press, 1995.

MONTANA

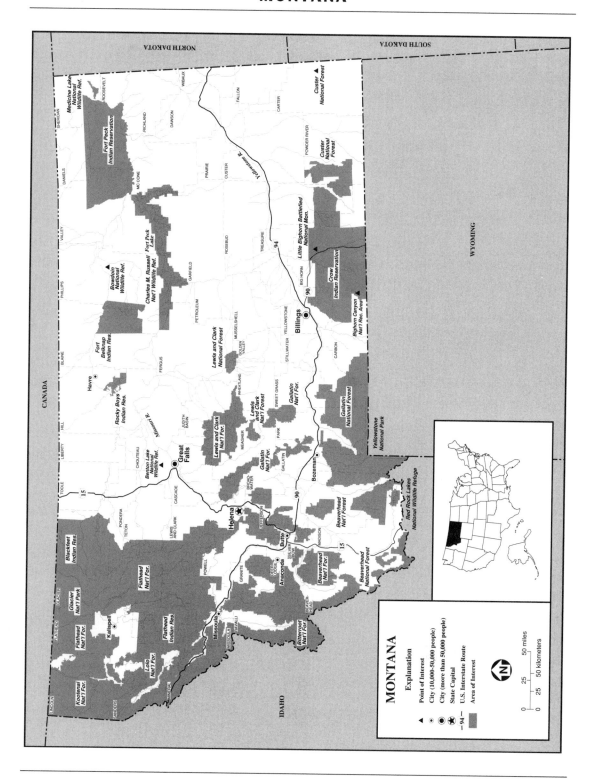

Explanation

- ▲ Point of Interest
- • City (10,000–50,000 people)
- ⊙ City (more than 50,000 people)
- ★ State Capital
- —94— U.S. Interstate Route
- ▨ Area of Interest

50 miles
25 50 kilometers
0 25

N

Glacier National Park, Glacier County.

resources and reclamation of strip-mined land. The Montana Environmental Policy Act, the Major Facilities Siting Act, and the Montana Resource Indemnity Trust Act (the latter imposes a tax on coal sales) reflect the determination of Montanans to protect the beauty of the Big Sky Country while maintaining economic momentum. The state had nine hazardous waste sites as of 1994.

6 POPULATION

According to the 1990 census, Montana ranked 44th among the 50 states, with a population of 799,065 and a density of only 5.5 persons per square mile (2 persons per square kilometer). The estimated population in 1995 was 862,000; the projection for the year 2000 is 920,000.

7 ETHNIC GROUPS

According to the 1990 census, there were approximately 48,000 Native Americans in Montana, of whom the Blackfeet and Crow are the most numerous. The black, Asian, and Hispanic populations are very small comprising 0.3%, 0.5%, and 1.5%, respectively.

8 LANGUAGES

English in Montana fuses Northern and Midland features, the Northern influence declining from east to west. In 1990, 703,198 Montanans spoke only English at home. Other languages spoken at home, and number of speakers, included German, 9,644; Spanish, 8,083; and various Native American languages, 8,207.

9 RELIGIONS

As of 1990, Protestant groups had 467,345 known members in Montana. Leading denominations included American Lutheran Church Association, 16,172; United Methodist, 19,461; and Latter-day Saints (Mormons), 28,620. Montana had 125,799 Roman Catholics and an estimated 310 Jews in 1990.

10 TRANSPORTATION

Montana is served by three major railroads, operating on about 3,315 rail miles (5,334 kilometers) of track. Amtrak operated one long-distance route (Chicago–Seattle/Portland) through the state, which served 12 stations. The total number of Montana riders in 1991/92 was 129,867.

Because of its large size, small population, and difficult terrain, Montana was slow to develop a highway system. As of the beginning of 1994, the state had 69,768 miles (112,257 kilometers) of public roads, streets, and highways. There were 939,220 registered motor vehicles. Late in 1995, Montana became the first state to abolish speed limits on certain highways. Montana had 206 airports, with the leading ones at Great Falls and Billings.

11 HISTORY

Montana's first European explorers were probably French traders and trappers from Canada who arrived during the 17th and 18th centuries. However, it was not until 1803 that the written history of Montana began. In that year, the Louisiana Purchase gave the United States most of Montana, and the Lewis and Clark expedition, dispatched by President Thomas Jefferson in 1804, added the rest. Soon afterwards, the first American trappers, traders, and settlers entered Montana.

The fur trade dominated Montana's economy until 1858, when gold was discovered east of the present-day community of Drummond, bringing with it a temporary gold boom. In 1863, the eastern and western sectors of Montana were joined as part of Idaho Territory. On 26 May 1864, President Abraham Lincoln signed the Organic Act, which created Montana Territory.

The territorial period was one of rapid and profound change. By the time Montana became a state on 8 November 1889, the remnants of Montana's Native American culture had been largely confined to federal reservations, following the surrender of the Nez Percé tribe to federal forces. As the Indian threat subsided, cattle ranchers wasted little time in putting the seemingly limitless open range to use. However, the "hard winter" of 1886/87, when perhaps as many as 362,000 head of cattle starved, marked the end of a cattle frontier based on the "free grass" of the open range and taught the stockmen the value of a secure winter feed supply.

Photo credit: Travel Montana/P. Fugleberg.

A statue at Fort Benton commemorating the explorers Lewis and Clark.

1880s–1990s

Construction of Montana's railroad system between 1880 and 1909 breathed new life into mining as well as the livestock industry. By 1890, the Butte copper pits were producing more than 40% of the nation's copper requirements. The struggle to gain financial control of the enormous mineral wealth of Butte Hill led to the "War of the Copper Kings," whose victor, Anaconda Copper Mining, practically controlled the press, politics, and governmental processes of Montana until the 1940s and 1950s.

The railroads also brought an invasion of agricultural homesteaders. Montana's population doubled between 1900 and 1920, while the number of farms and ranches increased form 13,000 to 57,000. Drought and a sharp drop in wheat prices after World War I brought an end to the homestead boom. Conditions worsened with the drought and depression of the early 1930s. Then the New Deal—enormously popular in Montana—helped revive farming and silver mining and financed irrigation and other public works projects.

The decades since the end of World War II have seen moderate growth in Montana's population, economy, and social services. Although manufacturing developed slowly, the state's fossil fuels industry grew rapidly during the national energy crisis of the 1970s. However, production of coal, crude oil, and natural gas leveled off after the crisis and even declined in the early 1980s.

12 STATE GOVERNMENT

The state legislature consists of 50 senators, elected to four-year terms, and 100 representatives, who serve for two years. Elected officers of the executive branch include the governor and lieutenant governor (who run jointly), secretary of state, and attorney general. Each serves a four-year term. To become law, a bill must pass both houses by a simple majority and be signed by the governor, or remain unsigned for five days, or be passed over the governor's veto by a two-thirds vote of both houses.

13 POLITICAL PARTIES

Since statehood, Democrats have generally dominated in contests for the US House and Senate, while Republicans led in elections for state and local offices and in national presidential campaigns (except during the New Deal years). In 1992 Montanans gave Democrat Bill Clinton 37.6% of the vote; George Bush, 35%; and Independent Ross Perot, 26%. The governor of Montana as of 1994, Marc Racicot, was a Republican. Republican Conrad Burns was reelected to the Senate in 1994, and Democrat Max Baucus won re-election in 1990. The sole US representative is a Democrat. In the 1994 mid-term elections, the Republicans gained control of the state senate for the first time in 40 years. There are now 31 Republicans and 19 Democrats. The Republicans continued to control the state house with 67 seats to the Democrats' 33.

Montana Presidential Vote by Major Political Parties, 1948–92

YEAR	MONTANA WINNER	DEMOCRAT	REPUBLICAN
1948	*Truman (D)	119,071	96,770
1952	*Eisenhower (R)	106,213	157,394
1956	*Eisenhower (R)	116,238	154,933
1960	Nixon (R)	134,891	141,841
1964	*Johnson (D)	164,246	113,032
1968	*Nixon (R)	114,117	138,835
1972	*Nixon (R)	120,197	183,976
1976	Ford (R)	149,259	173,703
1980	*Reagan (R)	118,032	206,814
1984	*Reagan (R)	146,742	232,450
1988	*Bush (R)	168,936	190,412
1992**	*Clinton (D)	154,507	144,207

*Won US presidential election.

** Independent candidate Ross Perot received 107,225 votes.

14 LOCAL GOVERNMENT

As of 1994, Montana had 56 counties, 128 municipalities, 578 special districts, and 544 school districts. Typically elected county officials are three county commissioners, an attorney, a sheriff, a clerk, and a recorder.

15 JUDICIAL SYSTEM

Montana's highest court, the supreme court, consists of a chief justice and six associate justices. District courts are the courts of general jurisdiction. As of 1994 there were 20 judicial districts. Justice of the peace courts are essentially county courts whose jurisdiction is limited to minor civil cases, misdemeanors, and traffic violations. Montana's crime rate in 1994 was 5,018.8 per 100,000.

16 MIGRATION

After a net gain of 16,000 from migration between 1970 and 1980, Montana had a net loss of 43,000 residents from migration during the 1980s. In 1990, 58.9% of all Montanans had been born in the state.

17 ECONOMY

Resource industries—agriculture, mining, lumbering—dominate Montana's economy, although tourism is of increasing importance. A lawsuit with the federal government, over the federal lands which have supplied much of the state's timber, has placed the timber industry's future in question. Residential construction grew in 1993 with a rise in population growth.

18 INCOME

With a per capita (per person) income of $17,824 in 1994, Montana ranked 41st among the 50 states. Total personal income increased to $15.3 billion in 1994. Some 14.9% of the state's population lived below the federal poverty level in 1993.

19 INDUSTRY

Montana's major manufacturing industries process raw materials from mines, forests, and farms. The total value of shipments by manufacturers in 1992 amounted to $4,137,000,000. Major industries include petroleum and coal products; lumber and wood products; and food products.

20 LABOR

Montana's labor force varies sharply with the season, swelling in the summer and shrinking in the winter. As of 1994, the civilian labor force totaled 437,000 persons. The unemployment rate was 5.1% in 1994. Some 18.8% of all workers in the state were union members in 1994.

21 AGRICULTURE

Montana's farms numbered 22,500 in 1994. Farm income totaled $1.8 billion in 1994. In that year, Montana was the nation's third-leading wheat producer, with an output of 170,590,000 bushels, valued at $646,000,000. Other major crops were sugarbeets, 1,307,000 bushels; hay, 4,540,000 tons; and barley, 52,800,000 bushels. Oats, potatoes, flax, and dry beans are also grown.

22 DOMESTICATED ANIMALS

Livestock production in 1994 was valued at $866.8 million, or 46.7% of Montana's farm income. At the end of 1994, the state had 2,700,000 cattle. Other livestock included 210,000 hogs and 490,000 sheep. Sales of livestock products in that year included cattle, valued at $774,000,000, which accounted for 39.6% of agricultural receipts.

23 FISHING

Montana's designated fishing streams offer some 10,000 miles (16,000 kilometers) of good-to-excellent freshwater fishing. Federal hatcheries distributed 1.3 million (136,482 pounds) of coldwater species fish and fish eggs (mostly trout) in 1992.

24 FORESTRY

Montana has about 22.4 million acres (9.1 million hectares) of forestland. There were ten national forests, comprising roughly 16,806,000 acres (6,801,000 hectares) in 1992. The lumbering industry produces about one billion board feet per year.

25 MINING

The estimated value of nonfuel mineral production for Montana in 1994 was $492 million. Metallic minerals—copper, gold, iron ore, lead, molybdenum, platinum group metals, silver, and zinc—accounted for 77% of the state's total nonfuel mineral production. In 1992, Montana ranked 18th nationally in the value of these minerals.

26 ENERGY AND POWER

In 1993, Montana produced 23.4 billion kilowatt hours of electricity, 41.3% from hydropower and 58.7% by coal-burning. The state has no nuclear power plants. Oil and natural gas supply about 60% of Montana's energy requirements. In 1993, the state produced 17 million barrels of crude oil. Natural gas production totaled 55 billion cubic feet. As of January 1992, coal reserves were estimated at 119.9 billion tons—first in the US and over 31% of the US total. Montana's energy expenditures were $2,091 per capita (per person) in 1992.

27 COMMERCE

Montana's wholesale sales totaled $5.9 billion in 1992; retail sales were $7.2 billion in 1993; and service establishment receipts were $2.6 billion in 1992. Montana's foreign exports in 1992 totaled $268 million.

28 PUBLIC FINANCE

The estimated revenues for the 1994/95 general fund were $616,049,000; estimated expenditures were $615,331,000. The state's debt as of 1993 totaled $1.7 billion, or $2,080 per capita (per person).

29 TAXATION

Montana taxes personal and corporate income and levies a property tax but no sales or use tax. State residents paid $1.9 billion in federal taxes in 1992.

30 HEALTH

Of the major causes of death in 1992, only the heart disease rate was below the national norm. There were 52 community hospitals in 1993, with 4,200 beds. The average expense of a hospital providing service was $481 per inpatient day, or $4,953 for an average cost per stay. There were 1,407 nonfederal physicians and 5,900 nurses as of 1993. Some 15.3% of state residents did not have health insurance in that year.

31 HOUSING

In 1993, Montana had an estimated 366,000 housing units. The state authorized 2,872 new housing units in 1993. In 1990, the median home value was $56,600. The median monthly cost for the owner (including a mortgage) was $575 that year. Renters had a median monthly cost of $311 in 1990.

32 EDUCATION

As of 1990, 81% of Montanans 25 years and older had completed high school, and 20% were college graduates. Public school enrollments in fall 1993 were 116,650 for grades Preschool–8 and 43,370 in grades 9–12. Expenditures on education averaged $5,459 per pupil (23d in the nation) in 1993. As of fall 1992, 39,582 students attended institutions of higher education. Of these, the University of Montana (Missoula) enrolled 10,614, and Montana State University (Bozeman) had 10,540.

33 ARTS

The C. M. Russell Museum in Great Falls honors the work of Charles Russell. Other fine art museums include the Museum of the Rockies in Bozeman, Yellowstone Art Center at Billings, the Montana Historical

Society Museum and Archives in Helena, and the Missoula Museum of the Arts.

34 LIBRARIES AND MUSEUMS

Montana had 6 public library federations in 1991/92, serving 56 counties. The combined book stock of all Montana public libraries was 2,605,999 and their combined circulation was 4,580,311. Distinguished collections include those of the University of Montana (Missoula) and Montana State University (Bozeman). Among the state's 66 museums are the Montana Historical Society Museum, Helena; World Museum of Mining, Butte; and Museum of the Plains Indian, Browning. National historic sites include the Little Big Horn battlefield.

35 COMMUNICATIONS

In March 1993, 94.4% of the state's households had telephone service. There were 106 commercial radio stations in 1993, and 21 television stations.

36 PRESS

As of 1994, Montana had seven morning dailies, five evening dailies, and seven Sunday newspapers. The leading papers and their circulations were the *Billings Gazette* (54,657 mornings, 61,822 Sundays) and the *Great Falls Tribune* (33,486 mornings, 40,009 Sundays).

37 TOURISM, TRAVEL, AND RECREATION

Many tourists seek out the former gold rush camps, ghost towns, and dude ranches. Scenic wonders include Glacier National Park in the northwest, and Yellowstone National Park, which also extends into Idaho and Wyoming. Bighorn Canyon National Recreation Area is another popular destination. In 1993, visitors spent $1.4 billion in Montana.

38 SPORTS

There are no major league professional sports teams in Montana. The University of Montana Grizzlies and Montana State University Bobcats both compete in the Big Sky Conference. Skiing is a very popular participation sport.

39 FAMOUS MONTANANS

Prominent national officeholders from Montana include US Senator Thomas Walsh (b.Wisconsin, 1859–1933), who directed the investigation that uncovered the Teapot Dome scandal; Jeannette Rankin (1880–1973), the first woman member of Congress and the only US representative to vote against American participation in both world wars. Crazy Horse (1849?–77) led a Sioux-Cheyenne army in battle at Little Big Horn.

Creative artists from Montana include Alfred Bertram Guthrie, Jr. (b.Indiana, 1901–91), author of *The Big Sky* and the Pulitzer Prize-winning *The Way West*; and Charles Russell (b.Missouri, 1864–1926), Montana's foremost painter and sculptor.

40 BIBLIOGRAPHY

Farr, William, and K. Ross Toole. *Montana: Images of the Past*. Boulder, Colo.: Pruett, 1984.
Spence, Clark C. *Montana: A Bicentennial History*. New York: Norton, 1978.
Toole, Kenneth R. *Montana: An Uncommon Land*. Norman: University of Oklahoma Press, 1984.
———. *Twentieth-Century Montana: A State of Extremes*. Norman: University of Oklahoma Press, 1983.

NEBRASKA

State of Nebraska

ORIGIN OF STATE NAME: Derived from the Oto Indian word nebrathka, meaning "flat water" (for the Platte River).

NICKNAME: The Cornhusker State.

CAPITAL: Lincoln.

ENTERED UNION: 1 March 1867 (37th).

SONG: "Beautiful Nebraska."

MOTTO: Equality Before the Law.

FLAG: The great seal appears in the center in gold and silver, on a field of blue.

OFFICIAL SEAL: Agriculture is represented by a farmer's cabin, sheaves of wheat, and growing corn; the mechanic arts, by a blacksmith. Above is the state motto; in the background, a steamboat plies the Missouri River and a train heads toward the Rockies. The scene is surrounded by the words "Great Seal of the State of Nebraska, March 1st 1867."

ANIMAL: White-tailed deer.

BIRD: Western meadowlark.

FLOWER: Goldenrod.

TREE: Western cottonwood.

GEM: Blue agate.

ROCK: Prairie agate.

GRASS: Little bluestem.

INSECT: Honeybee.

FOSSIL: Mammoth.

TIME: 6 AM CST = noon GMT; 5 AM MST = noon GMT.

1 LOCATION AND SIZE

Located in the western north-central US, Nebraska ranks 15th in size among the 50 states. The total area of the state is 77,355 square miles (200,349 square kilometers). Nebraska extends about 415 miles (668 kilometers) east-west and 205 miles (330 kilometers) north-south. The boundary length of Nebraska totals 1,332 miles (2,143 kilometers).

2 TOPOGRAPHY

Most of Nebraska is prairie; more than two-thirds of the state lies within the Great Plains. The elevation slopes upward gradually from east to west, from a low of 840 feet (256 meters) to 5,426 feet (1,654 meters). The main lakes in the state are mostly artificial. The Missouri, Platte, Niobrara, and Republican rivers flow through Nebraska.

3 CLIMATE

Nebraska has a continental climate, with highly variable temperatures. The central region has a normal monthly maximum of 76°F (24°C) in July and a minimum of 22°F (–6°C) in January. The record low for the state was –47°F (–44°C) in 1899; the record high of 118°F (48°C) was recorded in 1936. Normal yearly precipitation ranges from 17 inches (43 centimeters) in the west to 30 inches (76 centimeters) in the southeast.

4 PLANTS AND ANIMALS

Nebraska's deciduous forests are generally oak and hickory. Conifer forests are dominated by western yellow (ponderosa) pine. Slough grasses, needlegrasses, western wheatgrass, and buffalo grass are found in the prairies. Common Nebraska wildflowers include wild rose, columbine, and sunflower.

Common mammals native to the state are the pronghorn sheep, white-tailed and mule deer, and coyote. There are more than 400 kinds of birds, the mourning dove and western meadowlark (the state bird) among them. Carp, catfish, and trout are fished for sport. The bald eagle, Arctic peregrine falcon, and black-footed ferret are among the state's endangered species.

5 ENVIRONMENTAL PROTECTION

The Department of Environmental Quality protects the quality of Nebraska's water, air, and land resources. The state has 36 municipal landfills and four curbside recycling programs. There were ten hazardous waste sites as of 1994.

Nebraska Population Profile

Estimated 1995 population:	1,644,000
Population change, 1980–90:	0.5%
Leading ancestry group:	German
Second leading group:	Irish
Foreign born population:	1.8%
Hispanic origin†:	2.3%
Population by race:	
White:	93.8%
Black:	3.6%
Native American:	0.8%
Asian/Pacific Islander:	0.8%
Other:	1.0%

Population by Age Group

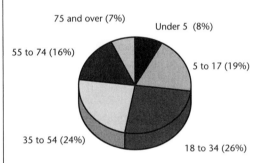

75 and over (7%)
Under 5 (8%)
55 to 74 (16%)
5 to 17 (19%)
35 to 54 (24%)
18 to 34 (26%)

Top Cities with Populations Over 25,000

City	Population	National rank	% change 1980–90
Omaha	339,671	48	6.9
Lincoln	197,488	78	11.7
Grand Island	40,036	681	18.7
Bellevue	30,994	902	42.0

Notes: †A person of Hispanic origin may be of any race. NA indicates that data are not available.
Sources: Economic and Statistics Administration, Bureau of the Census. *Statistical Abstract of the United States, 1994–95.* Washington, DC: Government Printing Office, 1995; Courtenay M. Slater and George E. Hall. *1995 County and City Extra: Annual Metro, City and County Data Book.* Lanham, MD: Bernan Press, 1995.

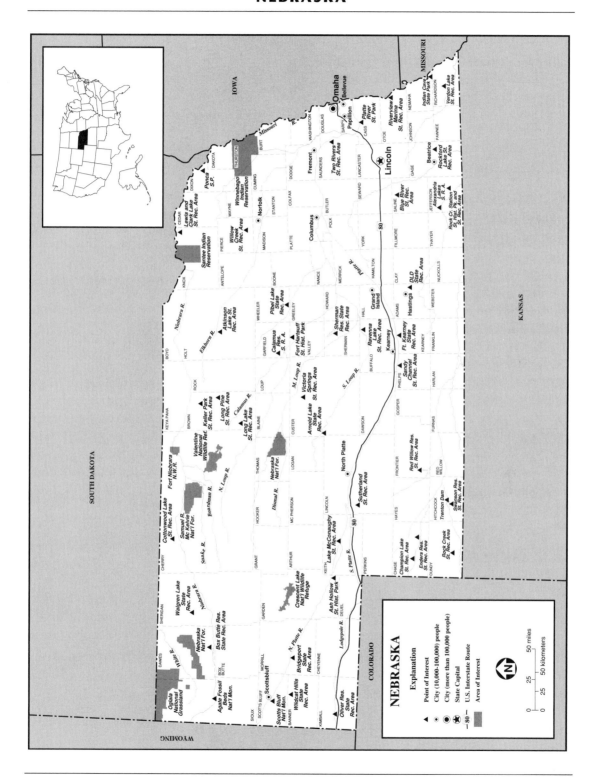

NEBRASKA

Explanation

▲ Point of Interest

⊙ City (10,000-100,000) people

◉ City (more than 100,000 people)

★ State Capital

—80— U.S. Interstate Route

▓ Area of Interest

| 0 | 25 | 50 miles |
| 0 | 25 | 50 kilometers |

Ⓝ N

SOUTH DAKOTA

WYOMING

COLORADO

KANSAS

IOWA

MISSOURI

Omaha
Bellevue
Papillion
Lincoln
Fremont
Norfolk
Columbus
Grand Island
Hastings
Kearney
North Platte
Scottsbluff
Beatrice

Ponca S.P.
Lewis and Clark Lake St. Rec. Area
Winnebago Indian Reservation
Willow Creek St. Rec. Area
Santee Indian Reservation
Two Rivers St. Rec. Area
Platte River St. Park
Riverview Marina St. Rec. Area
Indian Cave State Park
Verdon Lake St. Rec. Area
Rockford Lake St. Rec. Area
Blue River St. Rec. Area
Alexandria Lakes S.R.A.
Rock Cr. Station St. Hist. Pk. and S.R.A.
DLD State Rec. Area
Pibel Lake State Rec. Area
Atkinson Lake St. Rec. Area
Fort Hartsuff St. Hist. Park
Sherman Res. State Rec. Area
Ravenna Lake St. Rec. Area
Ft. Kearney State Rec. Area
Sandy Channel St. Rec. Area
Calamus S.R.A.
Victoria Springs St. Rec. Area
Long Pine St. Rec. Area
Keller Park St. Rec. Area
Long Lake St. Rec. Area
Arnold Lake State Rec. Area
Red Willow Res. St. Rec. Area
Nebraska Nat'l For.
Valentine National Wildlife Ref.
Fort Niobrara N.W.R.
Cottonwood Lake St. Rec. Area
Samuel R. McKelvie Nat'l For.
Sutherland St. Rec. Area
Lake McConaughy St. Rec. Area
Ash Hollow St. Hist. Park
Crescent Lake Nat'l Wildlife Refuge
Champion Lake St. Rec. Area
Enders Res. St. Rec. Area
Rock Creek St. Rec. Area
Swanson Res. St. Rec. Area
Trenton Dam
Walgren Lake State Rec. Area
Nebraska Nat'l For.
Box Butte Res. State Rec. Area
Bridgeport State Rec. Area
Wildcat Hills State Rec. Area
Oliver Res. St. Rec. Area
Oglala National Grassland
Agate Fossil Beds Nat'l Mon.
Scotts Bluff Nat'l Mon.

Niobrara R.
Elkhorn R.
Calamus R.
Dismal R.
N. Loup R.
M. Loup R.
S. Loup R.
Platte R.
N. Platte R.
S. Platte R.
Snake R.
Boardman R.
White R.
Lodgepole R.

Missouri R.

Counties: DAKOTA, DIXON, CEDAR, KNOX, BOYD, KEYA PAHA, CHERRY, SHERIDAN, DAWES, SIOUX, SCOTTS BLUFF, BANNER, KIMBALL, MORRILL, GARDEN, GRANT, HOOKER, THOMAS, BLAINE, LOUP, GARFIELD, WHEELER, ANTELOPE, PIERCE, WAYNE, THURSTON, CUMING, BURT, WASHINGTON, DOUGLAS, SARPY, CASS, OTOE, NEMAHA, JOHNSON, PAWNEE, RICHARDSON, GAGE, JEFFERSON, SALINE, LANCASTER, SEWARD, BUTLER, SAUNDERS, DODGE, COLFAX, STANTON, MADISON, BOONE, NANCE, MERRICK, POLK, YORK, FILLMORE, THAYER, NUCKOLLS, WEBSTER, CLAY, HAMILTON, HALL, HOWARD, GREELEY, VALLEY, SHERMAN, BUFFALO, ADAMS, FRANKLIN, KEARNEY, PHELPS, GOSPER, DAWSON, CUSTER, LOGAN, MC PHERSON, ARTHUR, KEITH, LINCOLN, DEUEL, CHEYENNE, PERKINS, CHASE, HAYES, FRONTIER, HITCHCOCK, RED WILLOW, FURNAS, HARLAN, DUNDY, MC PHERSON, ROCK, BROWN, HOLT

6 POPULATION

Nebraska ranked 36th in the US in 1990 with a census population of 1,587,385. The estimated population for 1995 was 1,644,000; a population of 1,704,000 is projected for the year 2000. The largest cities are Omaha, with a 1992 population of 339,671; and Lincoln, with 197,488.

7 ETHNIC GROUPS

In 1990, 794,911 Nebraskans identified their ancestry as German; 208,616, English; 272,185, Irish; 90,043, Czech; and 99,263, Swedish. The 1990 population also included 57,000 blacks; 12,000 Asians and Pacific Islanders; and some 12,000 Native Americans.

8 LANGUAGES

Nebraska English is almost pure North Midland, except for slight South Midland and Northern influences. In 1990, 1,389,032 Nebraskans spoke only English at home. The number of residents who spoke other languages at home included German, 13,927; and Spanish, 24,555. In 1990, about 1,300 Nebraskans spoke Native American languages.

9 RELIGIONS

In 1990, the state's Catholic population numbered 335,372. Lutherans constituted the largest Protestant group with 114,944 members of the Missouri Synod, 128,667 of the Lutheran Church of America, and 572 of the American Lutheran Churches Association. A total of 145,248 were United Methodists, and 48,591 were Presbyterians. The Jewish population was estimated at 6,732 in 1990.

10 TRANSPORTATION

In 1991 Nebraska had nine rail lines with 3,989 rail miles (6,418 kilometers) of track. Amtrak had a total of 58,477 Nebraska riders in 1992. The state's road system was estimated at 92,702 miles (149,158 kilometers) in 1993. A total of 1,439,026 motor vehicles were registered in 1993, of which 942,264 were automobiles and 490,968 were trucks. Eppley Airfield, Omaha's airport, is by far the busiest in the state, handling 19,316 aircraft departures with 1,057,836 passengers in 1991.

11 HISTORY

By 1800, the Pawnee, Ponca, Omaha, and Oto tribes, along with several others, were living in present-day Nebraska. The area was claimed by both Spain and France and was French territory at the time of the Louisiana Purchase in 1803, when it came under US jurisdiction. During the first half of the 19th century, the area was explored by Lewis and Clark, Zebulon Pike, and others.

Military forts were established in the 1840s to protect travelers from attack by Native Americans. The Kansas-Nebraska Act of 1854 established Nebraska Territory, which assumed its present shape in 1861. Still sparsely populated, Nebraska escaped the violence over the slavery issue that afflicted Kansas. However, from 1860 to the late 1870s, western Nebraska was a battleground for US soldiers and Native Americans, who moved onto reservations in Nebraska, South Dakota, and Oklahoma by 1890.

Chimney Rock on the Oregon Trail.

Statehood

Settlement of Nebraska Territory was rapid, escalated by the Homestead Act of 1862, under which the US government provided 160 acres (65 hectares) to a settler for a small fee. On 1 March 1867, Nebraska became the 37th state to join the Union. Farming and ranching developed as the state's two main enterprises. However, by 1890, depressed farm prices, high railroad shipping charges, and rising interest rates were hurting the state's farmers, and a drought in the 1890s worsened their plight.

When the dust storms of the 1930s began, thousands of people fled Nebraska for the west coast. However, the onset of World War II brought prosperity in other areas. Military airfields and war industries were placed in the state because of its safe inland location, bringing industrial growth that extended into the postwar years. Much of the new industry developed since that time is agriculture-related, including the manufacture of farm machinery and irrigation equipment.

Farm output and income increased dramatically into the 1970s. Many farmers took. on large debt burdens to finance expanded output, with their credit supported by strong farm-product prices and exports. When prices began to fall in the early 1980s, many found themselves in trouble. A 1982 state constitutional amendment prohibits the sale of land used for farming or ranching to anyone other than a Nebraska family farm corporation.

12 STATE GOVERNMENT

Nebraska's legislature is unique among the states. It is a single-chamber body of 49 members not elected by political party. Elected executives are the governor, lieutenant governor, secretary of state, auditor, treasurer, and attorney general. A bill becomes law when passed by a majority of the legislature and signed by the governor. If the governor does not approve, the bill is returned with objections, and a three-fifths vote of the legislature is required to override the veto. A bill automatically becomes law if the governor does not take action within five days after receiving it.

13 POLITICAL PARTIES

In 1994 there were 464,955 registered Republicans, or 49% of the total number of registered voters; 389,102 registered Democrats, or 41%; and 97,897 independents, or 10%. In the 1992 elections, Republican incumbent George Bush secured 47% of the vote; Democrat Bill Clinton, 29%; and Independent Ross Perot, 24%. In the November 1994 elections, Democrat Bob Kerrey was reelected to the US Senate and another Democrat, Ben Nelson, won the election for governor. However, Republicans won all three seats of the US House of Representatives in 1994.

14 LOCAL GOVERNMENT

In 1992, Nebraska had 93 counties, 471 townships, 534 municipalities, and 842 school districts. Municipalities are governed by mayors.

15 JUDICIAL SYSTEM

The state's highest court is the supreme court, consisting of a chief justice and six other justices. Below the supreme court are the district courts, trial courts of general jurisdiction. County courts handle criminal misdemeanors and civil cases involving less than $5,000. Nebraska's crime rate is well below the national average—in 1994 it was 4,440.4 per 100,000. In 1993, prison inmates in state and federal prisons numbered 2,518.

Nebraska Presidential Vote by Major Political Parties, 1948–92

Year	Nebraska Winner	Democrat	Republican
1948	Dewey (R)	224,165	264,774
1952	*Eisenhower (R)	188,057	421,603
1956	*Eisenhower (R)	199,029	378,108
1960	Nixon (R)	232,542	380,553
1964	*Johnson (D)	307,307	276,847
1968	*Nixon (R)	170,784	321,163
1972	*Nixon (R)	169,991	406,298
1976	Ford (R)	233,692	359,705
1980	*Reagan (R)	166,424	419,214
1984	*Reagan (R)	187,866	460,054
1988	*Bush (R)	259,235	397,956
1992**	Bush (R)	217,344	344,346

* Won US presidential election.
** Independent candidate Ross Perot received 174,687 votes.

16 MIGRATION

From 1930 to 1960, the state suffered a net loss of nearly 500,000 people, with more than one-third of the total leaving during the dust-bowl decade, 1930–40. This trend continues, with Nebraska experiencing a net out-migration of 27,400 for the period 1985–90.

17 ECONOMY

Agriculture is the backbone of Nebraska's economy. Cattle, corn, hogs, and soybeans lead the state's list of farm products. However, Nebraska is attempting to diversify and has been successful in attracting new business, in large part because of its location near western coal and oil deposits.

18 INCOME

Nebraska's per capita (per person) income was $20,824 in 1994, giving the state a rank of 23d in the nation. Total personal income rose to $33.8 billion in 1994. Some 10.3% of the state's population was living below the federal poverty level in 1993.

19 INDUSTRY

Nebraska has a small but growing industrial sector. In 1991, processing of food products was the leading industry, accounting for 28,600 jobs in manufacturing. Value of shipments by manufacturers in selected industries included meat products, $8.6 billion; grain-mill products, $1.6 billion; farm and other machinery, $786.6 million; and structural metal products, $445.5 million.

20 LABOR

Nebraska's labor force totaled 876,000 in 1994, of whom 2.9% were unemployed. There were three national labor unions operating in the state in 1993. Membership in unions totaled 10.7% of the labor force in 1994.

21 AGRICULTURE

With total farm marketings valued at over $8.5 billion in 1994, Nebraska ranked fourth among the 50 states. Farms in Nebraska are major businesses, requiring large landholdings to justify investments. The average Nebraska farm in 1994 had assets of $657,900. However, Nebraska farms still tend to be owned by single persons or families, rather than by large corporations.

In 1994, Nebraska ranked third among the states in production of corn and sorghum for grain. Crop production in 1994 (in bushels) included corn, 1,153.7 million; soybeans, 137.2 million; sorghum grain, 122.5 million; wheat, 71.4 million; oats, 7.5 million; and rye, 546,000.

22 DOMESTICATED ANIMALS

In 1994, Nebraska ranked second behind Texas in the US in number of cattle (6,150,000 head) and in quantity produced (3,905 million pounds). Nebraska's hog-raising business is the nation's fourth largest. The state had nearly 4.4 million hogs in 1994 and 105,000 sheep. Cattle marketings accounted for 51.1% of agricultural receipts in 1994; hog marketings, 8.7%.

23 FISHING

Commercial fishing is not significant in Nebraska. In 1991, the North Platte and Valentine State Fish Hatcheries provided 1.5 million fish for anglers.

24 FORESTRY

Arbor Day, now observed throughout the US, originated in Nebraska in 1872 as a

The Omaha skyline.

way of encouraging tree-planting in the sparsely forested state. Forestland occupies 1,029,000 acres (416,000 hectares), or 2% of all Nebraska. Ash, box elder, oak, walnut, elm, and willow trees are common to eastern and central Nebraska, while pine and cedar prevail in the west.

25 MINING

The value of nonfuel mineral production in Nebraska in 1994 was approximately $137 million. All nonfuel minerals produced in Nebraska, with the exception of gem stones, were basic construction materials. In 1992, mineral production included 11.8 million short tons of sand and gravel, 5.8 million short tons of crushed stone, and 189.4 metric tons of clay.

26 ENERGY AND POWER

Total energy consumed in Nebraska in 1992 amounted to 506 trillion Btu. Nebraska is the only state with an electric power system totally owned by the public, through cooperatives and municipal plants. In 1993, electrical output totaled 22.7 billion kilowatt hours. As of 1993, crude petroleum production in Nebraska was 5 million barrels. Natural gas production totaled 2 billion cubic feet in 1993. The state had two nuclear power plants as of 1993. Energy expenditures were $1,889 per capita (per person) as of that year.

27 COMMERCE

Nebraska's wholesale sales totaled $32.5 billion for 1992; retail sales were $13.3

billion for 1993; service establishment receipts were $6.5 billion for 1992. Nebraska's exports of goods totaled $1.2 billion in 1992.

28 PUBLIC FINANCE

Nebraska's constitution prohibits the state from incurring debt in excess of $100,000.

Total revenues for fiscal year 1992/93 were $2,905,787,000; total expenditures were $2,973,436,000.

29 TAXATION

A constitutional amendment in 1967 prohibited the use of property tax revenues for state government. This forced the passage of both a sales/use tax and an income tax, which had long been resisted by conservatives in the state. Nebraska's federal income tax burden in 1990 was $2.5 billion.

30 HEALTH

Nebraska had 90 community hospitals, with 8,400 beds, in 1993. The average expense to a hospital in the state per inpatient day was $626 in 1993, and the average cost per stay was $6,024. There were 3,000 nonfederal physicians and 13,300 nurses in 1993. Some 11.9% of state residents did not have health insurance in that year. Major causes of death in 1992 were heart disease, cancer, cerebrovascular diseases, accidents, and suicide.

31 HOUSING

According to the official 1993 estimate, there were some 679,000 housing units in Nebraska. Median value for owner-occupied homes was $50,400 in 1990, when owners with a mortgage had a median monthly cost of $610. Renters had a median cost of $348 per month. In 1993, 7,751 new privately owned housing units that were authorized by the state had a total value of $551 million.

32 EDUCATION

In 1993/94, there were 1,383 public schools in Nebraska: 1,000 were elementary schools, 354 were secondary schools, and 19 were special education schools. Public school enrollments for 1993/94 were elementary, 170,146; secondary, 113,119; and special education, 670. There was a total public school enrollment of 283,935 (preschool through 12th grade). Expenditures on education were $4,893 per pupil (35th in the nation) in 1993.

The University of Nebraska is the state's largest postsecondary institution, with campuses in Kearney, Lincoln, and Omaha. In 1993–94, there were also 3 state colleges, 17 independent colleges and universities, and 6 community colleges. In fall 1993, 19,496 students were enrolled at independent institutions of higher learning and 37,549 at community colleges.

33 ARTS

The Orpheum Theater in Omaha provides performance space for opera, symphony concerts, ballet, plays, and popular music. Opera/Omaha, Inc., presents three operas there each year, drawing an annual audience of 28,000. The state of Nebraska generated $9,289,333 from federal and state sources for the arts from 1987 to 1991.

The Great Plains Black Museum, the largest Black American historical and cultural center west of the Mississippi River.

34 LIBRARIES AND MUSEUMS

In 1993, the state had 9 county libraries, 16 regional libraries, and 270 public libraries. A total of 5,867,887 volumes were in the public library system in 1993. Total circulation was 10,031,992. The Joslyn Art Museum in Omaha is the state's leading museum. Other important museums include the Nebraska State Museum of History and the University of Nebraska State Museum.

35 COMMUNICATIONS

About 97.4% of the state's 625,000 occupied housing units had telephones in March 1993. In 1993, 94 FM stations and 52 AM stations were operating. There were 16 commercial TV stations and a network of 9 PBS stations. In 1993, there were three large cable television systems.

36 PRESS

In 1994, Nebraska had 5 morning dailies, 14 evening dailies, and 6 Sunday newspapers. The leading newspaper in 1994 was the *Omaha World–Herald,* with circulations as follows: morning, 128,055; evening, 95,693; and Sunday, 284,611. The *Lincoln Journal–Star* had a daily circulation of 35,721 and a Sunday circulation of 79,658.

37 TOURISM, TRAVEL, AND RECREATION

Expenditures by travelers in the state totaled about $1.7 billion in 1993. The 6 state parks, 9 state historical parks, 12 federal areas, and 55 recreational areas are main tourist attractions; fishing, swimming, picnicking, and sightseeing are the principal activities. Pawnee State Recreation Area and Fremont State Recreation Area are the most popular attractions.

38 SPORTS

There are no major league professional sports teams in Nebraska. The most popular spectator sport is college football. Horse-related activities, including racing and rodeos, are popular. Major annual sporting events are the NCAA College Baseball World Series and the World's Championship Rodeo, both held in Omaha. The University of Nebraska Cornhuskers compete in the Big Eight football conference.

39 FAMOUS NEBRASKANS

Nebraska was the birthplace of only one US president, Gerald R. Ford (Leslie King, Jr., b.1913). When Spiro Agnew resigned the vice-presidency in October 1973, President Richard M. Nixon appointed Ford, then a US representative from Michigan, to the post. Upon Nixon's resignation on 9 August 1974, Ford became the first non-elected president in US history.

William Jennings Bryan (b.Illinois, 1860–1925), a US representative from

Photo credit: Greater Omaha Convention & Visitors Bureau.

(Father) Flanagan's Boys Town in Omaha.

Nebraska, served as secretary of state and was three times the unsuccessful Democratic candidate for president. George W. Norris (b.Ohio, 1861–1944), who served 10 years in the US House of Representatives and 30 years in the Senate, promoted farm relief and rural electrification (his efforts led to the creation of the Tennessee Valley Authority).

Native American leaders important in Nebraska history include Oglala Sioux chiefs Red Cloud (1822–1909) and Crazy Horse (1849?–77), and Ponca chief Standing Bear (1829–1908). Father Edward Joseph Flanagan (b.Ireland, 1886–1948) was the founder of Boys Town, a home for underprivileged youth. Two native Nebraskans became Nobel laureates in 1980: Lawrence R. Klein (b.1920) in economics and Val L. Fitch (b.1923) in physics.

Writers associated with Nebraska include Willa Cather (b.Virginia, 1873–1947), who used the Nebraska frontier setting of her childhood in many of her writings and won a Pulitzer Prize in 1922; Mari Sandoz (1896–1966), who wrote of her native Great Plains; and author Tillie Olsen (b.1912). Composer-conductor

Howard Hanson (1896–1982), born in Wahoo, won a Pulitzer Prize in 1944.

Nebraskans important in entertainment include actor-dancer Fred Astaire (Fred Austerlitz, 1899–1984); actors Harold Lloyd (1893–1971), Henry Fonda (1905–82), and Marlon Brando (b.1924); and television stars Johnny Carson (b.Iowa, 1925) and Dick Cavett (b.1936).

40 BIBLIOGRAPHY

Creigh, Dorothy Weyer. *Nebraska: A Bicentennial History*. New York: Norton, 1977.
Hanna, Robert. *Sketches of Nebraska*. Lincoln: University of Nebraska Press, 1984.
State of Nebraska. Department of Economic Development. *Nebraska Statistical Handbook, 1993–1994*. Lincoln, 1994.

Glossary

ALPINE: generally refers to the Alps or other mountains; can also refer to a mountainous zone above the timberline.

ANCESTRY: based on how people refer to themselves, and refers to a person's ethnic origin, descent, heritage, or place of birth of the person or the person's parents or ancestors before their arrival in the United States. The Census Bureau accepted "American" as a unique ethnicity if it was given alone, with an unclear response (such as "mixed" or "adopted"), or with names of particular states.

ANTEBELLUM: before the US Civil War.

AQUEDUCT: a large pipe or channel that carries water over a distance, or a raised structure that supports such a channel or pipe.

AQUIFER: an underground layer of porous rock, sand, or gravel that holds water.

BLUE LAWS: laws forbidding certain practices (e.g., conducting business, gaming, drinking liquor), especially on Sundays.

BROILERS: a bird (especially a young chicken) that can be cooked by broiling.

BTU: The amount of heat required to raise one pound of water one degree Fahrenheit.

CAPITAL BUDGET: a financial plan for acquiring and improving buildings or land, paid for by the sale of bonds.

CAPITAL PUNISHMENT: punishment by death.

CIVILIAN LABOR FORCE: all persons 16 years of age or older who are not in the armed forces and who are now holding a job, have been temporarily laid off, are waiting to be reassigned to a new position, or are unemployed but actively looking for work.

CLASS I RAILROAD: a railroad having gross annual revenues of $83.5 million or more in 1983.

COMMERCIAL BANK: a bank that offers to businesses and individuals a variety of banking services, including the right of withdrawal by check.

COMPACT: a formal agreement, covenant, or understanding between two or more parties.

CONSOLIDATED BUDGET: a financial plan that includes the general budget, federal funds, and all special funds.

CONSTANT DOLLARS: money values calculated so as to eliminate the effect of inflation on prices and income.

CONTERMINOUS US: refers to the "lower 48" states of the continental US that are enclosed within a common boundary.

CONTINENTAL CLIMATE: the climate typical of the US interior, having distinct seasons, a wide range of daily and annual temperatures, and dry, sunny summers.

COUNCIL-MANAGER SYSTEM: a system of local government under which a professional administrator is hired by an elected council to carry out its laws and policies.

CREDIT UNION: a cooperative body that raises funds from its members by the sale of shares and makes loans to its members at relatively low interest rates.

CURRENT DOLLARS: money values that reflect prevailing prices, without excluding the effects of inflation.

DEMAND DEPOSIT: a bank deposit that can be withdrawn by the depositor with no advance notice to the bank.

ELECTORAL VOTES: the votes that a state may cast for president, equal to the combined total of its US senators and representatives and nearly always cast entirely on behalf of the candidate who won the most votes in that state on Election Day.

ENDANGERED SPECIES: a type of plant or animal threatened with extinction in all or part of its natural range.

FEDERAL POVERTY LEVEL: a level of money income below which a person or family qualifies for US government aid.

FISCAL YEAR: a 12-month period for accounting purposes.

FOOD STAMPS: coupons issued by the government to low-income persons for food purchases at local stores.

GENERAL BUDGET: a financial plan based on a government's normal revenues and operating expenses, excluding special funds.

GENERAL COASTLINE: a measurement of the general outline of the US seacoast. See also TIDAL SHORELINE.

GREAT AWAKENING: during the mid–18th century, a Protestant religious revival in North America, especially New England.

GROSS STATE PRODUCT: the total value of goods and services produced in the state.

GROWING SEASON: the period between the last 32°F (0°C) temperature in spring and the first

32°F (0°C) temperature in autumn.

HISPANIC: a person who originates from Spain or from Spanish-speaking countries of South and Central America, Mexico, Puerto Rico, and Cuba.

HOME-RULE CHARTER: a document stating how and in what respects a city, town, or county may govern itself.

HUNDREDWEIGHT: a unit of weight that equals 100 pounds in the US and 112 pounds in Britain.

INPATIENT: a patient who is housed and fed—in addition to being treated—in a hospital.

INSTALLED CAPACITY: the maximum possible output of electric power at any given time.

MASSIF: a central mountain mass or the dominant part of a range of mountains.

MAYOR-COUNCIL SYSTEM: a system of local government under which an elected council serves as a legislature and an elected mayor is the chief administrator.

MEDICAID: a federal-state program that helps defray the hospital and medical costs of needy persons.

MEDICARE: a program of hospital and medical insurance for the elderly, administered by the federal government.

METRIC TON: a unit of weight that equals 1,000 kilograms (2,204.62 pounds).

METROPOLITAN AREA: in most cases, a city and its surrounding suburbs.

MONTANE: refers to a zone in mountainous areas in which large coniferous trees, in a cool moist setting, are the main features.

NO-FAULT INSURANCE: an automobile insurance plan that allows an accident victim to receive payment from an insurance company without having to prove who was responsible for the accident.

NONFEDERAL PHYSICIAN: a medical doctor who is not employed by the federal US government.

NORTHERN, NORTH MIDLAND: major US dialect regions.

OMBUDSMAN: a public official empowered to hear and investigate complaints by private citizens about government agencies.

PER CAPITA: per person.

PERSONAL INCOME: refers to the income an individual receives from employment, or to the total incomes that all individuals receive from their employment in a sector of business (such as personal incomes in the retail trade).

PIEDMONT: refers to the base of mountains.

POCKET VETO: a method by which a state governor (or the US president) may kill a bill by taking no action on it before the legislature adjourns.

PROVED RESERVES: the quantity of a recoverable mineral resource (such as oil or natural gas) that is still in the ground.

PUBLIC DEBT: the amount owed by a government.

RELIGIOUS ADHERENTS: the followers of a religious group, including (but not confined to) the full, confirmed, or communicant members of that group.

RETAIL TRADE: the sale of goods directly to the consumer.

REVENUE SHARING: the distribution of federal tax receipts to state and local governments.

RIGHT-TO-WORK LAW: a measure outlawing any attempt to require union membership as a condition of employment.

SAVINGS AND LOAN ASSOCIATION: a bank that invests the savings of depositors primarily in home mortgage loans.

SECESSION: the act of withdrawal, such as a state that withdrew from the Union in the US Civil War.

SERVICE INDUSTRIES: industries that provide services (e.g., health, legal, automotive repair) for individuals, businesses, and others.

SHORT TON: a unit of weight that equals 2,000 pounds.

SOCIAL SECURITY: as commonly understood, the federal system of old age, survivors, and disability insurance.

SOUTHERN, SOUTH MIDLAND: major US dialect regions.

SUBALPINE: generally refers to high mountainous areas just beneath the timberline; can also more specifically refer to the lower slopes of the Alps mountains.

SUNBELT: the southernmost states of the US, extending from Florida to California.

SUPPLEMENTAL SECURITY INCOME: a federally administered program of aid to the aged, blind, and disabled.

TIDAL SHORELINE: a detailed measurement of the US seacoast that includes sounds, bays, other outlets, and offshore islands.

TIME DEPOSIT: a bank deposit that may be withdrawn only at the end of a specified time period or upon advance notice to the bank.

VALUE ADDED BY MANUFACTURE: the difference, measured in dollars, between the value of finished goods and the cost of the materials needed to produce them.

WHOLESALE TRADE: the sale of goods, usually in large quantities, for ultimate resale to consumers.

Abbreviations & Acronyms

AD—Anno Domini
AFDC—aid to families with dependent children
AFL–CIO—American Federation of
    Labor–Congress of Industrial Organizations
AI—American Independent
AM—before noon
AM—amplitude modulation
American Ind.—American Independent Party
Amtrak—National Railroad Passenger Corp.
b.—born
BC—Before Christ
Btu—British thermal unit(s)
bu—bushel(s)
c.—circa (about)
c—Celsius (Centigrade)
CIA—Central Intelligence Agency
cm—centimeter(s)
Co.—company
comp.—compiler
Conrail—Consolidated Rail Corp.
Corp.—corporation
CST—Central Standard Time
cu—cubic
cwt—hundredweight(s)
d.—died
D—Democrat
e—evening
E—east
ed.—edition, editor
e.g.—exempli gratia (for example)
EPA—Environmental Protection Agency
est.—estimated
EST—Eastern Standard Time
et al.—et alii (and others)
etc.—et cetera (and so on)
F—Fahrenheit
FBI—Federal Bureau of Investigation
FCC—Federal Communications Commission
FM—frequency modulation
Ft.—fort
ft—foot, feet
GDP—gross domestic products
gm—gram
GMT—Greenwich Mean Time
GNP—gross national product
GRT—gross registered tons
Hist.—Historic

I—interstate (highway)
i.e.—id est (that is)
in—inch(es)
Inc.—incorporated
Jct.—junction
K—kindergarten
kg—kilogram(s)
km—kilometer(s)
km/hr—kilometers per hour
kw—kilowatt(s)
kwh—kilowatt-hour(s)
lb—pound(s)
m—meter(s); morning
m^3—cubic meter(s)
mi—mile(s)
Mon.—monument
mph—miles per hour
MST—Mountain Standard Time
Mt.—mount
Mtn.—mountain
mw—megawatt(s)
N—north
NA—not available
Natl.—National
NATO—North Atlantic Treaty Organization
NCAA—National Collegiate Athletic Association
n.d.—no date
NEA—National Education Association or National
Endowment for the Arts
N.F.—National Forest
N.W.R.—National Wildlife Refuge
oz—ounce(s)
PM—after noon
PST—Pacific Standard Time
r.—reigned
R—Republican
Ra.—range
Res.—reservoir, reservation
rev. ed.—revised edition
s—south
S—Sunday
Soc.—Socialist
sq—square
St.—saint
SRD—States' Rights Democrat
UN—United Nations
US—United States

NAMES OF STATES AND OTHER SELECTED AREAS

	Standard Abbreviation(s)	Postal Abbreviation
Alabama	Ala.	AL
Alaska	*	AK
Arizona	Ariz.	AZ
Arkansas	Ark.	AR
California	Calif.	CA
Colorado	Colo.	CO
Connecticut	Conn.	CN
Delaware	Del.	DE
District of Columbia	D.C.	DC
Florida	Fla.	FL
Georgia	Ga.	GA
Hawaii	*	HI
Idaho	*	ID
Illinois	Ill.	IL
Indiana	Ind.	IN
Iowa	*	IA
Kansas	Kans. (Kan.)	KS
Kentucky	Ky.	KY
Louisiana	La.	LA
Maine	Me.	ME
Maryland	Md.	MD
Massachusetts	Mass.	MA
Michigan	Mich.	MI
Minnesota	Minn.	MN
Mississippi	Miss.	MS
Missouri	Mo.	MO
Montana	Mont.	MT
Nebraska	Nebr. (Neb.)	NE
Nevada	Nev.	NV
New Hampshire	N.H.	NH
New Jersey	N.J.	NJ
New Mexico	N.Mex.(N.M.)	NM
New York	N.Y.	NY
North Carolina	N.C.	NC
North Dakota	N.Dak. (N.D.)	ND
Ohio	*	OH
Oklahoma	Okla.	OK
Oregon	Oreg. (Ore.)	OR
Pennsylvania	Pa.	PA
Puerto Rico	P.R.	PR
Rhode Island	R.I.	RI
South Carolina	S.C.	SC
South Dakota	S.Dak. (S.D.)	SD
Tennessee	Tenn.	TN
Texas	Tex.	TX
Utah	*	UT
Vermont	Vt.	VT
Virginia	Va.	VA
Virgin Islands	V.I.	VI
Washington	Wash.	WA
West Virginia	W.Va.	WV
Wisconsin	Wis.	WI
Wyoming	Wyo.	WY

*No standard abbreviation